THE VICTORIAN RAILWAY
AND HOW IT EVOLVED

by the same author

Holiday Cruising in Ireland
Railways Revived
Waterways Restored
Your Book of Canals
The Archaeology of Canals
The Archaeology of Railways
Your Book of Steam Railway Preservation
The Archaeology of the Transport Revolution 1750—1850
Transport in Scotland through the Ages
Scottish Steam Today

The Victorian Railway
and How It Evolved

P. J. G. RANSOM

HEINEMANN : LONDON

William Heinemann Ltd
Michelin House, 81 Fulham Road, London SW3 6RB

LONDON   MELBOURNE   AUCKLAND
First published 1990
© P. J. G. Ransom 1990
ISBN 0 434 98083 8

Photoset by Rowland Phototypesetting Ltd
Bury St Edmunds, Suffolk
Printed in Great Britain by St Edmundsbury Press Ltd
Bury St Edmunds, Suffolk and bound by
Hunter and Foulis Ltd, Edinburgh

CONTENTS

ILLUSTRATIONS

AUTHOR'S NOTE

The course of events is sometimes strange and unexpected, and it has been particularly so during the interval between commencing to write this book and its eventual appearance in print. Since the opening paragraphs of chapter one were written, the antics of the prices of shares in Eurotunnel have demonstrated that it is once again possible for speculators to make – and lose – large sums of money in the shares of a railway still incomplete; and the privatization of all or part of British Rail, with the re-introduction of railway companies, has become a real possibility. Nevertheless it seems best to leave the text as written. The story here told of the original development of the railway system certainly contains lessons for the present day.

P.J.G.R.

1 : Early Railways and What Preceded Them

Jeames de la Pluche

The self-made man commands our respect, our admiration: the self-made millionaire more so, tinged perhaps with just a hint of jealousy. Such people make their pile, as everyone knows, out of property, or pop music. We cannot imagine that anyone might make a quick fortune out of railways. Railways? The railways we know are subsidised public services, or, if we are involved in railway preservation, something to be supported by public fund raising. Money is put into them, not made out of them.

It was not always so. When James Plush, footman to city banker Sir George Flimsy at £30 a year, announced hesitantly to his employer that he had saved a little money and wished to retire from service, it transpired on enquiry that, starting with £20 borrowed from the housemaid's savings, he had followed his master's example and speculated in railways. He had accumulated £30,000. The effect was as though he had today announced himself to be a multi-millionaire – Lady Flimsy promptly invited him to sit down and help himself to the breakfast he had just laid. The date was 1845 and the adventures of Plush were being revealed to the world by the pen of W. M. Thackeray through the pages of a new humorous magazine called *Punch*. James Plush is worth following – as he rises in the world he takes the precaution of discovering an ancestor who came over with the conqueror, and re-names himself Jeames de la Pluche – and we shall return to him.

Railways Young, Vigorous and Rapidly Expanding

To his original readers, the least implausible or exaggerated thing about Jeames was the bit about speculating in railways. They knew railways as

I

a young, vigorous and rapidly expanding industry – probably the most vigorous, the most rapidly expanding, that there had ever been, and that included the canal boom of fifty years earlier. Fortunes were being made, and indeed speculation in railways, the Railway Mania, was about to over-reach itself: hence the attention of the satirist. Certainly many people from humble walks of life who were briefly and on paper rich were going, like Jeames, to find themselves poor again when the crash came.

With the Railway Mania the pot boiled over. But there were real fortunes being made in those days – George Stephenson himself, son of a colliery worker and still illiterate at seventeen, was a very wealthy man before he died. Such fortunes were based on real, solid, achievement. In 1830 the Liverpool & Manchester Railway had demonstrated for the first time that steam trains linking cities would be not only much faster but also cheaper to travel on than road coaches – and by the early 1850s a railway system with over 7,000 miles of route had been built, by a host of different companies, throughout much of lowland Britain. Railways were on the up and up. Their position was totally different to that of railways in recent years during which, their technology overtaken by that of other means of transport, there has been a constant struggle to arrest and reverse a long-term decline – a struggle which, though heroic, has yet to be wholly successful. Indeed the atmosphere on railways in the middle of the last century – during the formative years of the system – was very much more akin to the railway preservation movement of recent decades: a young man's game, in which enthusiasm was all, success built on success and small beginnings had nationwide effect.

That being so, the early Victorian period deserves more attention than it gets from those interested in steam railways. We look back with nostalgia to the last days of steam in the 1950s and 60s, and indeed recreate them on railways such as the Worth Valley or the Severn Valley. We read with admiration, with awe, of the golden age at the turn of the century when everyone went everywhere by steam trains which were as yet unchallenged by road or air, and the railway companies were among the greatest, most prosperous and wealthiest commercial undertakings in Britain. Yet we tend to take for granted the emergence of a national railway system, fully equipped and more or less complete, by the mid-1870s, without considering very much how it had evolved. That is the gap which this book will, I hope, go some way towards filling. Its purpose is to describe steam railways in their formative years. The period starts, quite clearly, a few years before Victoria's accession to the throne, with the opening of the Liverpool & Manchester Railway in 1830. Its end is much less definite. With locomotives, for instance, most of the important features that were to develop during Victorian times had done so by the 1860s, but signals and telegraphs were still developing rapidly in the 70s and 80s. The book's emphasis, however, is very much on the early part of Victoria's reign.

Historic Relics and Lack of Them

Disregard of the period is aggravated by the sad lack of physical relics of it, of locomotives, rolling stock, permanent way and signalling equipment. In fact it is not by any means a total lack, but a comparative one – by comparison with the relics larger in size and very much greater in quantity which survive from the later periods. Queen Adelaide's coach of 1842 is there in the National Railway Museum all right, and worth detailed examination too, but it is overwhelmed by the greater and grander vehicles in which more recent monarchs travelled. Similarly the museum's Grand Junction Railway 2–2–2 *Columbine* of 1845 is reduced to apparent insignificance by the later and larger locomotives among which she is usually to be found, although in fact she represents a more important advance in locomotive design than most of them. The position has been alleviated to some extent by the construction of working replicas (a highly original concept) of some of the most notable locomotives and vehicles of the period, such as *Rocket* and, filling the most conspicuous gap of all, the Great Western Railway broad gauge 4–2–2 *Iron Duke* with two coaches. Apart from one small shunting locomotive of unconventional design, no original broad gauge locomotives survive, although throughout the period covered by this book the Great Western operated on track laid to the broad gauge of 7 ft 0¼ in.

With buildings and civil engineering works, however, the situation is much happier. Mid-Victorian railway architects and engineers, despite a need to satisfy investors thirsty for dividends, built substantial structures to last indefinitely. Later Victorian managements frequently catered for vastly increasing traffic not by replacement but extensions to buildings, quadrupling of tracks, duplication of routes. So stations large and small, tunnels, viaducts, cuttings, embankments and lesser engineering works all survive from our period, and many of today's fastest expresses operate from, through, and over them. Moreover, during Sir Peter Parker's chairmanship of British Rail, it was realised that restoration of historic buildings, particularly stations, was not merely desirable on historic and aesthetic grounds but in many cases also made commercial good sense, for restoration tended to be much cheaper than demolition and reconstruction, while having a similar effect in impressing on the travelling public that the railway intended to remain in business. Hence the handsomely restored stations through which we travel today.

Something else which has been drawing attention to the great period of railway expansion is the increasing frequency with which celebrations are held of railway 150th anniversaries. These started with the Stockton & Darlington in 1975, continued with the Liverpool & Manchester in 1979, and the period during which this book is being written, the mid-1980s, has seen not only widespread celebrations for the Great Western but also for lesser concerns such as the Newcastle & Carlisle and the London & Greenwich. The rapidly increasing number of railway 150th anniversaries which fall during the late 1980s and the 1990s serve to remind us just how quickly and extensively the railway system was spreading a century and a half before.

One of the few aspects of that period which has received much recent attention is the actual construction of the railways, and the people who built them. Brunel, little remembered thirty years ago, has become something of a demigod (he would not have relished either situation!), and much has been written of the Stephensons. Other engineers who laid out railways, the contractors who built them and the navvies who did the hard physical work in the days before mechanised earth-moving plant, all these have attracted the attention of other authors. So I will not be emphasising them here — although there are some largely forgotten notables of the period, such as W. Bridges Adams and, especially, W. F. Cooke, who deserve to be better remembered and whose reputations I endeavour to resurrect. But for the main part, however, I attempt rather to show what the railways themselves were like once built, how they appeared to the people who worked on them and the people who travelled on them, and how, from simple beginnings, they and their equipment evolved over a period of thirty to forty years into steam railways of the sort that remained commonplace until swept away under the modernization and reshaping plans of the late

1950s and the 1960s, and which are still a familiar memory in the minds of people who are yet reluctant to admit to middle age.

The Contemporary Viewpoint

To do so, however, it will be necessary to attempt to view railways through the eyes of contemporaries, rather than with the benefit of knowledge of subsequent history. As I pointed out in *The Archaeology of the Transport Revolution*, to us the *Rocket* appears primitive compared with later locomotives, but to contemporaries in 1829 she was an outstanding advance on any locomotive, on any other form of transport, that was then known. Before considering how railways themselves developed, therefore, it will be necessary first to consider in outline the earlier history of transport, for in 1829, when the practicability of the long-distance steam railway was first demonstrated at the Liverpool & Manchester Railway's Rainhill Trials, Britain was no primitive country so far as transport was concerned. Rather it was served by excellent and widespread networks of roads and waterways much of which had been built or greatly improved, and the services over them developed, over the previous century. They had enabled the industrial revolution to commence, and in turn had received the impetus for further improvement from it.

Road Transport, Pre-Rail

But advances in means of transport had not always been so rapid. From the earliest times until the sixteenth century, people travelled mostly on foot or on horseback, animals on the hoof, and light goods on packhorses. Late in the seventeenth century Thomas Pickford, who used packhorses to carry stone for road-mending, started to carry general goods with them also instead of sending them back to his quarry unladen – the origin of the well-known carrying business. Heavy goods went by barge along slow-flowing rivers, or by sailing ship along the coast. So did some people.

The Roman Occupation had for a few centuries brought an interlude of surfaced roads and wheeled vehicles – but in the Dark Ages Roman roads deteriorated and wheeled vehicles, waggons and carts, were little used. A road, the King's Highway, was no more than a right of passage across country along a track surfaced with earth or, more often, mud churned up by the hoofs of horses and cattle. Its maintenance was the task of nearby inhabitants, a task formalised in 1555 as 'statute labour' by an Act of Parliament which, in England and Wales, obliged the parishioners of each parish to spend several days each year working on their roads. Scotland followed suit a century later, and in due course many people were able to make money payments in lieu of physical labour.

The institution with the greatest need for communications was the Crown, and it was during the reign of Henry VIII that postmasters were first appointed, at towns and villages along important routes, to ensure that relays of horses were available for riders carrying royal dispatches. The system gradually came to be used for private letters too, and also by travellers requiring horses. Postmasters themselves often combined their position with that of innkeeper.

The first coaches in Britain were introduced from Europe in the second half of the sixteenth century. Lacking at first both springs and glazing, they were not so much a convenience for travelling as a status symbol. Queen Elizabeth I had one, and so in 1598 did the English ambassador to Scotland. King James I, on the other hand, on inheriting the throne of England as well as Scotland, progressed in 1604 from Edinburgh to London on horseback.

During the same period long-distance waggons, or 'stage waggons' carrying goods and passengers from stage to stage of their journeys, were also gradually introduced. The first stage coaches were introduced during the seventeenth century, and in 1734 for the first time relays of horses were provided for a stage coach. This enabled the journey time of the Newcastle-London Flying Coach to be reduced from twelve days to nine. The use of the term 'Flying' or 'Fly' to indicate speed is very old-established.

The increasing amount of wheeled traffic on the roads made it increasingly difficult for people working under statute labour to keep them in repair. The problem was tackled in two ways – on the one hand by a succession of legislative measures restricting the types of vehicles which might be used, and on the other by the introduction of turnpike trusts.

A few turnpike gates, at which travellers paid tolls to pay for road maintenance, were set up by Parliament in the late seventeenth century. In 1706, however, Parliament established the first turnpike trust, placing a length of road under control of trustees drawn from local landowners and others, and this arrangement became the usual one for main road maintenance for the next century and a half. Turnpike trusts borrowed capital to improve their roads, against the security of tolls. Originally it was thought that once improved the roads would revert to parishes for maintenance, so trusts were set up for limited periods, often twenty-one years; in practice trusts seldom if ever paid off their debts, and their powers were renewed at intervals by Parliament. The length of road for which an individual trust might be responsible was often quite short — twenty miles or so — but by 1750 most of the main roads radiating from London had been turnpiked, and during the period 1751–1772 a further 389 trusts were set up in England alone — William Albert in *The Turnpike Road System in England 1663–1840* calls it the 'Turnpike Mania'.

The Mail Coach System

Hand in hand with the gradual improvement of roads came gradual improvement of the vehicles that travelled over them and the services they provided. In this gradual process, however, one date, one event, stands out in importance above all the rest. The date is 1784, and the event the introduction of the mail coach system. Because of its effect on early main line railways — described in chapter five — this is worth consideration in some detail.

By the early 1780s stage coach services were widespread, but carriage of mails was a Post Office monopoly. Letters were still carried by 'post boys' on horseback, or even on foot, and only occasionally by cart. So the letter post was both slow and, since post boys were easy prey for highwaymen, insecure. Stage coaches could and did carry parcels, and since they were quicker than the mails, urgent letters were often wrapped up as parcels and sent by coach. Specifically, on the important Bath Road, a stage coach was running between Bristol, Bath and London in seventeen hours: the letter post took more than twice as long.

To John Palmer it was clear that the mails would be better carried by a swift coach with an armed guard. Palmer was not a Post Office man: he was manager and part-owner of theatres in both Bath and Bristol, and so had experience of travel and communications betwen those places and London. He made a detailed study of stage coach operation throughout England and Wales, and then with the support of young prime minister William Pitt, and in the teeth of entrenched opposition from Post Office officials, he was enabled to make a trial of his proposals at his own expense on the Bath Road. The first mail coach left Bristol at 4 pm on 2 August 1784 and, travelling overnight, reached London sixteen hours later.

The mail coach system was indeed an instant success, and mail coaches were introduced on many other routes over the next few years. The essence of Palmer's plan was this: on a mail coach the mail guard, with his blunderbuss and bags, provided the Post Office presence. The driver, the horses, the coach itself were all provided by contractors. The horse contractors were remunerated at a rate equivalent to that which the Post Office paid for horses for post boys. This was not sufficient for them to make a profit, but so that they might do so they were permitted to carry a limited number of passengers in the coach, and retain their fares. As Palmer rightly judged, such a swift, safe service proved very attractive to passengers.

The mail coaches left London in the early evening, and arrived there in the early morning, so a correspondent in London who wrote a letter in the afternoon, to any place of importance within say 150 miles, could rely on receiving a reply two mornings later.

The system was administered by men whom Palmer had brought into the Post Office, notably Thomas Hasker, who became Surveyor and Superintendent of the Mail Coaches, and Francis Freeling, who in due course became Secretary of the Post Office. To be reliable the mail coach system needed an extremely well-disciplined organisation. The principal instrument for achieving it was the time-bill. This printed form, along with a sealed timepiece, was carried by the mail guard on each journey: it detailed the times at which the coach was due at each stop, and the postmasters had to enter the actual times of arrival together with the reasons for any delays. The completed time-bill was then returned to the Post Office in London by the next coach, so that the performance of the system was constantly monitored. Not long before, stage coach operators had been disinclined to promise arrival on a particular day, let alone promising the time; now, quite suddenly, coaches running the length and breadth of the land were being scheduled throughout their journeys to the nearest minute.

Coach Design

The mail coach system was also made possible by improvements in vehicle design, and since the design of mail coaches was strongly to influence the design of early railway coaches, it is again worth going into it in some detail. The first coaches in Britain, private ones in the early seventeenth century, had had as their most important component the perch, a substantial longitudinal timber along, approximately, the centre-line of the vehicle, to which axles and wheels were attached. Together these formed the carriage, or as we would now say, the undercarriage or chassis. Above it, suspended from a wooden post at each corner by leather straps to reduce the jolts, was the body, containing seats for four (or sometimes six) passengers arranged so that two (or three) of them faced the other two (or three). Initially the lower part of the body was angular in shape; later it was rounded off with upswept curves at the ends – perhaps to make the leather straps easier to fix, perhaps just to look better. From the mid-seventeenth century leaf springs of steel started to replace the wooden uprights.

Stage coaches evolved differently, however. By the 1780s they had a driver's box mounted direct on the carriage forward of the body, and a large basket behind the body for parcels and low-fare passengers. The earliest mail coaches were similar to these (although the first one of all lacked the basket), but the intensive use to which they were put necessitated further improvements. By the turn of the century the improved mail coach had been developed and remained standard for the next four decades or so. The coachman's box seat and a rear boot in place of the basket were now combined with the main part of the body into a rigid structure. This enlarged body was suspended above the carriage by semi-elliptic springs. The carriage itself was still unsprung, for, when the mail coach was designed, springs mounted direct upon axles still lay in the future.

The mail guard's seat was external, mounted high upon the rear boot, facing forwards, and seats for outside passengers were placed on the front edge of the roof of the passenger compartment. The lower longitudinal edges of this retained the familiar upward curve, which was by now traditional and of little functional importance. Windows were glazed droplights fitted in the doors, with leather straps to raise and lower them. The rear wheels were of large diameter to smooth their passage over bumpy roads, with the body fitting between them; the front wheels, which swivelled about a central pivot, were of necessity of smaller diameter so as not to foul the body when turning. The wheels themselves were of wood with iron tyres, the components of the carriage of wood (ash was favoured) with iron fittings, the body of wood, canvas

9

and leather, protected by many coats of paint and varnish. Brakes of anything resembling the modern type were unknown: downhill, coaches were held back by the horses, with the assistance on the steepest descents of a metal skid placed under one of the rear wheels. This pattern of coach was also adopted for stage coaches.

Rivers and Canals

The improvements to road transport of the seventeenth and eighteenth centuries were matched by improvements to inland waterways. (Development of traditional forms of land and water transport during the eighteenth and early nineteenth centuries, and the contemporaneous development of steam power, form the theme of my earlier *The Archaeology of the Transport Revolution* where greater detail will be found than can be included here.) The wide, slow-flowing rivers of England had been used for transport since the middle ages and before, but alternating flood and drought often made passage difficult. Drought could be alleviated by dredging, and more so by constructing weirs to hold back sufficient water for boats, and locks for boats to pass the weirs. During the latter part of the seventeenth century, and the first half of the eighteenth, much was done in this way to improve large rivers for navigation, and to extend navigation up tributaries previously unnavigable. The work was at first undertaken by individuals under letters patent from the Crown, then, and more commonly, by commissioners appointed by an Act of Parliament, or companies of 'undertakers' incorporated under one, with powers to levy tolls on boats and their cargoes to pay for the work. Unlike turnpike trusts, their powers were perpetual, not limited to a period of time. By the middle of the eighteenth century river improvements were coming to include increasingly long sections of lateral canal which avoided shallows.

The canal which signalled the start of the canal era, however, was built by the Duke of Bridgewater, aided by his agent John Gilbert and millwright James Brindley, to carry coal from his mines at Worsley to Manchester seven and a half miles away. It was built between 1759 and 1765; later a branch longer than the original was completed to Runcorn where it entered the Mersey estuary, giving the duke a route between Manchester and Liverpool. But even while the Bridgewater Canal was being built, a much greater scheme was taking shape: a canal from the Trent to the Mersey, passing through the Potteries. To build it a joint stock company was incorporated by Act of Parliament in 1766, with powers to purchase the land compulsorily and to levy tolls upon goods eventually carried on the canal. The canal company was to provide a route which would be open for all to navigate. Such was to become the usual form of canal administration.

The Trent & Mersey Canal was engineered by Brindley and opened in stages between 1770 and 1777: it ran from the Trent near Derby to join the Bridgewater Canal above Runcorn. Brindley laid most of it out as a 'narrow canal' with locks only seven feet wide: this cheapened the costs of both construction and maintenance while the narrow boats that could use it could still carry loads large enough to show substantial economies over land carriage.

Promoters of canals had not rested with linking the Trent and the Mersey. To Brindley and others it seemed that these rivers should be linked also with the Severn and the Thames. Terrain had dictated that the T & M should be laid out in the form of a V: links to the two southerly rivers would turn it into an X, a cross. The south-western arm of the cross was provided by the Staffordshire & Worcestershire Canal, authorised on the same day as the Trent & Mersey to run from the T & M to the Severn at Stourport; the south-eastern by the Coventry Canal, to run from the T & M to Coventry, and the Oxford Canal to continue the line to the Thames. It was in fact a short part of the Coventry Canal which became the first narrow canal opened to traffic, in 1769. The first narrow locks to come into use, later the same year, were those of the Birmingham Canal, which was being built to link the town of its name with the Staffordshire & Worcestershire. Many other short branch canals were promoted at this period; so were some long strategic ones, notably Forth & Clyde, Leeds & Liverpool and, in the 1780s, the Thames & Severn.

Canal Mania

By the late 1780s many of the early canals were complete, and prospering visibly. The consequence was a new wave of canal pro-motion, the Canal Mania, a boom which reached its peak about 1792. During the years 1791 to 1795 inclusive, some forty-eight new canals were authorised, with a capital of more than £7 million. But from 1793 Britain was at war with France, and with the war came inflation. Construction of all these new canals cost more and took longer than expected. Some never were completed. But a great many canals of importance did date from this period. They included, notably, the Grand Junction, a wide canal from London direct to the Oxford Canal at Braunston, Northants; the Worcester & Birmingham, direct from Birmingham to the Severn, and the Rochdale and Huddersfield Canals, both of them to cross the Pennines. William Jessop, responsible for the Grand Junction and many other canals, was the greatest canal engineer of the 1790s; an up and coming young man was Thomas Telford.

Canal construction meant that existing skills had to be developed and new ones learned. For the first time, long continuous lines of communication had to be surveyed. Experience of river navigations and mills was useful for laying out watercourses, of mining for making tunnels, of architecture for bridges; but cuttings, embankments and aqueducts had in effect no precedents and appear on canals for the first time, small and tentative on the early ones, displaying greater confidence on the later. Materials for early structures were wood, local stone and brick; cast iron for bridges and aqueducts came into use early in the 1790s and enabled Pontcysyllte Aqueduct on the Ellesmere Canal to be built with nineteen cast-iron spans on stone piers which carry the canal 127 feet above the River Dee. It was completed in 1805.

Along this network of canals, horses towed boats carrying goods of all the classes needed by a nation undergoing the industrial revolution — and, on parts of it, carrying passengers as well.

Waggonways and Tramroads

There were during the canal era two other separate strands of development which were eventually to fuse and produce the steam railways that brought the canal era to an end. One was the development of steam pumps and stationary engines, the other the development of waggonways and tramroads. At the beginning of the nineteenth century however there was no indication of this, although simple railways had been developing gently for a couple of centuries.

The ancestors of the modern railway were trackways of wood used in the metal mines of central Europe in the late middle ages. Along them miners pushed wheeled tubs of ore; vertical guide pins projected below tub bodies to keep them on the track. The first railways in Britain were probably trackways of this type, used underground by Austrian miners working in the Lake District late in the sixteenth century. The first on the surface, of which there is definite record, was completed in 1604 by Huntingdon Beaumont. It ran about two miles from coal mines at Wollaton, west of Nottingham, to a point near that town from which the coal could conveniently be sold. Its rails were of wood, as they would continue to be on similar lines for the next one and a half centuries or so, and horses pulled the waggons along them. What, if any, means of guidance was provided to keep Beaumont's waggons on his track is not recorded: but later waggonways used flanged wheels, and it is probable that his did too.

Wooden railways or 'waggonways' were then built in slowly increasing numbers throughout the seventeenth century, and in more rapidly increasing numbers during the eighteenth. Individually they were never more than a few miles long, usually associated with extraction of minerals, particularly coal, and commonest in the coalfield of Northumberland and Durham. With the increasing scarcity of wood for fuel, this was supplying coal by sea to London in increasing amounts. To convey coal from pit to staith, where it was loaded into ships (or, in many instances, 'keels' or barges on the tidal Tyne or Wear which carried it downstream for transfer to ships), coal owners built waggonways. Often the mouths of coal pits were at some height above sea level, which enabled the waggonways to be laid out on a steady downward gradient which laden waggons descended by gravity; horses hauled them back again. The same circumstances no doubt discouraged construction of canals, which were unknown in the district, although by the time the canal era arrived waggonways were so well established that coal owners would probably have been reluctant to change.

The Newcastle waggonway of the mid- and late eighteenth century was advanced engineering for its day. Its track was well laid and well tended, and its wooden rails were pinned by wooden trenails to wooden sleepers. Usually the rails were between four and five feet apart, such a gauge being the most suitable for a waggon pulled by a single horse. Often the rails were doubled, one on top of the other, so that when the upper rail became worn it could be replaced without dismantling the track; sometimes to meet exceptional wear wrought iron plates were substituted for the upper rail of wood. Cuttings, embankments and bridges enabled the waggonway to maintain an even gradient, turntables were used to divert waggons from one track to another and the line terminated at high level above the water on a staith which enabled coal to be fed by gravity from waggons to vessels waiting below. This

13

arrangement led in turn to the characteristic shape of the chaldron waggons which ran on these lines (chaldron was a measure of coal): for gravity discharge, the floor contained a large trapdoor, and one or more of the sides sloped outwards from it. Wheels were made of wood until the 1730s after which cast iron started to replace it – and a brake block applied to one of them by a long lever kept the waggon's speed under control down grade.

The most remarkable relic of the waggonway era is Causey Arch, near Stanley, Co. Durham. This stone arch of 105 ft span was built about 1726 to carry the Tanfield Waggonway 80 ft above a stream at the bottom of a gorge. Now it forms the centrepiece of an extensive picnic area arranged by Durham County Council, and near to it a convincing full-size replica of a chaldron waggon has been placed on wooden rails. When built, Causey Arch had the longest span of any bridge in Britain; it was famous in its day, and so was a nearby embankment 100 ft high. Clearly a tradition of what would later be called civil engineering was growing up on the waggonways of North-East England, yet the canal pioneers do not seem to have benefited from it, presumably because Tyneside was remote from most parts of the country where canals were built.

Where a coal owner planning to build a waggonway did not also own all the land between the coal pit and the staith, he obtained wayleaves from the landowner. When coal owner Charles Brandling, who owned pits on Tyneside, wanted to build a waggonway into Leeds from his pit at Middleton, he obtained an Act of Parliament to reinforce his agreements for wayleaves. This Act, passed in 1758, was the first to authorise a railway.

East Shropshire was the other great area for wooden railways. Usually these were of narrower gauge than those of the North-East: early Shropshire coal mines often took the form of near-horizontal adits; small wooden railways ran continuously from within these to the bank of the River Severn where the coal was loaded into barges called trows. Their small waggons were often worked in trains, several to a single horse. In due course such railways were used to carry materials for the ironworks of the district. A stretch of wooden railway from one of these was unearthed at Ironbridge in 1986.

It was in Shropshire that iron was first used to form a continuous running surface. The first iron rails were cast at Coalbrookdale in 1767. These were simply bars of cast iron, laid along the tops of wooden rails.

A few wooden railways were laid as feeders of traffic to other navigable rivers and to canals, particularly in Nottinghamshire and Derbyshire. Iron rails of the Coalbrookdale type were used by the Trent & Mersey company on the branch, part canal, part railway, from its main line at Etruria to Caldon Low limestone quarries. This was authorised by Act of Parliament in 1776 and completed about 1779: it comprised rather more than seventeen miles of waterway as far as Froghall, followed by three and a half miles of railway which ascended some 670 feet en route to the quarries.

The natural development of making the rails wholly of cast iron seems to have occurred in South Wales: rails of this type were in use at Dowlais ironworks in 1791 and subsequently much used in the area. Waggons which ran on them probably had grooved, that is to say double-flanged, wheels. In Leicestershire, William Jessop laid out the 'Forest Line' of the Leicester Navigation partly as canal, where the route was level, and partly as railway, where steepish gradients could not be avoided. The railway parts were laid with iron rail of T-section, strong in proportion to their weight, on wooden sleepers during 1793–4.

Meanwhile John Curr had invented, for use underground in coal mines, iron rails of L-section upon which small vehicles with plain unflanged wheels could run. At that time the usual transport in coal mines was either sledges or small plain-wheeled vehicles running on 'barroways', flat wooden surfaces with, sometimes, raised wooden strips added as guide rails. Curr's first rails were installed in a mine at Sheffield about 1787. In 1788 they were used on the surface at the ironworks of Joseph Butler, Wingerworth (near Chesterfield), though still laid to a very narrow gauge appropriate to underground use; the Butterley Company, in which Jessop was a partner with Benjamin Outram, used them in 1793 laid to a gauge of 3 ft 6 in. at its quarry at Crich, Derbyshire, and when the northern part of the Derby Canal's line was built instead, on Jessop's recommendation, as a 'railway of cast iron', L-section rails were laid to a gauge of about 4 ft 4 in. upon stone blocks for sleepers. Or perhaps they were not, for although measurement of a waggon from this line which survives at the National Mining Museum, Lound Hall, Nottinghamshire, confirms that it ran on track of about this gauge, the gauge of 3 ft 6 in. is often given for this line and Outram himself is quoted* as advising the Ashby Canal Company that the Derby

* Clinker, C. R., and Hadfield, C., *The Ashby-de-la-Zouch Canal and its Railways*, Bristol, 1978.

Canal line was of this gauge, while recommending a gauge eight inches wider for lines for general use. Perhaps the Derby line was laid to 3 ft 6 in. – perhaps even on wooden sleepers – and subsequently widened.

At any rate the 'tramroad', or 'plateway', laid with L-section rails or 'plates' on stone blocks to a gauge of about 4 ft 4 in., and carrying waggons which had unflanged wheels revolving loose on their axles, then became the most popular form of railway for the next two decades or so. In part this was due to enthusiastic promotion by Benjamin Outram, engineer to the Derby Canal and the active partner in the Butterley Co. of which ironworks were the principal business. They tended to replace earlier types of wooden and iron railways, except in North East England, which remained mostly faithful to the wooden railway for the time being. There, in 1797, for the first time a wooden waggonway was re-laid with iron 'edge rails', held in cast iron chairs mounted upon stone blocks. Upon these rails flanged wheels continued to run, and other waggonways were subsequently re-laid similarly with increasing frequency. In North Wales in 1800–01 the Penrhyn slate quarries, Bethesda, were connected to Port Penrhyn by the Penrhyn Railway. This was built to a gauge of about two feet with edge rails of oval section, upon which ran wheels with concave treads invented by Benjamin Wyatt. One of his intentions was to avoid build-up of dirt and stones which was proving troublesome on L-section rails. Whether he was consciously copying earlier South Wales practice is not clear: certainly his oval rail wore its way into the wheels too quickly, and sections of both were altered so that double-flanged wheels with flat treads ran on a flat rail surface. Double-flanged wheels could run loose on their axles and accommodate themselves better than single-flanged wheels to variations in track gauge: their use became common in North Wales slate quarries and persisted until recent times. But in the early nineteenth century, throughout most of Britain the plateway became the commonest form of railway.

Such tramroads were particularly popular with canal companies, for though a horse could haul a greater load on a canal, tramroads were cheaper to build. Canal companies used them as temporary expedients to plug gaps in incomplete lines – notably the Grand Junction which built a tramroad over Blisworth Hill, Northants, pending completion of the long canal tunnel beneath – and even more they used them as permanent feeders of traffic. Canal company acts often contained powers to build feeder tramroads. In South Wales, where canals had been built up several of the industrial valleys in the 1790s, the extent of feeder tramroads eventually far exceeded that of the canals themselves.

With canals making greater and greater use of tramroads it is not surprising that in due course a tramroad was substituted for the entire course of a proposed canal. This happened in 1801 with the incorporation by Act of Parliament of the Surrey Iron Railway: a canal had been proposed from Croydon, then a country town, to the Thames at Wandsworth, but Jessop, as engineer to the project, found that water supplies would be inadequate and recommended a railway instead. If George Stephenson was, as he was eventually happy to be known, the father of railways, then William Jessop, the great canal engineer, was surely their grandfather.

The Surrey Iron Railway was built as a typical tramroad of its period with L-section rails laid on stone blocks. It was opened in 1803, for the use of the public on payment of appropriate tolls. The first public railway was operated in a manner analogous to contemporary canals and turnpike roads, with carriers using their own waggons upon it. It was the forerunner of several similar public horse railways built over the next two decades.

Stationary Steam

The earliest use of steam (so far as the direct ancestry of locomotives is concerned) was as a means to produce a partial vacuum, by condensing it within a cylinder; the application was the drainage of mines. Thomas Savery in 1698 patented a device in which atmospheric pressure would impel water from the mine bottom up a pipe past a valve into the cylinder, from which more steam under pressure would expel it up a further pipe. This did not work, at least not satisfactorily, and the field was left open to Thomas Newcomen. In Newcomen's atmospheric pump, steam was condensed beneath a piston in a vertical open-topped cylinder. The piston was linked by rod and chain to one end of a gigantic rocking beam: the other end was linked to a pump rod descending into the mine. Atmospheric pressure drove the piston downwards to raise the pump rod, after which more steam at minimal pressure was admitted beneath the piston while the weight of the pump plunger acted on the beam to draw the piston upwards. Then water was let into the cylinder to condense the steam – and so on, indefinitely. Newcomen's pump worked well and the first, installed in 1712, was the predecessor of many.

Yet Newcomen's pump offered scope for improvement. It was James Watt who realised that alternately heating up the cylinder, as steam was admitted, and then cooling it down again, when water was injected, was terribly inefficient. In 1765 the solution occurred to him that the steam should be condensed in a separate vessel, the 'separate condenser', while the cylinder was kept hot. But Watt at that date was instrument maker to Glasgow University, and not an engineer, so although he patented the separate condenser in 1769 it was not until 1774–5 that in partnership with Matthew Boulton he achieved a full-size pump working satisfactorily on his principle.

Pumps to Watt's patent then became extremely popular and were installed in many places, but particularly among the tin mines of Cornwall, where coal was expensive. The partnership drew a royalty based on the estimated coal saving, and as well as attending to the design and installation of pumps Watt continued to develop the principles upon which they worked. He placed the cylinder in a steam jacket and closed in its top, admitting steam to that end also to keep the cylinder warm and add a little pressure to that of the atmosphere pressing the piston downwards. He experimented with expansive use of steam, arranging the valve gear so that steam admission was cut off before the piston reached the end of its stroke, leaving the steam already in the cylinder to expand. He condensed steam alternately from above and below the piston, letting steam press the piston in both directions.

Such improvements building one upon the other evidently seemed to Watt more important than following the chimera of adapting the steam pump to produce rotary motion and so to power machines – yet there was certainly a demand for this. The task of Boulton & Watt's original engine had been to pump back, for re-use, water from the waterwheel which powered Boulton's metal-goods factory near Birmingham. Water wheels were then the principal form of power for factories and mills steadily increasing in number.

The principle of the connecting rod and crank, to convert reciprocating motion to rotary, was already familiar in, for instance, the treadle lathe: Watt was beaten in its application to the steam engine by James Pickard, who in 1780 produced the first steam engine with rotary motion obtained via a crank, and patented the application. But Pickard himself could of course only apply the crank to the atmospheric engine; within a couple of years Watt had steam engines to his own patent producing rotary motion through 'sun and planet' gearing which he substituted for the crank. Watt's first rotative engine for an outside customer was built in 1783, and in 1784 they were for the first time installed as winding engines at mines – tin in Cornwall and coal on Tyneside. From this time forward the steam engine started to become an accepted form of power for stationary machinery. By 1800 there were probably as many as 1,000 steam engines and pumps of various sorts in use in Britain; Watt's patent expired that year, and over the next couple of decades their numbers were to increase tenfold.

Inclined Planes

The various strands in transport history which have so far been mentioned were all in due course to become interwoven and to contribute features to the steam railway system, although for clarity it has been necessary to compromise with strict chronological accuracy and describe them to some extent subject by subject. With inclined planes, however, one despairs of doing this. Should they come under the heading of canals, of tramroads, or even of steam power? Their story, at any rate, is roughly this.

Originally, there were two distinct needs to be met. One was to restrain the waggons of wooden railways passing down a steep gradient, and to provide a means of getting them up again where the gradient was too steep for horse or human power. This was done by letting them down with a rope or hauling them up by it. The other need was for a means to allow boats to pass between one level of waterway and another, done by hauling them up (or letting them down) on rollers, or on a wheeled cradle guided along wooden or stone tracks. Examples of both were in use on the Continent by the late middle ages.

In Britain, the earliest Shropshire railways seem in several cases to have descended the side of the Severn gorge by inclines steep enough to require ropes or chains. By the third quarter of the eighteenth century, such inclines were being made self-acting: they were laid with double track and the rope attached to descending laden waggons passed round a braked winding drum at the top and then down again to the ascending empties, so that the weight of the laden waggons could draw these upwards. On Tyneside, such self-acting inclines are first recorded in

1784, but their main spread there was contemporary with the spread of iron-railed waggonways from 1798 onwards. Similarly, self-acting inclined planes formed part of many plateways built at this period.

In Shropshire a small canal, the Donnington Wood Canal, had been built in the 1760s to carry coal in 'tub boats' similar to those which the Duke of Bridgewater used at Worsley. In the 1780s ironmaster William Reynolds built another private canal nearby, the Ketley Canal, to carry coal and ironstone to an ironworks. Between its termini was a difference in altitude of 73 feet. This Reynolds overcame not by locks but by building a self-acting inclined plane up and down which tub boats were carried on wheeled cradles. These ran on iron railways laid with L-section plates, one of the earliest instances of their use on the surface, for the incline was completed and came into use in 1788.

In the same year the Shropshire Canal was authorised, to link both private canals with the Severn at Coalport. Reynolds was among the promoters. It was laid out through, by canal standards, rugged country, and there were three inclined planes along its route. But whereas at Ketley loaded boats passed downhill, on the Shropshire Canal loaded boats were expected in both directions, and at one incline, Wrockwardine Wood which had a rise of 120 ft and was 316 yards long, it was expected that the preponderance of loaded traffic would be uphill. The canal committee consulted Boulton & Watt, and installed steam winding engines at all three inclines to operate them. Wrockwardine was ready first, and came into use, probably, late in 1790.

This appears to be the first instance in which steam was used, other than on an experimental basis, as motive power for land transport.

The rest of the canal came into use in 1791, although men and horses worked the other two inclines until their steam engines were installed in 1793. At these two inclines most of the traffic was downhill, which meant that for much of the time they could be self-acting and the engines were used only intermittently. Part of the canal, including The Hay inclined plane, is now within the Ironbridge Gorge Museum Trust's Blists Hill Open Air Museum, and although both canal and plane have been disused since 1894 the trust has reinstated railway track on the incline. This has ordinary bullhead rail in chairs, for the usual railway track of this type replaced the original plate rails during the working life of the incline.

Tramroad inclined planes were just as likely to have an excess of upward traffic as those on canals, and steam engines were adopted equally to power them. Unfortunately as I pointed out in *The Archae-ology of the Transport revolution* there has been confusion about where and when this was first done. Certainly no one has yet contradicted the suggestion that I made there, that the steam-engine powered inclined plane installed at Avenham, Preston, in 1803 as part of the Lancaster Canal Co.'s tramroad may well have been the first instance. The canal company had every incentive to put in a powered plane here: the tramroad was built as a link, supposedly temporary, between completed sections of canal. It used inclined planes to descend into and then climb out of the valley of the River Ribble, in lieu of an aqueduct which in fact was never built. The principal traffic was coal, northbound, which meant that it had to be hauled up the incline which lay on the north bank of the Ribble. It is illustrated in my earlier book mentioned above.

In South Wales the Aber-nant Tramroad, a feeder to the Neath Canal, brought a steam-powered inclined plane into use in 1805. The first steam-powered incline on Tyneside came into use in 1809. It was the first of many.

Strong Steam

While Watt's separate condenser patent was still in force engine owners had naturally found payment of royalties based on notional coal savings increasingly irksome, and many engineers attempted to devise steam engines which would evade the patent. But only one was truly successful, and he was Richard Trevithick. Trevithick (born in 1771) was a Cornishman, son of a tin mine manager and by the 1790s a skilled engineer. About 1797 the obvious way to evade Watt's patent occurred to him: if he used 'strong steam' — that is to say, steam at a pressure of 30 lb per sq. in. or even more — to power an engine, the steam, once used, could simply be exhausted to the atmosphere and the condenser eliminated. He was not the first to think of this, but he was the first to put it into full-size practice. In 1799 the first Trevithick non-condensing beam engine came into use to wind the ore out of a tin mine, making for the first time the steam engine's characteristic puffing noise as it worked; and Trevithick went on to build a total of about thirty such engines.

Even as Trevithick built his first non-condensing engines, he grasped another vital point: that a steam engine using strong steam could, with its boiler, be made far more compact than existing beam engines. It could be compact enough to power a carriage. He commenced experiments to this end. Later he was also to experiment with one of his engines powering a boat.

Steam Boat and Vehicle Pioneers

Trevithick was not, of course, by a long way the first person to whom the idea of a steam-driven boat or carriage had occurred. Some had even been built. In France, as long before as 1770, N. J. Cugnot had built a steam vehicle intended to transport artillery, and in 1783 Marquis Jouffroy d'Abbans had built a steam boat which successfully ascended the River Saône against the current for fifteen minutes. In the USA, several years of experiments by John Fitch had culminated in construction of a steam boat so reliable that he operated a public service with it on the River Delaware throughout the summer of 1790 – unfortunately without attracting sufficient passengers for commercial success. In Britain, James Watt considered adapting the steam engine to power both ships and carriages – and rejected both notions, preferring the more practical task of developing the stationary engine. In early life, Watt seems to have dissipated his inventive energies too widely: his reluctance to experiment later may have been a reaction to this. Unfortunately the effect was, while his patent ran its course, to inhibit the inventiveness of others.

This affected paticularly William Murdock, who was Boulton & Watt's most skilled erector of pumps and engines and spent his entire working life with the firm. About 1784–6 he designed and built a model steam vehicle with a vertical cylinder driving, via a beam above it, a connecting rod and crank on the driving axle. This, the first self-propelled vehicle in Britain, worked well. Murdock intended to seek a patent and build a full-size version, but was persuaded by his employers to desist, so that he might concentrate on his work for them.

Earlier, in 1779, Murdock had commissioned a Boulton & Watt pump at Wanlockhead, Dumfriesshire. Here he met the local engineer William Symington: it is likely that together they discussed the prospects for a steam carriage. Symington subsequently planned such a vehicle, designed and built improved steam pumps which almost (but not quite) evaded Watt's patent, and eventually, after the patent had expired, built for the Forth & Clyde Canal the steam towing boat

Charlotte Dundas in 1803. This was technically satisfactory but wrang-lings within the canal company's directorate prevented her from going into service. Symington's experiments, however, were viewed by both Robert Fulton, who established the first commercially successful steam-boat service, in the USA in 1807, and Henry Bell, who brought successful steamboat operation to the Old World in 1812 with his *Comet* on the Clyde.

Trevithick

Murdock, after commissioning the Wanlockhead pump, had been moved by his employers to Cornwall. Here he had built his model vehicle. Here also Richard Trevithick came into contact with him, although since they were competitors it is not clear how closely, or how much, if anything, Trevithick's ideas owed to Murdock's model vehicle.

Certainly, having conceived the idea of building a steam vehicle, the models which Trevithick made during 1797–8 owed nothing to the layout of Murdock's model. The boilers of early steam pumps had often been of 'haystack' shape, or even with rectangular sides. Murdock's was of the latter type. Trevithick realised that for strong steam a stronger form of boiler was needed, and made his boilers cylindrical in shape, positioned horizontally. One of his models, preserved in the Science Museum, has a vertical cylinder recessed into the top of this cylindrical boiler: the piston rod emerges above the cylinder and connecting rods passing downwards either side of the boiler drive wheels which are attached to it. A large flywheel ensures continuity of motion. The full-size engines which Trevithick built subsequently – or which were built under licence from him – had similar features, although in some instances the cylinder was recessed into one end of the boiler. The fire was usually contained in a large-diameter fire tube within the boiler, with a single return flue leading from it to the chimney beside the firedoor.

In 1801 Trevithick built his first full-size steam carriage which worked well but, after a few trials, was regrettably destroyed by fire following an accident caused by the bad roads of the period. However Trevithick then sought a patent for his type of engine (granted in 1802) for use both stationary and in vehicles, and went to Coalbrookdale to experiment with higher steam pressures.

While there he mentioned in a letter that the Coalbrookdale

Company was building a steam carriage for use on its 'realroads', i.e. rail roads or tramroads. Unfortunately records of this, the first steam locomotive, are minimal. It is uncertain whether it was ever completed, or, if it was, whether it did any useful work.

In 1803 Trevithick built another steam carriage upon which he and his friends successfully steamed along the streets of London, without unfortunately arousing any commercial interest. In the same year Trevithick started to build the locomotive for which he is famous, the first steam locomotive known to have run satisfactorily. This was built for ironmaster Samuel Homfray of Merthyr Tydfil, whose ironworks was building Trevithick stationary engines. It was completed in 1804 and ran trials on the line variously known as the Penydarren or Merthyr Tramroad, of which Homfray was part-owner.

On 21 February 1804, in Trevithick's own words: '. . . we proceeded on our journey with the engine; we carry'd ten tons of Iron, five waggons, and 70 men riding on them the whole of the journey. Its above 9 miles which we perform'd in 4 hours & 5 Mints, . . .'

From a performance point of view, the locomotive was a success. Unfortunately from another point of view it was not. The Penydarren Tramroad was laid with the usual cast iron L-section rails: the weight of the locomotive was too great for them, and too many of these brittle rails were broken for it to be put into regular use.

Remarkably perhaps the next locomotive of Trevithick's type was intended for track which would have been even less suitable. These were the wooden rails of the Wylam Waggonway in Northumberland, which ran more or less level from Wylam colliery along the valley of the Tyne to the river's navigable limit at Lemington. Horses had to haul waggons laden with coal down to Lemington, as well as the returning empties, which gave owner Christopher Blackett a strong motive to seek improved and cheaper means of traction. Having seen the locomotive in 1805, however, he must have realised its unsuitability, for he refused to accept it.

Trevithick made one further attempt to promote the steam locomotive. For several weeks during the summer of 1808 he demonstrated a locomotive, called *Catch me who can* on a circular track in North London. Once again there was no immediate outcome, although J. U. Rastrick, of Hazledine & Rastrick who built the locomotive, became in due course a noted railway engineer, and the demonstrations doubtless helped to impress on the public mind the practicability of steam locomotion.

Blenkinsop and Murray

On the Middleton Waggonway, as at Wylam, it was for the most part necessary for laden waggons as well as empties to be hauled by horses, and at both places escalating prices of horse fodder, caused by the Napoleonic wars, were making operation increasingly uneconomic. John Blenkinsop, the 'viewer' or manager at Middleton, thought that a locomotive so light that it would not break cast iron rails would be too light to haul a worthwhile load by adhesion without constant slipping. The way to avoid this, he thought, would be by what we today call a rack railway, with teeth cast into the sides of the rails and a pinion on the locomotive to mesh with them. He patented his scheme in 1811.

To put it into practice he approached the established Leeds firm of Fenton Murray & Wood, engineers and builders of stationary engines. Matthew Murray of this firm then designed and built for him a locomotive closely based on *Catch me who can*. A royalty was paid to the owners of the Trevithick patent, which Trevithick himself had sold. Murray designed a locomotive with, for the first time, two cylinders. The pistons drove the rack pinion, through rods, cranks and gear wheels, and the cranks were arranged at right angles to one another. This meant that the locomotive would be self-starting in whatever position it had come to rest. Meanwhile the waggonway, upon which iron edge rails had started to replace wood about 1807, was re-laid on one side with rails with cast-in teeth to Blenkinsop's patent – and from now on we must call it the Middleton Railway.

After trials during the summer of 1812, the first locomotive went into regular service on 12 August. It was the first locomotive ever to do so. And it was satisfactory, hauling a useful load, and was soon joined by another locomotive and later two more.

Blenkinsop's locomotives ran on the Middleton Railway for more than twenty years. An eye-witness account of one of them is left to us by David Joy. Joy, a native of Leeds, became a locomotive engineer of note, and his reminiscences survive in the care of the Science Museum. In 1832, however, he was still a child and, as he later recalled:

. . . the old coal railway from the Middleton Pits into Leeds ran behind our house a few fields off, and we used to see the steam from the engines rise above the trees. Once I remember going with my nurse . . . to watch the engine with its train of coal-wagons pass.

We were told it would come up like a flash of lightning, but it only came lumbering on like a cart.

On the Liverpool & Manchester Railway, as we shall see, there were indeed by 1832 locomotives which moved at a speed that seemed to contemporaries akin to that of lightning, and famous they were too. But the Middleton locomotives were becoming old fashioned and wearing out, and from 1835 when horse fodder was cheap and coal prices depressed, their use was discontinued and horses reintroduced. A few other lines which had been built on the same principle had already ceased to operate. The Middleton locomotives in their early years, however, did have a lasting influence on steam locomotive design, and today the preserved Middleton Railway maintains a steam presence in the locality in which they ran.

Wylam

Meanwhile at Wylam, Christopher Blackett had re-laid his wooden waggonway with iron rails, the work being completed in 1808. He had chosen, probably uniquely on Tyneside, to use the L-section plate rails then at their zenith of popularity elsewhere in Britain. Blackett seems to have been particularly well-informed about engineering developments, perhaps a consequence of his being proprietor of the *Globe* newspaper.

It occurred to Blackett's viewer William Hedley that if the wheels of a locomotive, intended to be driven by adhesion, were connected together, then any tendency of one pair to slip would be overcome by the others. Trevithick's locomotives of 1804 and 1805 had been arranged so. Hedley however carried out experiments, first with a model, and then with a full-size weighted test carriage powered by men who turned handles. These experiments, according to Tomlinson (*The North Eastern Railway*), were to establish what relation the weight of an engine bore to the greatest load it was capable of moving from rest. With Hedley satisfied on this point, the full-size test carriage was then used to form the chassis of a locomotive of basically Trevithick type, although, like the Middleton locomotives but unlike the Trevithick originals, its fire tube passed but once through the boiler. It was completed early in 1813. This locomotive was not satisfactory. Its single cylinder gave it a spasmodic and intermittent action and, like many another new class of locomotive to follow, it was shy of steam.

Hedley therefore had another locomotive built, at Wylam by, for the most part, Timothy Hackworth, the foreman smith, and Jonathan Foster, principal engine wright. This time they used a return-flue boiler and placed two vertical cylinders outside it, which in turn enabled them to be enlarged. Drive was through overhead rocking beams, connecting rods and cranks to gears which drove the wheels. The result can be seen by visitors to the Science Museum in the form of *Puffing Billy*, and by visitors to the Royal Museum of Scotland in Edinburgh in the form of *Wylam Dilly*, for the design proved successful enough for more than one locomotive to be built. The two survivors are now to be seen carried on four flanged wheels: these date probably from the 1830s when the Wylam line was re-laid with edge rails. Initially – the first of these locomotives was completed about March 1814 – they were carried on four unflanged wheels for plateway track.

Unfortunately despite Hedley's experiments they still damaged the track, and to reduce the load on each wheel they were rebuilt so that each was carried on two four-wheeled bogies. Bogies were the particular brainchild of William Chapman, who had worked with Jessop and had had built at Butterley about 1812 a locomotive which was to haul itself along a chain. Four of its six wheels were mounted upon a bogie. This locomotive was tried out on a Tyneside waggonway and, though the chain arrangement proved ephemeral, the bogie did not and survived to become a familiar part of locomotive design. Initially it enabled the Wylam locomotives to perform satisfactorily until the line was eventually re-laid.

George Stephenson

On to the stage now appears to the most famous of all people in railway history, George Stephenson. Stephenson had been born on 9 June 1781: his father was fireman of the stationary engine at Wylam colliery and he spent his early years in a cottage, which still stands, beside the Wylam Waggonway. The family in due course moved, but remained in the district. George followed his father into colliery work, starting with the humblest of tasks: but clear mechanical talent had led, despite limited formal education, to quick promotion so that by 1812 he had reached the position of engine-wright in charge of all the machinery of the 'Grand Allies'. This was the combination of coal-owning families Wortley, Liddell and Bowes, which for the best part of a century had taken the leading part in exploitation of the coalfield. His base was at Killingworth, north of Newcastle, where the colliery was served by a waggonway laid with cast iron edge rails.

Late in 1813 George Stephenson's employer Sir Thomas Liddell asked him to construct a steam locomotive in the colliery workshops for the waggonway. At this time a Blenkinsop-type locomotive was being tried out on the nearby Kenton & Coxlodge Railway (owned by the Brandlings), and Stephenson saw this. He was also familiar with locomotive developments at Wylam. The locomotive which he designed and built at Killingworth during 1813–1814 was similar in many respects to Blenkinsop's – it had two vertical cylinders recessed into the boiler and its furnace tube passed but once through it. However, benefiting, probably, from Wylam experience, no rackrail was used. The locomotive entered service on 25 July 1814.

As we have seen, George Stephenson did not invent the locomotive, nor yet the railway. He was, however, the first to build a locomotive driven by adhesion, and carried on flanged wheels which ran on edge rails – the arrangement which became the conventional one, and remains so to this day and indeed for the foreseeable future.

Stephenson's first locomotive, the *Blucher*, was, not surprisingly, far from perfect, tending both to be short of steam and to damage the track. Nevertheless she became the start of a continuing process of development during which locomotives were built and re-built while their defects one by one were alleviated. But apart from this, the surge of interest in steam locomotives died away: for a decade or so, Stephenson alone worked on their development.

2 : From Horse to Steam

Coach Road Improvements

We know now that Stephenson's developments were to have more far-reaching effect than any other in transport at this period – but to his contemporaries this was far from clear, if indeed they knew of them at all. For the period was the great age of road improvements. Two great names were associated with this: John Loudon McAdam and Thomas Telford.

What both had realised, in an age when road surfaces commonly included a mixture of materials ranging from earth and dirt through stones to small boulders, was that to make a good surface, carefully graded material was needed. Stones about one inch across were ideal. Such material, when constantly traversed by iron-tyred vehicles, compacts to form a smooth, water-resistant surface. The tyres grind the stones and the resultant dust fills the gaps, bound there by surface tension of rain water. (There was no tar in McAdam's roads, or Telford's – that was a development of the early twentieth century, when pneumatic tyres started to damage road surfaces by sucking out the dust and stones.)

McAdam also found that turnpike trusts were usually incompetent where not actually corrupt, and their reform became as high a priority with him as improvement of maintenance methods. Eventually McAdam and members of his family were directly responsible, at one time or another, for a total of about 3,700 miles of turnpike roads, and his influence spread far wider still. By the early 1830s, 1,100 turnpike trusts were responsible for about 25,000 miles of road, which was a greater mileage than that of the railway system at its most extensive a century later.

Telford by contrast was more concerned with the engineering aspects

29

of road improvement. His road surface was placed upon a foundation layer of larger stones, carefully positioned and placed on edge. This in turn was carried on a course supported by bridges and embankments, buttressed against the sides of hills or dug through cuttings, for Telford carried out much of his road work in rugged parts of the country, between Glasgow and Carlisle, and between Shrewsbury and Holyhead. The Holyhead Road formed part of the route between London and Dublin, the inadequacies of which had impressed themselves markedly upon MPs from Ireland obliged after the Union of 1801 to travel to Westminster. The most important piece of road engineering upon it, indeed of this whole era of road improvements, was Telford's great suspension bridge across the Menai Strait, completed in 1826, but he also carried out many improvements to the route between London and Shrewsbury, easing gradients and eliminating sharp corners. Telford's improvements to the Holyhead Road were carried out between 1815 and 1830.

Upon it was instituted in 1825 the Shrewsbury *Wonder*, a fast stage coach which covered the 158 miles between Shrewsbury and London by day in fifteen and a half hours. It was the first of many fast day coaches which Telford's and McAdam's improvements made practicable. These brought London into daytime contact with many places which had previously been accessible only overnight. The general effect of the road improvements at this period was to halve journey times, more or less: and although coach travel at 10 mph seems laughable when viewed from the supersonic smugness of the late twentieth century, to those who travelled then it was a marked improvement on the 5 or 6 mph which had been normal not long before. It was achieved only by spectacular skills, such as four-in-hand driving over long distances, and spectacular performances, such as prompt and quick changes of horses at the end of every ten-mile stage. Coaching required widespread and detailed organisation on a scale unknown before. It was for the most part based upon inns whose keepers frequently provided horses under contract to coach proprietors or the Post Office. At coaching inns passengers booked their tickets at the coach office and, in mid-journey, were allowed a brief interval for refreshment. By the second and third decades of the nineteenth century the whole of Britain was covered by networks of fast, efficient mail and stage coach services. They were the wonder of the age.

City transport was improved by the introduction of omnibuses – the first ran in London in 1829 – which avoided the delays of coach offices by picking up and setting down passengers in the street. On these vehicles, rear doors gave access to lengthways seating; from the mid-1840s passenger seats were provided on the roof also.

The nobility continued to use their travelling chariots, the luxurious bodies of which were suspended above traditional perch-based carriages, and the merely wealthy used similar vehicles hired out as post-chaises. But a breakthrough in carriage design had come in 1804 when Obadiah Elliot patented a method of mounting coach bodies on elliptical springs attached directly to the axles. The consequence was greatly to encourage construction of lightweight private carriages: the first of such vehicles, the phaeton, had been introduced in the 1780s, and now they came in many and varied types, on two wheels and four, to be driven not only by coachmen but also, for sport, by their owners. Such vehicles made travel a pleasure where previously it had been a chore.

Not that to some people at least there was not room for further improvement still. W. Bridges Adams (1797–1872) was brought up in a coachbuilding family, and in his book *English Pleasure Carriages* (1837) he has not only left us a detailed description of coaches and the techniques for building them, but also his proposals for improvements. A point which concerned him particularly was that the small front wheels inevitable on carriages of traditional design were an unsound feature, and so was the swivelling front axle itself. He proposed to alleviate this by making the body in separate parts, front and back, and (as we would now say) articulated together at the mid point, with each part of the body mounted on semi-elliptical springs attached to the axles and with all wheels of the same size. Bridges Adams's 'equirotal phaetons' were indeed built on this principle, and did show an improvement in both comfort and safety over vehicles of traditional layout. But Bridges Adams also by the mid-1830s was aware of the coming importance of railways and their vehicles: to these he increasingly turned his attention, and we shall meet him again.

But carriages of any sort were only for the well-off. Most people did not travel at all. If they did, they walked, or travelled by carrier's waggon. Such vehicles had been carrying goods and people since the sixteenth century, and the spread of turnpike roads had meant a spread of carrying services by waggon, and a corresponding decline in carriage by pack horse. Waggons moved slowly, at perhaps two and a half mph, and by the early nineteenth century 'fly vans' were carrying light goods at a faster rate. Both also carried passengers who could not afford coaches but preferred not to walk.

Inland Waterways

The alternative to road transport, for both goods and passengers, was transport by water: by inland waterways and by coastal shipping. By the second decade of the nineteenth century central England was served by an interconnected system of inland waterways – canals, navigable rivers and tideways – which extended from Portsmouth to Ripon, from Maidstone to Liverpool, from Hull to Bristol. Elsewhere, separate river navigations and canals connected ports with their hinterlands. Two canals, the Forth & Clyde and the Caledonian, crossed Scotland and enabled small ships to pass from coast to coast. The main English system was handicapped by the varying dimensions of locks, and therefore of vessels, on different sections.

Along inland routes the waterways, aided by their feeder tramroads, were the principal means of transport for bulk commodities such as coal and limestone. But they conveyed all other forms of goods too, including merchandise and parcels. The latter particularly were carried by 'fly boats' hauled by relays of horses between London, Birmingham and Manchester. Carriers such as Pickford operated both road waggons and canal boats.

Passengers had travelled by river barges for centuries, and the Duke of Bridgewater had started passenger boats on his canal about 1767. Passenger boats then became a smooth, comfortable, dust-free alternative to stage coaches in many parts of Britain, particularly in North West England and on the Scottish canals, and also in Ireland. Throughout most of the canal era, passenger boats were not fast, averaging perhaps four or five mph. Only towards the end of the era was it found that long, lightweight, shallow draft boats hauled by two horses would plane on their own bow waves and could travel at about nine mph.

These 'swift boats' were part of a continuing process of canal improvement. Other examples were construction under Telford of improved sections of canal. The Birmingham new main line, a wide canal with dual towpaths, one each side, followed a direct and largely lock-free course made possible by deep cuttings and long embankments: it replaced the old line which the engineer considered, in a quotation well known but meriting repetition, 'little better than a crooked ditch'.

On the Trent & Mersey at Harecastle, Telford supervised construction of a new and enlarged tunnel duplicating Brindley's original bore.

Gaps in the canal map were being filled: the Edinburgh & Glasgow Union Canal, for instance, completed in 1822 provided an all-canal route between those cities by linking Edinburgh with the Forth & Clyde Canal at Falkirk. The most conspicuous gap on the map, however, was a direct route between the industries of the Midlands and the port of Liverpool. To fill this the Birmingham & Liverpool Junction Canal was authorised in 1826, to run from the Staffs & Worcs Canal near Wolverhampton to Nantwich, whence the Ellesmere & Chester Canal, then isolated from the main system, ran down to Ellesmere Port on the Mersey. A branch of the E & C was authorised to Middlewich on the Trent & Mersey, to provide an improved route from Birmingham to Manchester. Construction commenced under Telford as engineer, using as on the Birmingham new main line the most advanced techniques. Unlike early canals, where the details of layout and construction were left very much to the whim of craftsmen on the spot, the B & LJ with its 39-mile main line was designed as an entity, with standardised (but not inelegant) structures, locks laid out in flights, and construction undertaken by contractors each responsible for about one third of the total.

Coastal Shipping

Over the centuries, development of ships had taken place at a different rate to that of land transport. The breakthrough had come early in the fifteenth century when the ship design traditions of Northern Europe and the Mediterranean had merged to produce the highly manoeuvrable three-masted ships in which the great explorers of the period first crossed the Atlantic and rounded the Cape of Good Hope. Subsequently ships had grown steadily in size, complexity and refinement of design. By the end of the eighteenth century a full-rigged ship had about thirty-seven sails and might carry a load greater than 1,000 tons. Allied to this, the eighteenth century had seen steady increase and improvement in harbour facilities, and in construction of docks.

When Jane Austen removed Mrs Dashwood and her daughters from Sussex to Devon in the opening pages of *Sense and Sensibility* (1811), 'The furniture was all sent round by water. It chiefly consisted of household linen, plate, china and books, with an handsome pianoforte. . . .'

Today we tend automatically to think of ships as a means of crossing seas and oceans where such passages are unavoidable, and forget that in the early nineteenth century, as for centuries before, coastwise shipping provided an alternative to land transport which was in many cases preferable. We have already seen how collier brigs supplied London with coal by sea from North East England throughout the eighteenth century, a trade which would have been impracticable overland at that period. Coastal shipping was also used by travellers, for instance between London and Leith, despite uncertainties which were inescapable when progress was dependent upon the fluctuations of wind and tide. The vessels used were much smaller than those used for ocean voyages, usually carrying less than 100 tons.

Steam Boats in Service

Coastal and estuarial shipping was the first large-scale application of steam power for transport. Once Henry Bell had shown in 1812 that a steam boat could proceed directly into a head wind – a revolutionary feature to those accustomed to sailing ships – and given sufficient power would be largely independent of the tides, there was a rush to build steam boats and put them into coastal service (they were, at first, too small for the open sea). By 1818 there were eighteen steam boats working on the Clyde and nine on the Thames estuary, and they had also reached the Firths of Forth and Tay and the estuaries of the Mersey and the Trent.

All of these vessels were driven by paddle wheels (satisfactory screw propellers were not developed until the late 1830s) and most used low pressure steam; most also carried sails for use when the wind was fair. Canals benefited little from steam propulsion at this stage, for vessels small enough to pass along most of them were too small for bulky steam plant to be fitted; the Caledonian Canal, large enough for ships, was an exception. The first successful sea-going steamer services were introduced in 1818 across the Irish Sea, and by 1821 there were services also between Dover and Calais, Glasgow and Liverpool, and Leith and London. From this period onwards ships propelled partly by steam and partly by sail (to save coal when the wind suited) were starting to make occasional ocean voyages.

The rapid spread of steam boats on estuarial and coastal services was contemporary with coach road improvements and fast coaching inland,

and preceded the development of main line railways by a couple of decades. Indeed Inverness, which got a steamer service to the South as soon as the Caledonian Canal was completed in 1822, had already been enjoying the advantages of mechanical long-distance transport for thirty-six years when its first rail link to the South was completed in 1858.

Horse Railways and Cable Traction

While all these diverse and conspicuous means of transport were increasing and expanding, a much smaller, less conspicuous one was doing likewise in a limited way. Horse railways were on the increase, for both private and public use. Eventually their total mileage was probably between 1,500 and 1,600. New lines used iron rails, usually of L-section but sometimes now edge rails, laid upon stone sleeper blocks. Rails were still of cast iron and short – three feet or so; edge rails, for maximum strength, had their lower edges curved downwards into the form known as 'fish belly'. Their ends butted against one another, held usually in a common chair.

One horse on a tramroad could haul as much as ten on an ordinary road, yet on an edge railway he could haul as much again. Horses and gravity remained the principal form of motive power, but increasing use was made of inclined planes, both self-acting and powered. By judicious selection of route a line could be laid out as a succession of cable-worked inclined planes.

Benjamin Thompson, a Tyneside coalowner, in 1821 developed powered cable haulage into a means of traction for level or near-level sections of line: with a steam engine at each end of a section of waggonway, he arranged that when one engine drew a train of waggons towards it, there was attached to the rear of the train the cable from the other engine, its drum running out of gear. When the train reached the engine towards which it was travelling, the other's cable was ready to be attached to a train about to depart in the opposite direction. This system of 'reciprocal working' was installed continuously over five miles of the Brunton & Shields Railroad, a colliery line on the north bank of the Tyne completed in 1826, where it conveyed trains of waggons at ten mph, or six mph average including stoppages for changing cables.

Here is how a visitor to the region in 1842 described the scene on its cable-hauled railways:

You saw careering over the plain, long trains of coal-waggons, without horses, or attendants, or any apparent cause of motion, but their own mad agency. . . . they were accompanied by the most comical whistlings, and warblings, screamings and chucklings, imaginable. When you came up to one of these mad dragon trains, it was then only that you became aware . . . [that they] . . . were impelled by stationary engines . . . A huge rope running over . . . pulleys or rollers, all in busy motion on their axles, made the odd whistlings and warblings that were heard.*

Back in the early 1820s in the North-East of England, railways were still serving their specialised, coal-carrying function. Elsewhere and with increasing frequency they were being authorised by Act of Parliament, independently of canals. Baxter, in *Stone Blocks and Iron Rails*, notes twenty-two public railways authorised between 1803 and 1821 inclusive, of which only three were not built.

Of those that were, one of them, the 'Oystermouth Railway or Tramroad' which ran westwards out of Swansea, was the first railway upon which passengers were carried. The coach in which they travelled was, of course, horse-drawn, and was started by Benjamin French, a member of the railway company, who paid an annual fee in lieu of tolls. The service started in 1807, but the earliest known description of it, according to C. E. Lee, *The First Passenger Railway*, is that of Elisabeth Spence in 1809: 'This car contains twelve persons and is constructed chiefly of iron, its four wheels run on an iron railway by the aid of one horse, and is an easy and light vehicle.' Other railways gradually followed the Oystermouth example.

This was, too, a time when visionaries started to make serious proposals for extensive tramroad networks. William James, who was thinking of a tramroad from Liverpool to Manchester as early as about 1803, in 1808 proposed a 'General Railroad Company'; in 1819–20 he was proposing a 'Central Junction Railway or Tram-Road' from Stratford upon Avon (he controlled the Stratford Canal) to Cheltenham and London. Only the section from Stratford to Moreton in Marsh was built, as the Stratford & Moreton Railway, in effect an extension of the canal.

---

* William Howitt, *Visits to Remarkable Places;* . . . , quoted by F. D. Klingender, *Art and the Industrial Revolution.*

Thomas Gray published *Observations on a General Iron Railway* in 1820, proposing a system powered by Blenkinsop rack locomotives, and also recommending a line from Liverpool to Manchester.

Stephenson, Stockton & Darlington and Liverpool & Manchester

It was against this background that an Act of Parliament was obtained in 1821 (at the second attempt) for the Stockton & Darlington Railway. This was intended to run from coal mines near Bishop Auckland to Darlington and onwards to the navigable estuary of the Tees at Stockton. For over fifty years there had been proposals for a canal or a tramroad over the route. What the S & DR promoters now intended was a horse-worked plateway similar to those in South Wales, for that was what the engineer who surveyed their line had experience of building. On the same day that the Act received royal assent, however, Edward Pease, one of the principal promoters, received a visit from George Stephenson: Stephenson's ideas on railways were clearly so much more advanced that he was asked to re-survey the line and eventually became its engineer.

For the previous seven years Stephenson had been steadily improving his steam locomotives, with the aid and support of Ralph Dodds and Nicholas Wood who were successive head viewers at Killingworth. Some improvements, such as steam springs formed by pistons working in vertical cylinders let into the boiler bottom, turned out to be blind alleys off the path of progress; others, such as connection of the coupling rods to the wheels directly by crank pins instead of through gears became lasting features of locomotive design (Stephenson seems to have been unaware that Trevithick had used this arrangement on *Catch me who can*). For the time being, however, the wheels were coupled together by chains.

Stephenson's attempts to improve locomotive suspension were complemented by attempts to improve the track. Stone block sleepers often tilted when they settled, producing in effect steps at each joint: to eliminate these he introduced rails with chamfered ends carried in chairs with convex seats. The breakthrough came, however, with development of rails made from malleable iron. Such rails of T-section were patented by John Birkinshaw, manager of Bedlington ironworks, Northumberland, in 1820 – malleable iron rails were already in use on the waggonway which supplied the works with coal from a colliery of which Stephenson was part-owner. In due course he recommended them to the Stockton & Darlington directors: made by passing heated bars of iron between rollers, rails of malleable iron could be made much longer than cast iron rails – up to fifteen feet long or even more – and lacked their brittleness. Here was material to make track fit for locomotives.

Since 1819 George Stephenson had been building the Hetton Colliery Railway in Co. Durham. This was the first railway built to be operated independently of animal power: its eight-mile length included two near-level sections which were operated by Killingworth-type locomotives and totalled three and a half miles; the remaining sections were inclined planes, either powered or self-acting. It was completed in 1822.

In surveying the Stockton & Darlington Railway George Stephenson was assisted by his son Robert. Robert Stephenson had been born in 1803 and George Stephenson ensured that Robert received a formal education such as he himself had missed. In 1822 however he was sent to assist William James survey a railway from the port of Liverpool to Manchester, where the cotton industry was undergoing a phenomenal boom – the 503 bags of American cotton imported through Liverpool in 1792 increased to 412,020 in 1823. There were by this date three waterway routes between Liverpool and Manchester. The oldest used the Mersey estuary and the Mersey & Irwell Navigation, parts of which dated back to the 1730s. The second option was the Mersey estuary as far as Runcorn, and thence the Bridgewater Canal. The third, longer but entirely on still water, involved the Leeds & Liverpool Canal: this had just opened, in 1821, a branch to Leigh where it met the Bridgewater Canal's line to Worsley and Manchester. But rapidly increasing traffic was straining the capacities of all three routes and the carriers upon them.

We shall return to the Liverpool–Manchester route shortly. In the meantime the Stockton & Darlington was being built under George Stephenson alone as engineer, and in 1823 the company obtained a further Act which not only authorised it to adopt deviations which Stephenson had recommended should be made from the intended route, but also authorised it to use 'loco-motive or moveable engines'. The latter clause had a narrow escape from being struck out of the bill by a parliamentary official unable to comprehend its meaning.

The same year George and Robert Stephenson, Edward Pease and Michael Longridge (owner of Bedlington ironworks) joined together as partners to set up a company to build locomotives: Robert Stephenson & Co. of Newcastle. Robert Stephenson himself, who had just returned from Edinburgh University, was appointed managing partner. A year later, however, he had fallen out with his father and left for South America in June 1824. Three eventful years were to pass before he returned and father and son were reconciled. Meanwhile William James too had largely disappeared – or been removed – from the scene, bankrupt in 1823 and imprisoned for debt at the instance of his brother-in-law. In May 1824 the promoters of the Liverpool & Manchester Railway appointed George Stephenson as their engineer in his place.

The L&MR was now gathering valuable support, including William Huskisson, a Liverpool MP and President of the Board of Trade, and John Moss, a prominent Liverpool banker and industrialist. But when in 1825 the promoters went to Parliament for an Act, Stephenson's survey – produced by subordinates and not properly checked – was shown to be grossly inaccurate, and this in the face of strong opposition was enough to cause the bill to be lost. The main opposition had come from landowners and proprietors of inland waterways: there was only limited opposition from a turnpike trust and none at all, it appears, from coach proprietors or carriers. The railway was still seen as a means of transport for bulk commodities at speeds of four to eight mph.

The Stockton & Darlington Railway Open

The Stockton & Darlington Railway was opened on 27 September 1825. It was a long railway for its period, twenty-six miles, of which some twenty-five were complete by the opening day. At its western end successive pairs of cable-worked inclined planes carried it over two ridges, with a section in between worked by horses. Then at Shildon began the relatively level line to Darlington and Stockton: here horses, gravity and locomotives were to be used. Most of the railway was laid with malleable iron rails, though some cast iron survived in sidings; both stone and wooden sleepers were used.

Its first locomotive, *Locomotion*, had been built by Robert Stephenson & Co. in Newcastle: in the absence of Robert Stephenson himself, Timothy Hackworth had come temporarily from Wylam to supervise construction. Then, after a brief return to Wylam, he moved to Shildon to take charge of the S&DR's stationary engines and locomotives.

39

Locomotion was the first locomotive to have her wheels coupled by rods, and with George Stephenson himself driving hauled a triumphant opening-day special train: hundreds of people squeezed on board the coal wagons of which, with the company's single passenger coach, it was comprised; many thousands more came to watch.

Regular coaching traffic on the S&DR started a few days later, on 10 October. The coach was horse-drawn, the driver providing the horse with money loaned to him by the company. Both passengers and parcels were carried. The following spring a contractor took over operation of the coach; other coaches were put on the line and became so popular that within fifteen months of the opening of the railway there were seven coaches operating between Stockton and Darlington. All were horse-drawn, their operators paying tolls to the railway company. It was 1834 before they eventually gave way to company-operated steam passenger trains.

With goods traffic too the company started out by carrying goods itself, then after three months withdrew from the trade and let carriers undertake it, some of them using the company's wagons. So far as horse-drawn coal traffic was concerned, it seems to have been 'led' by contractors from the start; with locomotive-hauled coal trains, the company once again vacillated between paying the drivers fixed wages, which meant that they did not bother to economise on fuel and materials, and contracting with them to haul the coal at a rate per ton, paying their firemen's wages and providing their own materials – which meant they tended to help themselves to coal from laden wagons when no one was looking.

More serious was the poor performance of the locomotives (*Locomotion* had been joined by three more like her). They were, however, being expected to work continuously over a far greater length of run (twenty-one miles) than any locomotives built previously, and they were far removed from the watchful and kindly eye of their designer. But in Timothy Hackworth, responsible for day-to-day running and improvements arising out of experience, they found a worthy substitute. Hackworth, for instance, discovered that drivers were tying down the lever of their weighted safety valve to prevent intermittent loss of steam whenever a jolt bounced it open: the results were explosive, and his reaction was to invent the spring safety valve. Bad riding and shortage of steam were two of the locomotives' particular faults. George Stephenson attempted to produce an improved design of locomotive in the form of the *Experiment* delivered, probably, early in 1828. Its two cylinders were recessed horizontally into the rear of the boiler, driving the front wheels through rocking levers and inclined coupling rods. This meant the locomotive could be mounted on springs. Water tubes were fitted in the firebox to increase the heating surface. Originally this locomotive was placed on four wheels; too heavy for the track, she was soon fitted with six, all coupled by rods.

Meanwhile Hackworth too was developing an improved locomotive. For this he used a large boiler from another locomotive which had been unsuccessful on trial, but which had been purchased for the sake of the boiler. Whether this originally had a return flue, or whether Hackworth now fitted one, is no longer clear: but the effect was to produce a boiler with more than twice the heating surface of *Locomotion*. Hackworth placed two cylinders vertical and inverted beside the rear of the boiler: this meant that drive could be direct, connecting rods to the rear pair of wheels, which were coupled by rods to the other two pairs, for this locomotive had six wheels from the start. The front two pairs were carried on springs. Despite the inconvenient layout dictated by the return flue, which meant that the coal tender had to be propelled at the front of the locomotive where the firedoor was, while the water tender followed in the usual way, ample steaming capacity and plenty of adhesion from her heavy weight meant that this locomotive, the *Royal George*, was well adapted to hauling the heavy, slow-moving coal trains of the Stockton & Darlington Railway: Hackworth used her as the basis of a design of which many more examples were built, with progressive improvements in detail.

Railway Speculations

The period 1824–1826 was one of economic boom and speculative fever. Among the dock companies, insurance companies, turnpike trusts and so on which were promoted at this time, railways had their share of attention and possibly more than their share. Some proposals were no more than speculative promotions designed to relieve the gullible of their money; such no doubt was the London Northern Railroad Company, to link London with Birmingham, Derby, Nottingham, Hull and Manchester. Others, such as a line from Birmingham to Liverpool, went into abeyance when an improved waterway line was successfully promoted. Others yet again were to take root and within a few years grow into railway companies which were authorised and lines which were built – such were proposals for railways from Leeds to Hull and from Newcastle to Carlisle. The latter, like the Stockton & Darlington, was to put paid to proposals for a canal between those places.

Out of all the speculation there emerged, during those three years, Acts of Parliament for perhaps a couple of dozen railways. Many of them were for lines associated with water transport: the Monkland & Kirkintilloch (authorised in 1824), the Cromford & High Peak and the Bolton & Leigh (both 1825) were all originally closely associated with canals, and the Canterbury & Whitstable and Nantlle (1825) and Dundee & Newtyle (1826) connected ports with hinterland. Two railways authorised in 1826, however, were to be in direct competition with existing inland waterways. These were the Garnkirk & Glasgow and the Liverpool & Manchester: and though the L&M was intended as a port-to-hinterland line, the G&G which ran parallel to the Monkland Canal had minimal contact with waterways.

The Marquess of Stafford

We left the Liverpool & Manchester promoters having failed to get an Act of Parliament in 1825. This they took as a setback rather than a total defeat, and sought a replacement for George Stephenson as engineer. They appointed as their engineers in chief the brothers George and John Rennie whose father had been one of the greatest of canal engineers, and they in turn chose Charles Blacker Vignoles as chief surveyor to survey a new route. C. B. Vignoles (1793–1875) had been orphaned in infancy and brought up by his grandfather, who was professor of mathematics at the Royal Military Academy, Woolwich. After training in mathematics and to some extent law, he had quarrelled with his grandfather and set out to seek his fortune in America where he surveyed large areas of South Carolina and Florida. By the mid-1820s he had returned to England and done surveying work for the noted civil engineer James Walker on London docks and Fen drainage, and then, in 1825, for the Rennie brothers on a railway proposed from London to Brighton. For the Liverpool & Manchester, Vignoles's route avoided the estates of the principal land-owning objectors, and terminated in Salford rather than Manchester to avoid a crossing of the navigable Irwell, but it increased the estimated cost of the line by one quarter, from £400,000 to £500,000.

At this stage it was clearly necessary for the railway promoters to come to terms with the canal interest, and a new prospectus avoided the anti-waterway polemic which had been a feature of the earlier one. The key figure was the Marquess of Stafford, nephew of the Duke of Bridgewater, who had died in 1803, and recipient of the income from the trust set up under the duke's will to administer his Worsley estate, of which the Bridgewater Canal formed the most important part. Early financial struggles by the duke to build the canal were now long past: by the 1820s profits from the canal were enormous – £80,697 in 1824 – and with the estate's other income had made the marquess one of the wealthiest men in Britain, perhaps the wealthiest. But the marquess had no say in the management of the trust which produced his income. Under the duke's will, this was vested entirely in R. H. Bradshaw, Superintendent and one of the three trustees.

Approaches to Bradshaw by the railway promoters had been met by implacable opposition. They therefore decided to approach Stafford direct. In this they had two remarkable pieces of good fortune. The first was that their principal counsel before Parliament, Mr Adam, was a relative of James Loch, Principal Agent of the Marquess of Stafford. Loch was a liberal and in favour of the railway: through him, negotiations were opened with the marquess. The second piece of good fortune was that William Huskisson, who had come into the railway scheme to support his commercial constituents, was an old associate of Stafford since the time when the marquess had been British ambassador in Paris during the French Revolution and Huskisson his secretary. It was Huskisson who talked round not only the marquess but his second son on whom the income from the estate was entailed – the full fascinating story emerges in F. C. Mather's *After the Canal Duke*. The consequence was that, more or less simultaneously, the marquess not only released substantial capital for improvements to the Bridgewater Canal, and invested in the Birmingham & Liverpool Junction Canal which would bring traffic to the Bridgewater and serve his industrial interests in east Shropshire, but he also agreed to invest in the Liverpool & Manchester Railway to the extent of £100,000 with the power to appoint three of its fifteen directors. James Loch became one of them.

So the railway promoters simultaneously eliminated the core of the opposition and raised the substantial additional finance they needed. It was a coup compared with which the efforts of today's city financiers pale into insignificance. The Liverpool & Manchester Railway's bill went through Parliament in 1826 and received the Royal assent on 5 May.

Stephenson Returns to the L&M

The terms required by the Rennies to act as engineers for construction of the L&MR proved unacceptable to the board and George Stephenson was appointed in their place. Despite his poor performance earlier there was still a faction among the directors who believed, correctly, that he possessed the practical railway engineering experience they now needed. Vignoles, too, after starting to stake out the line, soon parted company with Stephenson who by now would have little to do with the civil engineering establishment and anyone connected with it. For Vignoles, this rejection at such a promising stage in his career was the last thing he needed, and, as I shall mention below, various subsequent developments in the evolution of the railway system suggest continuing animosity between Vignoles and Stephenson. For the moment, however, Stephenson had experience of building railways, and Vignoles had not: the line that he had laid out was built by George Stephenson and his assistants. Some of these, notably Joseph Locke, were to become famous railway engineers in their own right. Construction was undertaken by a system akin to direct labour, with Stephenson acting in effect as both engineer and contractor to the company, responsible with his assistants for deciding how much the labourers should be paid for what we would now call piecework. Telford, sent to inspect by the government from which the company had requested a loan, was highly critical, for such an arrangement was inefficient and open to abuse. Perhaps Stephenson, mindful of the loss of the 1825 bill largely through his lack of attention to detail, was now determined to keep everything closely under his own control.

The railway they built included some notable engineering works — more ambitious than anything built previously for a railway, and on a par with those built for canals. They included the 2,250-yard tunnel beneath Liverpool itself, up from the docks to Edge Hill, the two-mile-long rock cutting at Olive Mount, as much as 70 ft deep, and the viaduct over the Sankey valley and the Sankey Brook Navigation with nine arches of 50 ft span and a height of some 70 ft. In 1829 the company obtained a further Act which did enable it to cross the Irwell by a two-arched skew bridge and terminate in Manchester at Liverpool Road, close to the Bridgewater Canal basin. The length of the railway was to be about thirty-one miles and its track was laid with malleable iron fish-belly rails fifteen feet long, weighing 35 lb per yard, carried in places upon stone blocks and elsewhere upon wooden cross-sleepers. As with Stephenson's earlier railways, and based on the usual sort of gauge of Newcastle waggonways, the gauge of the track was 4 ft 8 in. The additional half-inch to produce the British standard gauge was introduced later.

Horses, Locomotives or Cable Haulage?

While the Liverpool & Manchester Railway was being built, the Bolton & Leigh Railway nearby was completed and opened, for goods traffic, in 1828. It had been laid out by George Stephenson, although he did not supervise construction, and included two powered inclined planes; elsewhere locomotives and horses were employed. At Leigh the line connected with the Leeds & Liverpool Canal, to provide a route to Liverpool: but with the L&MR under construction not far away, a further Act was obtained in May 1829 for the Kenyon & Leigh Junction Railway to link the two railways. The same day an Act was obtained for another branch of the Liverpool & Manchester, the Warrington & Newton Railway, and shortly afterwards an Act was obtained by the Newcastle & Carlisle Railway. At sixty-three miles this was by far the longest railway so far authorised: but its Act restricted it to haulage by horses.

Indeed there was at this period a reaction against the use, actual or potential, of steam locomotives. Railway promotion had now had so much publicity that people feared that the country was about to be filled by monstrous locomotives lumbering along and, when they did not actually explode, obliterating everything beneath their smoke. The promoters of the Liverpool & Manchester Railway, who had earlier taken use of steam locomotives almost for granted, eventually kept very quiet about them during the course of their successful application to Parliament.

Furthermore, during the 1820s the spotlight was again on possible use of steam carriages on ordinary roads: no doubt the improving roads of this decade provided encouragement. Although road steam carriages were meeting the same sort of opposition that railway locomotives were meeting, during the mid-1820s their technicalities made faster progress. Their arch-protagonist was Goldsworthy Gurney: by 1829 he had developed a steam 'drag', or light tractor, with a water-tube boiler and horizontal cylinders between its frames driving a cranked rear axle. On trial in July that year one such vehicle ran from just outside London to Bath, hauling a barouche with four passengers, at an overall speed of six mph including all stops for water, fuel and so on. Gurney planned a network of steam carriage services.

On rails, the inadequacies of the Stockton & Darlington locomotives, prior to the introduction of *Royal George* late in 1827, were well known: it was rumoured that locomotive traction was to be abandoned in favour of horses. On the Hetton railway one of the locomotive-worked sections had indeed been converted to reciprocating cable haulage in 1825. By the middle of 1828, as the works of the Liverpool & Manchester Railway began to progress towards completion, successful operation of railways elsewhere by stationary engines and cable haulage was manifest: successful operation by locomotives was not.

The company's directors found themselves in a dilemma, one faction favouring cable haulage, another locomotives. They agreed only that the amount of traffic anticipated would be too great for horses, and obtained powers from Parliament to provide the whole mechanical power necessary for working the railway. Successive delegations were dispatched to examine methods used in North-East England, and reported in favour, to a greater or lesser extent, of cable haulage. The most notable of these delegations comprised engineers James Walker and John Urpeth Rastrick. Their conclusion was that if the railway was to be equipped to carry the whole of the anticipated traffic from the opening day it should have reciprocating cable haulage: only if traffic was to be built up gradually might locomotives be used.

The chief protagonists of the locomotive were the company's treasurer, Henry Booth, and its engineer, George Stephenson. It is often suggested (in for instance Rolt's *George & Robert Stephenson* and Carlson's *The Liverpool & Manchester Railway Project*) that Stephenson was at this period resolutely opposed to cable haulage. Yet his stance was a curious one and would merit further investigation. Certainly he had plenty of personal experience of cable haulage: he had engineered more than one line employing it, and he was closely involved with the Canterbury & Whitstable Railway even then under construction, with most of its route comprised of cable-worked inclined planes on gradients so easy that in the future the whole line was to be worked by locomotives without difficulty. He indeed provided the Liverpool & Manchester itself with a complex but well-designed cable haulage installation at Edge Hill, to work the tunnels down to the docks and upwards to the passenger terminus at Crown Street.

Maybe he had sufficient experience of railways operated by cable haulage to be all too well aware of its defects − notably that a single breakdown anywhere on the line would bring all traffic to a halt. He was certainly better placed than anyone else on the Liverpool & Manchester to appreciate the steam locomotive's potential for improvement − for just this had been the main pre-occupation of Robert Stephenson since his return from South America late in 1827. In its development, and the future prosperity of Robert Stephenson & Co., George Stephenson had a strong personal interest: they would clearly have been hampered if the L&M had chosen cable haulage: yet he may equally have been motivated by a genuine belief that the locomotive would be much superior to cable haulage − earlier he had not hesitated to recommend malleable iron rails for the Stockton & Darlington despite personal financial interest in a patent for rails of cast iron.

Robert Stephenson was aware of the progress made by the road steam carriage engineers, particularly Gurney, and he was also aware of the areas in which steam locomotive design most needed improvement: better steaming and better riding. His first locomotive looks as though he took *Experiment*, built during 1827 for the S&DR but possibly not delivered until early in 1828, as his starting point. Robert Stephenson retained the inclined connecting rods but removed the cylinders from within the boiler and placed them outside, to the rear of the locomotive. They were mounted not vertically, as on Hackworth's locomotives, but at an angle approaching forty degrees to the horizontal, to align with the connecting rods − through them the pistons drove the front pair of wheels directly. This arrangement meant that, like *Experiment*, all wheels could be mounted on springs. To increase the heating surface, rather than have a return firetube, two parallel single-pass firetubes each containing a furnace were used. This locomotive was ordered by the Liverpool & Manchester Railway in January 1828 but transferred before delivery to the Bolton & Leigh, where she had arrived in time for the opening on 1 August, and where she was named *Lancashire Witch*. She seems to have performed satisfactorily, but evidently the mechanical

47

arrangements were better than the boiler, for while Robert Stephenson then built a series of locomotives with cylinders similarly inclined, he experimented with various different types of boiler without great success.

Rainhill – The Entrants

It was against this background that the directors of the Liverpool & Manchester Railway sought a way out of their dilemma by holding a prize competition: a premium of £500 over its price was offered for the most improved locomotive engine. Their concept of what the most improved engine might be expected to do seems modest in retrospect, and is indeed an indication of contemporary inadequacies. If it weighed six tons (the maximum to be permitted) it was to haul day by day on the level a train weighing twenty tons, or less in proportion to its weight, at a speed of ten mph.

The idea had originated with James Walker: the competition became famous as the Rainhill Trials of October 1829. Along one and three-quarter miles of completed track at Rainhill, some nine miles from Liverpool, contestants' locomotives were to run up and down ten times – equivalent to a journey from Liverpool to Manchester, and then after re-fuelling do the same again to represent the return journey. The average speed, it was eventually decided, should be not less than ten mph – one eighth of a mile was allowed at each end of the course for speeding up and slowing down. A working pressure of 50 lb per sq. in. was envisaged, and in accordance with the railway's Act of 1826, locomotives were to 'consume' their own smoke – in practice this meant that they burned coke instead of coal.

Announcement of the competition seems to have prompted every crank in the land to approach the company with his proposals, and ten locomotives were later said to be in preparation for it. Four steam locomotives and the *Cycloped*, worked by a horse upon a sort of treadmill, eventually appeared, and the performance of one of the locomotives was so abysmally bad that it was withdrawn. That left three serious entrants: *Rocket*, entered by George Stephenson, Robert Stephenson and Henry Booth in partnership, *Sans Pareil* entered by Timothy Hackworth, and *Novelty* entered by partners John Braithwaite and John Ericsson. *Rocket* had been built at Newcastle, tried out at Killingworth, and taken in parts by road to the Solway and thence by sea to Liverpool. *Sans Pareil* was built at Shildon and tried out briefly on the S&DR before being taken to Rainhill by road. *Novelty* was built in London and was probably delivered to Liverpool by Pickford, by canal: on arrival at Rainhill she was untried. Nevertheless, at the start of the trials, she was popularly considered the favourite.

Ericsson was a Swede with an inventive turn of mind, who had come to England to seek his fortune three years earlier, and entered into partnership with Braithwaite, who had an engineering works in London. Here they had built in 1828 the first practical steam fire engine, and on the layout of this was based *Novelty*, which was built in six weeks. Vignoles helped to finance her, and rode on her at Rainhill. As a vehicle, she was probably the best of the three locomotives: her frame was mounted by springs on four equal-sized wheels, and one pair of wheels had a cranked axle driven by near-horizontal connecting rods. These were driven from two vertical inverted cylinders through bell cranks. Her boiler had in effect two components: one was large, vertical and cylindrical, mounted at one end of the frame, with an internal firebox, which had water all round it and was fed with fuel from a hopper above; the other, branching from the vertical component, was a horizontal cylinder of much smaller diameter which extended to the far end of the frame: through it a small-diameter tube carried hot gases from the fire, turning back on itself twice to traverse the length of this cylinder three times before emerging as a vertical exhaust pipe. Bellows driven by the engine delivered a forced draught to the furnace. Supplies of water and coke were carried aboard the locomotive.

Hackworth's *Sans Pareil* was a small version of his Stockton & Darlington goods locomotives – though not small enough in that she was over the stipulated maximum weight, but was allowed to take part. Vertical inverted cylinders drove one pair of wheels directly and these were coupled to the others. The boiler had a return-tube furnace. Axle bearings were mounted direct on the boiler and no springs were fitted – another non-compliance with the conditions – but cylinders which are unusually long in relation to piston stroke suggest they may have been envisaged. As it was, an observer commented that she 'rolls about like an empty beer butt on a rough pavement'.

The appearance of *Rocket*, the most successful and famous of the three locomotives, is familiar to everyone: but the secret of her success lay hidden within her multi-tubular boiler. This was Henry Booth's idea (though Marc Seguin in France was simultaneously and independently working on the same principle) – that to raise the greatest quantity of steam in a short time and a small space, the hot gases from the fire should be taken not through a 12 in. diameter tube of half-inch thick iron but rather through a multitude of 2 in. or 3 in. diameter tubes of $1/16$ in. thick copper. The Stephensons accepted the idea and Robert, not without some difficulty, built the boiler with twenty-five tubes of 3 in. diameter. A water-jacketed firebox was added at the rear of the boiler barrel, and at the front a tall chimney. The boiler/firebox assembly was mounted on frames of wrought iron bars, which were in turn carried on springs supported by the axles. The cylinders, inclined like *Lancashire Witch*'s, drove the front wheels, 4 ft 8½ in. diameter; the rear wheels, uncoupled, were smaller 'wagon wheels' (amongst her many other distinctions, the practice of making the unpowered carrying wheels of a locomotive smaller than the driving wheels seems to have originated with *Rocket*). For adhesion, the greater part of *Rocket*'s weight was concentrated on the front wheels: but this, the thrust from the inclined cylinders and the tall chimney combined to make her sway badly at speed.

Steam was distributed to *Rocket*'s two cylinders by slide valves. These were worked by rods from loose eccentrics on the driving axle, which were themselves driven by pegs fitted to it and positioned appropriately for forward or reverse running. Each valve was connected by a short rod to a small rocking lever or handle, so that their positions could be altered manually to reverse her. When running, notches in the ends of the two eccentric rods fitted over pins on the handles so that the valves were worked automatically: while the locomotive was being reversed, the ends of the eccentric rods had to be lifted to disconnect them from the handles. A disadvantage of this system was that whenever the locomotive was in motion, there were two levers rocking to and fro on the footplate.

A wooden tender, with water barrel and coal space, was provided by the railway company for the locomotives which needed it. It was built by Liverpool coachbuilders Worsdell & Son.

Rainhill – The Results

The event that was the Rainhill trials has often been described. A good recent description appears in Rolt's *George and Robert Stephenson*; a detailed contemporary description appeared in successive issues of

Mechanics' Magazine in October 1829, complete with engravings of the entrant locomotives and echoes of the controversies that the contest aroused – although from the favourable opinion repeatedly expressed of *Novelty* one is left with the impression that the editor must have been in Ericsson's or Vignoles's pocket!

The judges appointed were Nicholas Wood, J. U. Rastrick and John Kennedy, a Manchester manufacturer of machinery. Crowds estimated as large as between 10,000 and 15,000 gathered to watch the fun. A grandstand was provided.

The first few days were occupied by trial runs and demonstrations of each of the three locomotives. During these *Novelty* achieved a speed of 28 mph: so, running light, did *Rocket*. However when the locomotives were put through their 'ordeal', *Rocket* alone was able to do all that was required, and considerably more. On 8 October *Rocket*, almost certainly driven by George Stephenson, alternately pushed and pulled the wagons of stone which represented her train up and down the course nineteen times at speeds around 14 mph; then, on her last run (when she had already in effect made a continuous journey of some sixty-six miles, far longer than any journey made by a locomotive previously) she was opened up to run the one-and-a-half mile course in 3 minutes 44 seconds – a little over 24 mph.

Sans Pareil when put to the ordeal on 13 October trundled up and down methodically for a couple of hours covering about twenty-five miles when she failed from a cause reported at the time as being a 'burst feed pipe' but which was in fact probably a defective cylinder casting which allowed steam to blow through to exhaust. *Novelty* fared even worse: during an early test run, the boiler feed pipe gave way, with the result that the water level fell and the internal flue pipe was damaged by overheating. To get access to this to mend it, joints on the boiler and the flue had to be broken and re-made, with cement which took a week to harden. So anxious, however, were her builders to get on with the ordeal that they prevailed upon the judges to let their locomotive undertake it within a few days, although the joints were, as Ericsson put it, 'rather green'. The consequence was that soon after *Novelty* started her third round trip, when she was running at fifteen mph, the joints started to blow so badly that the ordeal had to be abandoned.

The company therefore made its award for *Rocket*. Although dissension rumbled on for some time afterwards, the die was cast in favour of the locomotive, the Stephenson locomotive.

Rainhill – The Consequences

Rocket was purchased by the L&MR and, modified to improve her performance still further, became part of Robert Stephenson's continuing process of improvement in locomotive design. The story of this is continued in chapter seven. *Sans Pareil* too was purchased by the company, though in 1831 she was sold for use on the Bolton & Leigh Railway where, in circumstances less demanding than those of the L&MR, she ran successfully for many years. Braithwaite & Ericsson did not sell *Novelty* to the L&MR, but kept her there for some time for modifications and improvements. It seems unlikely that her bellows-driven forced draught arrangement would ever have enabled her to steam adequately over a distance, and M. G. Satow surmises (*Railway Magazine*, November 1980) that the modifications included fitting some form of centrifugal blower, to enable her to reach speeds claimed to have been as high as 40 mph. Certainly two later locomotives, *William the Fourth* and *Queen Adelaide* which Braithwaite & Ericsson built for the L&MR in 1830 were so fitted – these however despite enlarged boilers were unsuccessful in traffic. *Novelty* herself was subsequently used on the St Helens and North Union Railways – which will be mentioned below – and fitted with a multi-tubular boiler in 1833. I speculated in *The Archaeology of the Transport Revolution* that Ericsson might have then re-used the original boiler during experiments with a steam-propelled canal boat also called *Novelty*.

Parts of the original *Novelty* locomotive survived to be included in a non-working replica now at Greater Manchester Museum of Science & Industry; *Rocket* and *Sans Pareil*, or what is left of them, are to be seen in the Science Museum. Working replicas of all three were built for the 150th anniversary celebrations in 1980, that of *Rocket* becoming the property of the National Railway Museum.

The real significance of Rainhill, however, was far greater than simply to establish the form of motive power for the Liverpool & Manchester Railway. Rainhill demonstrated that man was now freed from the constraints of animal power for land transport, that he was going to be able to travel two or three times faster than animal power had ever permitted, with consequent reductions in journey times. Liverpool and Manchester, four and a half hours apart by coach, would be separated by less than two hours by rail, and the effect would be repeated wherever steam railways were built. This was widely understood at the time (though not invariably accepted immediately). All the improvements made to transport over the preceding century with so much effort were insignificant by comparison: and no subsequent advance in transport (with the possible exception of that of Wilbur and Orville Wright) has had so great a significance as that provided by George and Robert Stephenson and Henry Booth at Rainhill in 1829.

3 : How the Railway System Grew

Into the 1830s

So far in the development of railways their various aspects – track, vehicles, motive power, the extent of railways themselves and the influences upon them of other forms of transport – have been so closely interwoven that it has been possible, indeed necessary, to consider them together. Their story now becomes too complex to be treated in this way. So this chapter and the next describe only the mainstream historical development of the railway system, and particular aspects and influences are described in those which follow them. The story is taken to about 1860; but it is so diverse in its components and their rates of development that a specific cut-off date is scarcely practicable.

In the two decades prior to 1829 the well-to-do were leading a secure and settled existence, benefiting from the results of a long period of improvements in technology and in transport. The period has un-comfortable similarities to the years pre-1914: the coming change was to be mercifully neither so catastrophic nor so tragic – but its effects in changing everyday life were to be almost as great. Not that the effect was immediate: when the Cromford & High Peak Railway was opened (the first section in the summer of 1830 and the rest the following year) it was very much the mixture as before – horse traction and inclined planes, cast iron rails and stone blocks, and a canal link at each end. When the Canterbury & Whitstable Railway was opened in May 1830, however, passenger trains were for the first time regularly hauled by a steam locomotive – for Robert Stephenson's latest locomotive *Invicta*, which is described in chapter seven, hauled them (none too satisfactorily, it seems) over the short section of that line which was not operated by cable haulage.

As Manchester prospered on cotton, so Leeds prospered on cloth, and

1 Remains of a wooden railway were excavated at Ironbridge in 1986, having been found within a layer of iron furnace slag. Traces of two sleepers and two rails are seen here, the rails butting against one another as a joint supported by a sleeper. This has had an additional timber pegged to it, top left of picture, probably to enable horse's hoofs to grip.
(*Ironbridge Gorge Museum Trust*)

2 (*below*) A short length of narrow gauge plateway of Curr's type is preserved on its original location at Cheddleton Flint Mill, Staffordshire.
(*Author*)

3 Opening the Stockton & Darlington Railway, 1825.
(*Trustees of the Science Museum, London*)

4, 5, 6 The principal contestants in the Rainhill Trials, as depicted in the contemporary *Mechanics' Magazine: Novelty, Sans Pareil* and *Rocket*. (*Mary Evans Picture Library*)

7 Opening of the Liverpool & Manchester Railway was celebrated by
commemorative pottery: the mug depicts Ericsson's *Novelty* and the
Stephensons' *Northumbrian*, and the jug shows the railway at Edge Hill,
Liverpool.
(*Elton Collection: Ironbridge Gorge Museum Trust*)

8 The ordered confusion of the London & Birmingham Railway under
construction through north London, vividly described in words by Dickens in
Dombey and Son, is here illustrated by J. C. Bourne in his lithograph.
(*Elton Collection: Ironbridge Gorge Museum Trust*)

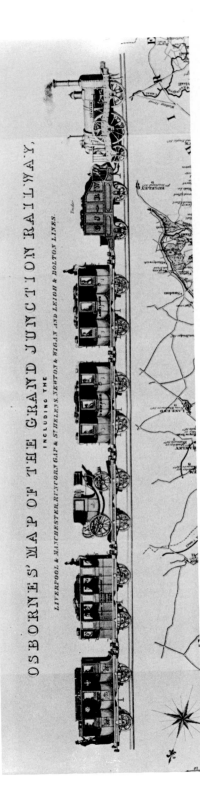

OSBORNE'S MAP OF THE GRAND JUNCTION RAILWAY,

INCLUDING THE

LIVERPOOL & MANCHESTER, RUNCORN GAP & ST HELENS, NEWTON & WIGAN AND LEIGH & BOLTON LINES

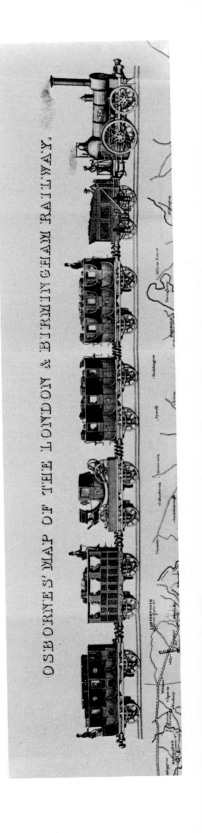

OSBORNE'S MAP OF THE LONDON & BIRMINGHAM RAILWAY.

9, 10 Trains of the Grand Junction and London & Birmingham Railways were illustrated on the borders of the maps accompanying Osborne's guides to these lines. Locomotives of Stephenson's and Bury's types are respectively shown hauling trains comprising two first class carriages, a carriage truck carrying a private carriage, a second class carriage, and a mail coach with the Post Office mail guard seated aloft facing his mail boxes on the roof.

(Trustees of the National Library of Scotland)

equally needed improved communication with the coast. The Leeds & Selby Railway was authorised in May 1830: steam boats on the tidal River Ouse would, it was considered, extend the line to Hull. James Walker was its engineer, and had laid it out so that either horses or locomotives might be used. Two railways to be connected with the Liverpool & Manchester Railway also received their Acts of Parliament in May 1830: the Wigan Branch Railway and the St Helens & Runcorn Gap Railway. For both, C. B. Vignoles became engineer: and while the Wigan line was a straightforward branch of the L&M, the St Helens, en route from St Helens itself to the Mersey, was to cross over the L&M by a bridge, perhaps the first instance where two public railways with conflicting routes were separated in this way. A curve linked the two lines.

Opening Day on the Liverpool & Manchester

During the first half of 1830 the Liverpool & Manchester Railway approached completion. New and improved locomotives were delivered by Robert Stephenson & Co., carriages and wagons were built, and many trial trips were run, some of them with passengers – directors, shareholders, public. With experience gained, 15 September was settled as the date for the ceremonial opening. The Duke of Wellington as prime minister was the principal guest: Sir Robert Peel attended, and so did William Huskisson. Around 700 people were carried in eight special trains: 50,000 gathered along the line to watch.

The railway was laid with double track and the special train carrying the duke travelled on the southern line: all the rest travelled in procession on the northern. At Parkside, the half-way point, locomotives were to take water, the duke's special remaining stationary while the other trains overtook it one by one. Passengers in the duke's train had been requested to stay on board: but many got down on to the track. When the third train on the northern line approached, drawn by *Rocket* which was driven by Joseph Locke, those on the track scattered: Huskisson, who is said to have been accident-prone, seems to have gone first one way and then back again, to attempt to climb into the duke's carriage. He slipped and fell with a leg doubled across one of the rails: it was run over by the locomotive and several carriages and he was seriously injured.

The locomotive *Northumbrian* was detached from the duke's train

55

and, driven by George Stephenson, carried the wounded man at the unprecedented speed of thirty-six mph to Eccles, to which place surgeons were brought from Manchester in an attempt to save Huskisson's life. Sadly this was in vain: he died later the same evening. The event was doubly tragic in that, as we have seen, without Huskisson there would probably have been no Liverpool & Manchester Railway, at least not in the same form.

After the accident the special trains continued sombrely to Manchester and eventually safely back to Liverpool, but in the confusion that had naturally resulted it was 11 pm before some of the passengers reached their destination.

Liverpool & Manchester Railway Traffic

The following day a special train carried fare-paying passengers for the first time from Liverpool to Manchester and back, and on the day after, 17 September, timetabled passenger services commenced. The company had powers both to charge tolls for use of its line by others, and also to carry on its own behalf: in practice, it had decided to exercise the latter powers, to own and operate its own trains. Deputy chairman John Moss was largely responsible for this move, and additional capital had been raised to set up a carrying department, with the rolling stock, warehouses, etc. which it would need. Back in 1826, what the company had expected that it would eventually carry was principally cotton, coal and merchandise. But Rainhill had changed all that: plans to carry goods were laid aside for the time being, and the company concentrated on passengers.

At first, locomotive-hauled trains of first class coaches ran over the line three times a day; second class was soon introduced, and the number of trains increased. They had to be: rail travel was not only much quicker than road, it was also cheaper, and provided a journey (according to *The Times*'s correspondent) 'performed more easily, equably, steadily, and comfortably'. It had cost twelve shillings inside and seven shillings outside to travel by coach from Liverpool to Manchester: now it cost seven shillings first class and five shillings second by train. The consequence was not merely that passengers deserted the road for the railway, but that far more people travelled. Before the railway was opened, the twenty coaches which ran daily between Liverpool and Manchester had a total capacity of 108,000 passengers a year, if they had all been full. The railway, in its first year, carried 460,000 passengers between its termini. By 1832 all the coaches had been withdrawn but one, which carried mostly parcels. Takings at turnpike gates slumped. Over the next couple of decades, this was to be an increasingly familiar story wherever the steam railways were built.

During the first year, passenger trains averaged seventeen mph, taking about two hours for the journey. The speed was imposed by the condition of the track (of which more in chapter nine): enginemen could, and did, achieve quicker times between the termini, for which they were reprimanded. On the other hand, many unforeseen circumstances could make a journey take longer: the company publicised the departure times of its trains, but not their arrival times. Sunday travel was a matter which exercised the consciences of the directors: they decided eventually that trains should not run during the hours of church services, which in practice meant most of the morning and the early afternoon. It was the sort of compromise which many subsequent railways were to make. The first connecting passenger train service came in June 1831 when the line from Kenyon Junction to Bolton was opened to passenger traffic.

Liverpool & Manchester Railway passenger trains seem to have carried parcels from the start, and from early in November 1830 they also carried the mails. This was the start of a long-lasting and by no means invariably harmonious relationship between railways and the Post Office, which is described in chapter five.

It was early in December 1830 before the L&MR was opened to freight traffic. One reason for the delay was that the directors had been waiting for delivery of more locomotives, particularly *Planet*. Robert Stephenson's *Planet*, with her firebox within the boiler shell, her chimney mounted upon an opening smokebox for ease of access to the boiler tubes, and her horizontal cylinders beneath it, was both the culmination of his immediate line of development (of which *Rocket* had been a stage reached in passing) and the prototype of all subsequent conventional steam locomotives. Of all this, there is more in chapter seven.

The first freight train carried nearly fifty-two tons of merchandise, including cotton, flour and oatmeal, in eighteen wagons, and regular goods trains were then introduced. But they did not see the same immediate outstanding success of the passenger trains: water transport proved a more effective rival than road to the new railway. Although the journey by goods train took three hours compared with twelve to fifteen by barge, this in effect only meant delivery the same day instead of the day following. By lowering tolls and charges, waterways and their carriers remained competitive; and though goods traffic on the L&M railway increased over the ensuing years, so, in general, did traffic on the Bridgewater Canal. The canal's profits, however, did not. Even the canal's passenger traffic continued and was not decimated as the road coaches were – it seems that although the waterway journey between Liverpool and Manchester took longer than the rail journey, it was cheaper. The eventual ascendency of railways over waterways was a much more gradual affair than their ascendency over roads, and the continuing interaction between rail, road and canal is described in chapter ten.

Local Lines

So the rapid development of the steam locomotive during the period when the L&MR was being built meant that this railway, which had been promoted for port-to-hinterland goods traffic, found its immediate success with passengers, mails and parcels, and became the prototype for city-to-city trunk railways soon to be built. Nevertheless the momentum of existing practices meant that for a while some lines continued to be built in ways which came to seem increasingly old-fashioned. The Edinburgh & Dalkeith Railway, opened in 1831, was a horse railway, and so were the associated Bristol & Gloucestershire and Avon & Gloucestershire Railways opened between 1832 and 1835. The Festiniog Railway was authorised in 1832 and the Whitby & Pickering in 1833: both were completed as horse railways as late as 1836. Of these the E&D and W&P operated horse-drawn passenger traffic, the Festiniog, using the North Wales two-foot gauge, was operated largely by gravity, and the E&D, Festiniog and Whitby & Pickering all included inclined planes operated by cables. George Stephenson himself in 1830 or 1831 (wrote Gordon Biddle in the Journal of the Railway & Canal Historical Society for November 1963) despite Rainhill recommended no less than five cable-worked inclined planes in an improved route for the Lancaster Canal Tramroad.

It was not built, but away in the North East of England Robert Stephenson was consulting engineer for the Stanhope & Tyne Rail

Road. When this was opened in 1834 its motive power included self-acting inclined planes, stationary engines with cable traction, and horses as well as locomotives. This railway, which had evolved out of the waggonway traditions of the region, was built using the old system of wayleaves, by a company which was in effect a partnership with unlimited liability – and when it collapsed in 1839 almost ruined Robert Stephenson who had been rash enough to accept shares in lieu of a fee. In the same region the Durham & Sunderland Railway, a public line opened in 1835 (though it never reached Durham), was laid out for cable traction throughout, with several miles of reciprocal working; this was used not only for goods and mineral trains but also for passenger trains which were soon being operated by cable traction over nearly ten miles of its line. Much further south the London & Blackwall Railway was opened in 1840 with cable haulage of passenger trains throughout its near-level line: but to control operation of its obsolescent method of traction it used the latest in communications equipment – the electric telegraph. From this it gains its place in history, and so is described more fully in chapter six.

Other railways were less hesitant about adopting the new locomotive technology demonstrated on the Liverpool & Manchester Railway. The Warrington & Newton and Wigan Branch Railways, which connected with it and were opened in 1831 and 1832 respectively, were locomotive lines from the start. The Wigan Branch Railway subsequently amalgamated with the then unbuilt Wigan & Preston to form the North Union Railway, successfully completed to Preston in 1838. The Garnkirk & Glasgow Railway obtained two Planet-type locomotives from Robert Stephenson & Co. for the opening of its line in 1831, though horses also were used. The Leicester & Swannington Railway, opened in 1832–3, had George Stephenson as a substantial shareholder and Robert Stephenson as engineer, and so was a locomotive line, although it included two powered inclined planes, and much of its traffic was coal transferred to canal boats at Leicester. The Bodmin & Wadebridge Railway, the first locomotive-worked railway in Cornwall, was opened in 1834, and the Dublin & Kingstown Railway, the first steam railway in Ireland, had Vignoles as its engineer and was opened in December the same year.

Those were short lines, but the twenty-one-mile Leeds & Selby Railway benefited fully from the experience of the Liverpool & Manchester, and was built as a double track main line for locomotive working without inclines. It opened for passenger trains in September 1834; goods traffic started three months later.

Steam trains ran into a London terminus for the first time in 1836 with the opening in December of the first section of the London & Greenwich Railway. It was completed to Greenwich in 1838; meanwhile powers had already been obtained for the London & Croydon Railway, which was laid out as a branch from the London & Greenwich and opened in 1839. Its trains ran over the London & Greenwich for one and three-quarter miles from the terminus at Tooley Street (which later became London Bridge) to the junction at Corbett's Lane, and tolls were paid by the Croydon company for use of this section.

When the first section of the Newcastle & Carlisle Railway was ceremonially opened to passenger traffic, from Blaydon near Newcastle to Hexham in March 1835, steam locomotives hauled the trains. This produced an injunction from one of the landowners; the company had to revert temporarily to horse traction and obtain a further Act of Parliament to permit the use of locomotives. The remainder of the line was opened by stages, Carlisle being reached in 1838.

There was a fever of railway promotion in North East England in the 1830s, of which the Stanhope & Tyne, Whitby & Pickering and Durham & Sunderland Railways were but three results. Much of it was connected with development of coal ports at South Shields, Sunderland and Hartlepool, and with the extension to the East Coast of the Newcastle & Carlisle Railway. Rival groups of promoters battled their way through intricate negotiations and disputes, juggling routes and powers, potential and actual. The most important outcome of all this was the Brandling Junction Railway, successfully promoted by members of that ancient coal-owning family to complete a link between the N&CR, Gateshead, the Stanhope & Tyne, South Shields and Monkwearmouth, which is on the Wear opposite Sunderland. The junction railway was authorised in 1836 and opened to goods and passenger traffic in 1839. With its opening there was railway communication from Carlisle through to South Shields, and the nucleus of a local system of interconnected railways in North East England was established. But it was already clear that very soon these would become part of a far greater, national, system.

The Grand Junction

The effect of the success of the Liverpool & Manchester Railway on subsequent local lines was great, but even greater was its effect on proposals for long-distance railways. What had seemed to most people fanciful and unnecessary in the mid-1820s was now clearly both practicable and desirable. So the early and mid-1830s were the period when the first great trunk railways were surveyed, authorised and eventually built: but building them was a much greater task than building the local railways just mentioned, so the decade was nearing its end before the first of them was completed.

One immediate effect of the L&M was to put new heart into promoters of railways to link Liverpool with Birmingham, and Birmingham with London, and committees for both were soon formed. Early in 1831 a committee was formed for a railway from London to Southampton, and early in 1833, after various false starts, for a railway between London and Bristol. For clarity it is necessary to consider separately how these schemes developed, though many of the events were contemporaneous. Indeed by the time the London–Southampton committee was formed, the Liverpool–Birmingham promoters had already made two unsuccessful applications to Parliament and were putting the final touches to the survey for a third. This line, to be called the Grand Junction Railway, was to start from the Warrington & Newton Railway at Warrington, and run by Stafford and near Wolverhampton to Birmingham, seventy-four miles. George Stephenson was engineer, with Joseph Locke doing the detail work on the northern part of the line and J. U. Rastrick on the southern. Likely objectors were either bought off or their lands avoided: and the Grand Junction Railway Act received the Royal Assent on 6 May 1833.

John Moss was chairman of the Grand Junction Railway Company, and many of his associates from the Liverpool & Manchester Railway were among its proprietors. The 'Liverpool party' were to finance many railways up and down the country – George Stephenson raised much of the money needed for the Leicester & Swannington in Liverpool – and became correspondingly influential in railway circles. The position with the Grand Junction's engineers was less happy: Locke and Stephenson were becoming incompatible with one another. In 1833 Stephenson and Rastrick were the principal engineers and Locke assistant on the northern half of the line, but the situation deteriorated by stages so that eventually in 1835 Locke, at just thirty years of age, became engineer-in-chief for the railway and Stephenson nominally consultant, while Rastrick had, perhaps tactfully, withdrawn. Precise causes of dispute seem not to be recorded, but it may have had something to do with Stephenson's and Locke's respective attitudes towards construction by contract. Stephenson, who had built the Liverpool & Manchester to Vignoles's plans by direct labour, seems on the southern part of the Grand Junction to have had difficulty in providing plans and specifications to enable contractors to tender. Locke, on the other hand, had made himself at home with construction of the line in sections by contract, the system perfected earlier by the canal builders, and the building of the Grand Junction went ahead in this way. The pupil seemingly had excelled the master. In 1835 the company took over the Warrington & Newton Railway, so that its line would extend from Birmingham to the L&MR at Newton Junction.

London & Birmingham

As early as the summer of 1830, George and Robert Stephenson were asked to report on the respective advantages of two routes proposed for the railway from London to Birmingham, and were then engaged to survey their preferred route via Rugby and Coventry. Early in 1832 the London & Birmingham Railway had a bill before Parliament. But although the idea of railways was becoming accepted north of Birmingham, in the region between Birmingham and London it was still a novelty. Landowners were strongly opposed to invasion of their acres. Moreover the proposed route closely paralleled, mile after mile, not only the great Grand Junction Canal, but also the Holyhead Road: the product of fifteen years of improvements by Telford, the route of the Shrewsbury *Wonder*, the greatest coach road in the kingdom. So to opposition from canal interests was added, at last, strong opposition from turnpike trusts and coach proprietors.

It is worth noting too that landowners had a vested interest in horse-drawn transport, for it was on their land that fodder for the horses was grown, while individually many were also turnpike trustees. Their opposition was strong enough to stifle development of steam road coaches at this period, which were in any case now being rapidly outclassed by railways, and it was to be several decades before serious attempts were made to reintroduce mechanical transport on to British roads.

The bill for the London & Birmingham Railway had an extremely rough ride in Parliament, yet passed the Commons only to be thown out by the Lords, many of their lordships being personally among the landowners opposed to it. Yet others were in favour, notably Lord Wharncliffe, one of the Grand Allies of the coal-owning North East: and when the bill was re-presented in the following session, it passed almost without opposition, receiving the Royal Assent in 1833 on the same day as the Grand Junction Railway. The promoters, like their northern counterparts, had been busy 'conciliating', or buying off, the opposition. The cost of land needed had risen from the original estimate of £250,000 to some £622,500; the capital required for the railway had originally been put at £1,500,000, but the capital authorised by the Act had risen to £2,500,000. The cost of obtaining the Act was itself almost £73,000. High parliamentary expenses were to become an all-too-familiar story, hindering development of the railway system and leading to companies which were overcapitalised.

For the unhappy shareholders in the London & Birmingham, however, this was no more than the beginning. For whereas Joseph Locke was finding construction of the Grand Junction none too difficult a task – the principal obstacles were the crossings of the Mersey and (twice) the Weaver – Robert Stephenson, engineer responsible for building the London & Birmingham at the age of twenty-nine, had very much more difficult country to contend with. Here, too, George Stephenson had either withdrawn or, perhaps, been quietly usurped by his son. But as his assistant on the London & Birmingham, Robert Stephenson had George Parker Bidder. As a child Bidder had been the prodigy known as 'The Calculating Boy' from the facility with which he performed complex calculations in his head by self-discovered methods. Robert Stephenson had first met him at Edinburgh University. Before long he was working directly for Robert Stephenson, and became his right-hand man, associated with him in numerous engineering enterprises, and becoming particularly skilful as a Parliamentary witness.

The immediate problem on the London & Birmingham arose from the fact that George Stephenson had left his son with the considered opinion that the railway should be built with a ruling gradient no steeper than 1 in 330 – through country much of which comprised a series of ranges of hills, and intervening low ground, lying transversely across the route. The consequence was that he had to build a series of long and deep cuttings, at Tring, for instance, and Roade, and long tunnels – Primrose Hill, Watford, and, longest and through quick-sands by far the most difficult to build, Kilsby – interspersed by long and high embankments. Only the first mile or so from Euston to Camden Town was steeper, and that was worked by cable haulage. The London & Birmingham Railway was 112¼ miles long and was probably the greatest and most extensive work of civil engineering that had ever been undertaken. By the time it was complete the company had been back to Parliament more than once to raise its authorised capital to £5,500,000.

The most vivid near-contemporary description of the L&B under construction is the famous passage in which Charles Dickens in *Dombey and Son* describes the scene as the first railway is built in North London:

> Traces of its course were visible on every side. Houses were knocked down; streets broken through and stopped; deep pits and trenches dug in the ground; enormous heaps of earth and clay thrown up; buildings that were undermined and shaking, propped by great beams of wood. Here, a chaos of carts, overthrown and jumbled together, lay topsy-turvy at the bottom of a steep un-natural hill; there, confused treasures of iron soaked and rusted in something that had accidentally become a pond. Everywhere were bridges that led nowhere; thoroughfares that were wholly impass-able; Babel towers of chimneys, wanting half their height; tempor-ary wooden houses and enclosures, in the most unlikely situations, carcases of ragged tenements, and fragments of unfinished walls and arches, and piles of scaffolding, and wildernesses of bricks and giant forms of cranes, and tripods straddling above nothing. . . .
>
> In short, the yet unfinished and unopened Railroad was in progress; . . .
>
> But as yet the neighbourhood was shy to own the Railroad. One or two bold speculators had projected streets; and one had built a little, but had stopped among the mud and ashes to consider farther of it. A bran-new Tavern, redolent of fresh mortar and size, and fronting nothing at all, had taken for its sign The Railway Arms; but that might be rash enterprise – and then it hoped to sell drink to the workmen. . . . The general belief was very slow. There were frowzy fields, and cow-houses, and dunghills, and dustheaps, and ditches, and gardens, and summer-houses, and carpet-beating grounds, at the very door of the Railway.

Dickens wrote this in 1846 or thereabouts, recalling the scene of ten or a dozen years earlier. How he describes the same scene, nearer the date of writing, we shall see below.

Navvies and Contractors

The Grand Junction and London & Birmingham Railways were built by pick and shovel, with minimal mechanisation. Temporary track was laid for horse-drawn tipping wagons which took spoil from cuttings to be dumped where embankments were needed. Most of the physical labour was done by navvies: formerly 'navigators', their description inherited from those who had built canals, they were men who could shovel twenty tons of muck a day, developing immense appetites and greater thirsts. Railway construction brought them together in hordes – 3,000 along five miles of the L&B at Blisworth, 1,000 at Kilsby alone – living in shanty towns, some with wives and many with women, they were ignorant of religion and the use of money, they drank their pay, terrorised the villagers and died young, all too often in accidents at the workings; or, in a few cases, prudently saved their pay, became first sub-contractors and then contractors and died old and rich. Railway navvies became a familiar phenomenon throughout the Victorian era wherever railways were built.

So did railway contractors. When the GJR and the L&B were built they were still in a fairly small way of business – construction of the former was let in lengths no greater than ten miles, the latter only six – and even then many of the L&B contractors failed financially. On the GJR one of the small men was Thomas Brassey, successful tenderer for and builder of Penkridge viaduct. It was the start of a railway-building career which was eventually to make him the greatest of all railway contractors able, like other great contractors such as S. Morton Peto and Joseph Firbank, to build entire railways and command an army of navvies.

Southampton and Bristol

The London & Southampton Railway was wanted not only by commercial interests but also by the Admiralty, which felt that in time of war ships could load and unload at Southampton and avoid the dangerous narrow seas leading to and from London, and by the War Office which saw its value for deploying troops in similar circumstances. It was authorised by Parliament in 1834; its engineer was Francis Giles, previously of canals and the Newcastle & Carlisle Railway, who nevertheless seems to have been unequal to his task, and Locke was called in in his place.

If the London & Southampton's original choice of engineer was dull, the choice of engineer for the London-to-Bristol railway was spectacular, inspired: Isambard Kingdom Brunel. Brunel, son of a French émigré father and an English mother, was aged twenty-six when appointed – a brilliant workaholic, yet a man of spirit and character, already set to become perhaps the greatest of all Victorian engineers, not only in railway building but in ship building too. Brunel laid out a route of easy curves up the Thames valley and a ruling gradient of 1 in 344, steepened to 1 in 100 for a few miles of the descent from the Cotswold escarpment, through the long Box Tunnel, towards Bath. The line was given the title Great Western Railway; opposition in Parliament came from landowners, coach proprietors, the Thames Navigation and the Kennet & Avon Canal, and also from the London & Southampton Railway Company which was thinking in terms of a line to Bristol which would diverge from its own at Basingstoke. Opposition by one railway company to the proposals of another was soon to become a very familiar story. But the GWR it got its Act, in 1835.

The most famous feature of Brunel's Great Western Railway was its broad gauge. Most railways were being built to the Stephenson gauge of 4 ft 8½ in. – only a few varied from it, and that usually only by a few inches and they were far away in Scotland. Generally the gauge was specified in a railway's Act of Parliament, but it was omitted, probably by oversight, from the London & Southampton Act (although this was built to 4 ft 8½ in. gauge) and again from the GWR Act, this time at Brunel's instance. For Brunel had decided the gauge between the rails should be wider – it was eventually settled at no less than 7 ft 0¼ in. In his own words:

> Looking to the speeds which I contemplated would be adopted on railways, and the masses to be moved, it seemed to me that the whole machine was too small for the work to be done, and that it required that the parts should be on a scale more commensurate with the mass and velocity to be attained.*

* Evidence of I. K. Brunel to the Gauge Commissioners, 25 October 1845.

He was, of course, absolutely right. But the drawback lay in the difficulties of interchange wherever his railways met another. As the railway system spread the gauge question would within a few years become a matter of national controversy and concern. One immediate effect was that the GWR was unable to share the London terminus of the London & Birmingham at Euston, as had been planned, and had to build its own at Paddington.

Another effect of establishment of the broad gauge was that the 4 ft 8½ in. gauge became known, at this period, as the 'narrow gauge'. It does not seem to have become known as the 'standard gauge' until after the Gauge of Railways Act 1846, which we shall encounter in due course. But because 'narrow gauge' has subsequently come to mean gauges of less than 4 ft 8½ in., and 'standard gauge' is the term now familiar, I shall be using it here to describe the 4 ft 8½ in. gauge, except where quoting contemporary sources.

The Boom of 1836

Now the pace of railway promotion hotted up. By 1835, Henry Grote Lewin tells us in *Early British Railways*, there were in the British Isles 41 different railway companies (excluding horse tramroads) authorised to construct 970 miles of railway, of which 338 were complete. With the evident success of these, and a favourable financial climate, there were then 57 railway bills put before Parliament in 1836, with the result that 35 Acts were passed, of which 29 were for new companies, involving a total of 955 miles of line.

Some of these Acts were for railways which were in effect segments of great trunk routes. The route from the South to Newcastle was to be formed by the Midland Counties Railway which would run from Rugby, on the London & Birmingham, to Nottingham and Derby; the North Midland, from Derby to Leeds; the York & North Midland, from Normanton on the North Midland to York, and the Great North of England from York to Newcastle. To be connected with these were to be the Birmingham & Derby, the Birmingham & Gloucester and, in the North, the Manchester & Leeds which would in fact join the North Midland at Normanton. Elsewhere the Cheltenham & Great Western Union and Bristol & Exeter Railways would extend the GWR, the Hull & Selby would extend the route of the Leeds & Selby to Hull, and the Eastern Counties was to run from London to Norwich and Yarmouth, while the Northern & Eastern was to diverge from it at Stratford and go to Cambridge, with hopes of eventual extension to York. In Ireland the Ulster Railway was authorised to build from Belfast to Armagh, and the Dublin & Drogheda between the places of its name.

Parliamentary activity continued on a lesser scale in 1837. The London & Brighton Railway, after a fierce battle in Parliament between competing schemes, was authorised to run from Croydon, to which point railway communication from London was already authorised, to Brighton; and the route of the South Eastern Railway, which had obtained an Act the previous year to run from Croydon to Dover, was altered so as to leave the London & Brighton at Redhill. The Lancaster & Preston Junction was authorised to extend the route under construction from Euston to Lancashire, the Sheffield, Ashton-under-Lyne & Manchester Railway obtained its Act over a route for which a canal had long been proposed, and two short associated lines were authorised in Scotland, the Glasgow, Paisley & Greenock and the Glasgow, Paisley, Kilmarnock & Ayr.

The great engineers were at work on these railways. George Stephenson was associated with the North Midland, particularly, and with the Birmingham & Derby, York & North Midland and Manchester & Leeds. J. U. Rastrick was engineer to the London & Brighton, Brunel to the broad gauge lines which extended the Great Western, and C. B. Vignoles to the Midland Counties and the Sheffield, Ashton-under-Lyne & Manchester. Vignoles and Braithwaite surveyed the Eastern Counties, and Braithwaite and Ericsson were involved in building it until Ericsson left for the USA in 1839; and the Northern & Eastern was surveyed by James Walker. The Glasgow, Paisley & Greenock employed as secretary Mark Huish, who although only twenty-six had already served ten years in the East India Company's army, latterly as quartermaster. It was the first railway company appointment of a man who was before long to become the most notable, and perhaps the most controversial, of early railway managers.

In Ireland, government commissioners had been appointed in 1836 to 'enquire into the manner in which railway communication can be most advantageously promoted in Ireland'. The whole of Ireland was at this date part of the United Kingdom, and in terms of population a relatively far more important part of the British Isles than now, for the population of Ireland was then approaching 8 million, while that of Great Britain was some 18 million. The commissioners employed

Vignoles to assist them over the southern part of the country, and John MacNeill (who had learned his engineering under Telford on the Holyhead Road) over the northern; and in 1838 produced a comprehensive report with proposals for a series of trunk lines throughout the country.

The track gauge which was recommended for these was 6 ft 2 in. This almost certainly originated from Vignoles who, like Brunel, had come to the conclusion that a broader gauge than 4 ft 8½ in. would be desirable. He considered that a gauge of 6 ft would give useful additional space for the machinery of locomotives, and enable coaches to have wider bodies. He would have liked to have used it on the Dublin & Kingstown, but had been over-ruled by the directors who, since they would be obtaining rolling stock from England, preferred the gauge prevailing there (one of the locomotives was tried out on the Liverpool & Manchester before shipment). Besides, they said, on such a short line the gauge could easily be altered if necessary. . . . Vignoles would have liked 6 ft for the Eastern Counties, too, but Braithwaite would go no wider than the 5 ft gauge to which the line was built. In Ireland, however, the Ulster Railway was built to the commissioners' 6 ft 2 in. gauge.

In 1838 the Edinburgh & Glasgow Railway was authorised, and then for a few years there was very little activity in promotion of further railways. This was a period of financial depression, and available financial resources and engineering skills were fully stretched in construction of railways already authorised — indeed in some instances, notably the Eastern Counties and Northern & Eastern, great plans proved over-ambitious and only parts of such lines were actually built.

London to Preston by Train

Throughout most of the speculative period of the mid-1830s none of the trunk lines promoted in the image of the Liverpool & Manchester was complete, and in *English Pleasure Carriages* published in 1837 W. Bridges Adams could still write, 'As yet there is no existing railroad which can be considered more than experimental'. That same year saw two great steps forward, however: the openings of the Grand Junction Railway, and of the first section of the London & Birmingham.

The Grand Junction Railway commenced operations on 4 July 1837: there had been trial runs earlier, and on and from that date a full service of trains for passengers, parcels and mails commenced between Birmingham and Manchester, and Birmingham and Liverpool. I put it that way intentionally, for although great crowds gathered at the lineside there was remarkably little by way of opening ceremony: the GJR's chairman, deputy chairman and engineer had all-too-vivid eye-witness memories of the Huskisson disaster, and furthermore King William IV had recently died, and the railway commenced operations during the period of mourning which followed his death. To us in retrospect it seems perhaps more significant that this, the first long-distance trunk railway, came into use within a fortnight of Queen Victoria's reaching the throne.

The first northbound train of the GJR reached speeds as high as forty mph, and conveyed portions for both Liverpool and Manchester. It was divided at Warrington, and both parts reached their termini after a journey of about four and a half hours, at an average speed of about twenty-two mph. This speed, which sounds so modest by present-day standards, was of course more than double that to which people were accustomed. The pattern of operation became the usual one: the Grand Junction paid tolls to the Liverpool & Manchester Railway for passengers and parcels which it carried over the L&M line. Similar arrangements were made for freight traffic which, on the GJR as on the L&M, commenced later than passenger traffic, in February 1838. Whishaw notes that the Grand Junction had its own booking offices at the Liverpool and Manchester termini of the L&MR, and also its own goods depots; and at Edge Hill, Liverpool, were the Grand Junction's coach-building establishment and one of its two 'chief locomotives-establishments' (sic), the other being at Birmingham.

The very much more difficult and extensive engineering works of the London & Birmingham Railway, compared with the Grand Junction, caused many delays to its completion. The first section from London to Boxmoor, however, was opened to passengers on 20 July 1837, two and a half weeks after the Grand Junction, and was extended to Tring in October. In the same year George Carr Glyn, influential city banker, became chairman. The following April the railway was extended to Denbigh Hall, where it crossed over the Holyhead Road north of Bletchley, and at the same time the line was brought into use between Birmingham and Rugby: a service of stage coaches, operated by noted coach proprietors Chaplin & Horne, was introduced between Denbigh Hall and Rugby to link the trains. The principal feature causing delay on the incomplete section was Kilsby tunnel, into which the last brick was eventually inserted with ceremony on 21 June 1838. On Sunday 24 June one train in each direction ran through between London and Birmingham: this service was advertised on Sundays and may have run on some weekdays also according to the state of the continuing construction works. Finally on 17 September 1838 the London & Birmingham Railway was formally opened throughout and a full train service instituted.

London was now in direct railway communication not only with Birmingham, but also with Liverpool and Manchester. When the North Union Railway was opened just over a month later (Vignoles brought *Novelty* out for a triumphant opening run) there was railway continuously from London as far north as Preston, 218 miles from Euston. On the L&BR, those early trains were for first and second class passengers: goods traffic seems to have started in November 1838, and third class passenger traffic not until 1840.

South Western and Great Western

Earlier than this, in May 1838, the first section of the London & Southampton Railway was opened, from Nine Elms to Woking: it was extended by stages, with at one period the gap caused by an intermediate and incomplete section being filled, London & Birmingham style, by connecting coaches, until the whole line was opened in 1840. By then the company had decided to build a branch to Gosport, for Portsmouth, and diplomatically changed its name to the London & South Western Railway.

The first section of the Great Western Railway was opened in 1838 too, in June from Paddington to Taplow, following a ceremonial inaugural special on 31 May. Among the 250 guests was William Fothergill Cooke, who in uneasy partnership with co-inventor Charles Wheatstone was about to install the first electric telegraph line, alongside the railway from Paddington to West Drayton. Of the remarkable story of the invention of the electric telegraph at this date, and its development and mutual influence with the new trunk railways, there is more in chapter six. The broad gauge was already coming in for criticism – though much of this seems to have been politically inspired by investors of the Liverpool party. With the gradual elimination of defects in track and locomotives, speeds of 40–50 mph became common, compared with 30 to 40 on the standard gauge Grand Junction. Higher speeds were obtained on trial, on both gauges. The Great Western was eventually completed through to Bristol in 1841, by which date the Bristol & Exeter was also open as far as Bridgwater.

By that date indeed many other railways were open, and the nucleus of a national English system established, for many of the railways authorised during 1836–7 were completed during the years 1839 to 1841. During this period were opened the lines which were to link, to each other and to the existing London–Birmingham–Preston route, Derby, Sheffield, Hull, York, Darlington, Leeds, Lancaster, Chester, Birkenhead, and Gloucester. Traversing the Pennines the Manchester & Leeds Railway was opened in 1841, but Woodhead tunnel delayed completion of the Sheffield, Ashton-under-Lyne & Manchester Railway until 1845, the line being completed by Locke after Vignoles found himself in financial difficulties from investing in the railway too heavily, to get it started during the depression. Elsewhere the Taff Vale, first of many steam railways in the South Wales valleys, was opened in 1840; so was the Chester & Crewe Railway, which was absorbed by the Grand Junction before opening. It diverged from the older company's line at Crewe: this was the origin of the railway importance of that place, until then open Cheshire countryside, which was confirmed with the removal thither in 1841 of the Grand Junction's locomotive works from Edge Hill. The year 1841 also saw completion of the London & Brighton Railway. The two Paisley lines were opened by stages during 1839–1841, and owned the Glasgow–Paisley section jointly: joint ownership of a line by two (or more) companies was later to become a common practice.

Competition and Amalgamation

The most important route completed at this period was that which linked York with the London & Birmingham, and the first part of this to be opened, in 1839, was the northern section of the York & North Midland, from York as far as a junction with the Leeds & Selby. Here for the first time we encounter George Hudson (1800–1871), the former draper's apprentice who had inherited a fortune of £30,000 and elevated himself to become Lord Mayor of York, following the dubious financial practices customary in local government at this period. He had also become chairman of the YNMR.

The following year saw the YNM extended to join the North Midland Railway near Normanton: with the North Midland opened from Derby to Leeds, this meant that there were two routes between York and Leeds of which that via the North Midland, though longer than via the Leeds & Selby, contained the greater mileage of YNM track. Therefore competition broke out between the companies for the York–Leeds traffic, and also, with the Hull & Selby Railway opened, for the Hull–Leeds traffic. Hudson's response was for the YNMR to take a lease of the Leeds & Selby (which had never been very profitable) and close it between Leeds and the junction, forcing all passengers on to his own longer route.

The success of this manoeuvre must have encouraged Hudson on his meteroric career of railway financing, construction and company manipulation which was to gain him the name of the Railway King – prior to an even more sudden downfall in the late 1840s. It was only after that that the Leeds & Selby line, which was also closed to freight for a few years, was eventually re-opened. But Hudson's longer route remains available when engineering works temporarily close the direct line – as in the author's recent experience when travelling from Leeds to York on a Sunday.

To revert to the late 1830s: in the corridor between the London & Birmingham Railway and Leeds, continuing conflict between Charles Vignoles and George Stephenson is evident. The first railway in this district was Stephenson's Leicester & Swannington Railway, and coal supplied by it to Leicester was cheaper than coal brought by water from the Erewash valley, Leicester's previous source of supply. The Erewash coal owners therefore promoted their own railway to Leicester: this eventually materialised as the Midland Counties Railway. On its board were James Cropper and Theodore Rathbone – both of whom had been among the promoters of the Liverpool & Manchester Railway, but were by no means supporters of George Stephenson. Cropper in particular had been the great proponent of cable traction, and subsequently supported Braithwaite and Ericsson. It comes as no surprise, therefore, that Vignoles was chosen to engineer the line.

The Midland Counties as authorised and built ran from the London & Birmingham at Rugby via Leicester to the viaduct over the Trent near Sawley, where it divided, one line going to Nottingham, the other to Derby. It therefore missed out altogether the Erewash valley, which runs northwards along the Nottinghamshire–Derbyshire border, but Vignoles surveyed the route north along it.

This brought the line into conflict with Stephenson's North Midland (Derby–Rotherham–Leeds), the London traffic of which it would have abstracted. The North Midland therefore prevailed upon the adjoining Birmingham & Derby – also in the Stephenson camp – to alter its name to Birmingham & Derby Junction and, more important, its route, diverting south to join the London & Birmingham at Hampton-in-Arden and so providing an alternative to the Midland Counties. Birmingham was eventually reached by a branch.

Although the three companies (and the two engineers) managed to co-operate sufficiently to build a joint station at Derby, the inevitable consequence, once all these lines were open, was ruinous competition between the Midland Counties and the Birmingham & Derby Junction for the traffic from London to the North East. It was to be alleviated only in 1844 when George Hudson, who had got himself on to the Midland Counties board, successfully promoted amalgamation of the two railways together with the North Midland to form to Midland Railway. That is to jump ahead: in the meantime passengers had found themselves able to travel from London to York in eleven hours, and London had been supplied with its first rail-borne coal – from mines developed by George Stephenson at Clay Cross, Derbyshire, where coal had been found during construction of the North Midland's tunnel at that place.

To Scotland and Ireland

By 1840, passengers could travel from Euston to Lancaster, 238 miles, in through carriages in 11 hours – a journey which, four years earlier by coach all the way, took 26 hours. For two years they had also been able to travel by steam all the way from Euston to Glasgow – by train from Euston to Liverpool, and thence by steamer; then in 1840 a new steamer service went to Ardrossan, whence passengers continued to Glasgow over the new Glasgow, Paisley, Kilmarnock & Ayr Railway. In fact, although this service was claimed to bring London within 24 hours of Glasgow, it was not a success, passengers still preferring traditional land routes. But ever since the Grand Junction Railway had been authorised, it had been thought of not merely as a link between

Birmingham, and Liverpool, but as part of future links between London and Scotland, and London and Ireland.

The routes that these links should take, however, had become matters of controversy. Locke had surveyed routes through Cumberland, Westmorland and Southern Scotland in the late 1830s. In 1839 government commissioners in the form of Lt Col. Sir Frederick Smith, RE, and Professor Peter Barlow were appointed to enquire into the best means of communication between London, Dublin, Edinburgh and Glasgow. Barlow, of the Royal Military Academy, Woolwich, had already served on the 1836 commission on railways for Ireland. They considered in detail possible Anglo-Scottish routes ranging from the extreme East Coast to the extreme West, and then in 1840 reported:

> We are led to believe that the amount of traffic which . . . may be expected between Edinburgh and Glasgow and the South is not such as would be likely to afford an adequate return for the outlay of two distinct lines of railway, the one from Darlington to Edinburgh and the other from Lancaster to Glasgow . . .

Therefore they proposed that the route should be northwards from Carlisle and over Beattock, thence dividing into lines to Glasgow and Edinburgh. Time would eventually show that the commission had got its route right, if not its projections of traffic.

The commission was similarly awry in its preference for the Irish route. Here the big obstacle was the Menai Strait: the commission preferred what was basically the route eventually built, from Chester to Holyhead, but to avoid the need for a second bridge across the Menai it proposed that a railway should be laid across Telford's suspension bridge and carriages drawn across by horse or stationary engine. All of this meant that for years the mainland harbour of Porthdinllaen, on the north side of the Lleyn Peninsula and almost as far west as Holyhead, was a strong and plausible contender for the rail/steamer interchange on the route to Dublin. Its drawback was that its approach, through North and Mid-Wales, lay through much more rugged country than the Chester and Holyhead route along the North Wales coast. Nevertheless several routes were proposed and surveyed, the engineers involved including both Vignoles (at the behest of the Irish Railway Commissioners of 1836) and, later, Brunel. The latter's route, broad gauge, would have gone from Didcot via Worcester and Newtown. For both

Scotland and Ireland it was to be some years before the routes were finally settled.

Inspectorate, Clearing House and Royal Journeys

By the late 1830s the old concept of a railway as a sort of public highway was finally breaking down – it had become clear that the complexities of operating a railway were so great that they must remain the responsibility of the owning company. The position of carriers, however, continued to remain equivocal for some years and is described in chapter ten. In 1840 'An Act for Regulating Railways' obliged railway companies to give notice of opening lines to the Board of Trade, and also obliged them to make returns to the board of accidents attended with personal injury. The Board of Trade was given power to appoint inspectors; a further Act in 1842 reinforced its powers. Thus was established the Railway Inspectorate – a corps of government inspectors whose principal tasks, then as now, were to inspect and approve new railways before they were opened, and to investigate the causes of railway accidents with a view to preventing repetition. This department's principle of supervision without interference was established with the support of some noted engineers – such as George Stephenson – and the distrust of others – such as Brunel. It remains an outstanding example of how the Victorians could get things right.

With more and more railways coming to form part of a connected system, the principal railway companies themselves in 1842 set up the Railway Clearing House to apportion the receipts from through traffic, both passenger and freight, and to record the movements of wagons and carriages away from the lines of their owning companies. It was to become an enduring feature of inter-railway co-operation.

The new form of transport received the seal of royal approval when Queen Victoria travelled by rail for the first time in June 1842. The journey was from Slough to Paddington, 'in half an hour, free from dust and crowd and heat, and I am quite charmed with it', wrote the young queen to her uncle, the King of the Belgians. Prince Albert, and the dowager Queen Adelaide, were already regular travellers by train.

The Atmospheric Railway

At this period an alternative to the steam locomotive appeared which would, it seemed, offer not only better speed, cleanliness, acceleration and gradient-climbing ability but also freedom from collisions. This was the atmospheric system of traction demonstrated by the brothers Jacob and Joseph Samuda and their partner Samuel Clegg on a section of the West London Railway in 1840–1. Its principles are pretty well known: a large-diameter cast iron pipe, with a longitudinal slot along the top, was laid between the rails, and the train attached by an arm through the slot to a piston within this pipe. A stationary steam engine exhausted the air from the pipe ahead of the piston which, with the train, was then propelled forward by atmospheric pressure: the slot was kept air-tight by a leather flap which an apparatus on the train opened ahead of the arm and subsequently re-sealed.

As demonstrated this system produced good enough results to attract the attention of the principal engineers of the day. The Stephenson camp stood aloof – not, it appears, because they foresaw any great technical problems in the system's achieving what it set out to do, but because dependence on successive stationary engine houses and a 'rope of air' was too close for comfort to the principles of cable traction which they had defeated at Rainhill a dozen years previously. Other engineers – notably Vignoles and Brunel – were, as we can say with the benefit of hindsight, taken in.

The atmospheric system was therefore installed on the Dalkey extension of the Dublin & Kingstown Railway, for which Vignoles was engineer. This was one and three-quarter miles long, uphill all the way, terminating with a length of 1 in 57; trials were held on it from August 1843 onwards, and it was opened in March 1844. It worked very well: trains at half-hourly intervals averaged 26 mph up to Dalkey by atmospheric power, and returned by gravity. On trial, speeds over 50 mph were attained deliberately, and into the eighties when the carriage attached to the piston escaped and was drawn away by mistake.

The results achieved by the Dalkey railway were impressive enough for the atmospheric system to be adopted for longer railways to be built in Britain and France. The story of the system's rise, however, and subsequent rapid decline, will be continued in the next chapter. By comparison with the attention it received there went almost unnoticed an early demonstration of the system which was eventually to achieve most of what was hoped for from the atmospheric system, and more besides: in 1842 Robert Davidson demonstrated on the Edinburgh & Glasgow Railway a locomotive driven by 'electro-magnetic engines' or, as we would now say, electric motors. It hauled a load of about six tons at four mph. But electric power at that date could be drawn only from batteries, and it was to be another four decades or so before — following the invention of the dynamo — the electric railway became truly practicable.

The Edinburgh & Glasgow Railway was opened in 1842; so were the Manchester & Birmingham, in the form of a line from Manchester direct to Crewe, and the South Eastern from Redhill as far as Ashford. The Newcastle & Darlington Junction Railway, formed under Hudson's auspices, was authorised to complete a route which the earlier Great North of England Railway had failed to do. So there was little activity in railway promotion and construction at this date: it was a situation, however, which would not last.

4 : The Railway Mania, and After

Railways in Equilibrium

By 1843 the depression in trade had been both long and severe, but distressing though this may have been for contemporaries, it has the advantage for us that the railway system at that date can be viewed in a state of near-equilibrium. A basic railway network already existed in England, and most large towns and cities were served by it, although routes between them were in some cases circuitous. Other lines had yet to be connected to it, notably the Newcastle & Carlisle and the Edinburgh & Glasgow.

Authorities differ over the exact length of line open – Grote Lewin in *Early British Railways* gives us about 2,050 route miles, Acworth in *The Railways of England* 1,829 miles, evidently for the whole of the UK. According to Acworth, the capital authorised was about £70 million, of which £60 million had been spent; about 300,000 passengers were being carried each week, and total weekly receipts from all sources were rather more than £100,000. Average speeds, excluding stops, of the fastest trains were 33 to 36 mph on broad gauge lines, 25 to 30 mph on standard gauge; the average speed on all lines was said to be 21½ mph. Speeds were restricted by the state of the track and the simple signalling as much as by the power of locomotives, though locomotives at this date could only run twenty-five or thirty miles without stopping for water.

It was a year in which amalgamations between companies first came to the fore – not only the companies which formed the Midland, but also the North Union with the Bolton & Preston, and the Great Western with the as yet incomplete Cheltenham & Great Western Union. Amalgamations (which had to be sanctioned by Parliament) were to be a continuing feature of the railway scene for decades to come. The Eastern Counties, in 1843, leased the Northern and Eastern.

79

Of new construction, in the South the South Eastern Railway reached Folkestone in 1843 and Dover the following year: while in London the South Eastern and Croydon companies opened a new terminus at Bricklayer's Arms, to avoid running into London Bridge, for which the London & Greenwich was charging excessive tolls. In the North, the Newcastle & Darlington Junction Railway was opened in 1844: this filled the gap between Darlington and the Durham Junction Railway, so that there was continuous railway communication from Euston as far as Gateshead, just across the Tyne from Newcastle.

The speeds mentioned above referred to trains of first and second class carriages. Passengers travelling third class fared much worse, both in speeds and in the type of vehicles provided. In this the new railways reflected contemporary road transport practice: first and second class accommodation corresponded to inside and outside positions on road coaches, and for those who could not afford these the choices were the stage waggons or Shanks's pony. In the vehicles provided for third class railway passengers, roofs or seats or both were often absent; they were run either in trains by themselves, or incorporated into goods trains, and in either case travelled very slowly, if only to prevent excessive exposure of their passengers to the weather. The numbers of passengers travelling third class were in any case, on the long-distance lines, very small: according to Gourvish (*Mark Huish and the London & North Western Railway*), during the year July 1841–July 1842, receipts from third class passengers on the London & Birmingham Railway were only 4.6% of the total passenger receipts, and 8.8% on the Grand Junction. Only on short lines in industrial areas were third class passengers found to be a useful source of railway revenue, and better facilities provided for them.

The plight of third class travellers was drawn to public attention on Christmas Eve of 1841. On the Great Western, which had had a remarkably accident-free record, a goods train with two third class coaches coupled next to the locomotive ran into an earth slip in Sonning Cutting between Twyford and Reading. The locomotive overturned and the coaches — open, low-sided vehicles — were crushed against locomotive and tender by the weight of the following train. Eight passengers were killed and seventeen severely injured.

This resulted in the government's starting to take an interest in third class travel, which culminated with provisions in W. E. Gladstone's Act of 1844. The Act obliged railways to run one train at least over each trunk, branch or junction line, at least once each way daily at a minimum of 12 mph, stopping if required at all stations, and carrying passengers for one penny a mile or less in carriages with seats and protected from the weather. The Act applied to all railway companies 'incorporated in the present session or hereafter', or which 'by Act of the present or future session obtain amending powers', so that within a few years there can have been few if any railways to which it did not apply.

The term *Parliamentary train* then entered the language, to describe trains operated under this Act – trains which in due course came to seem slow and inconvenient to the extreme. Although the Parliamentary train is now largely forgotten, it was still well known in the 1880s: at least, W. S. Gilbert's Mikado, seeking a punishment to fit the crime for 'the idiot who, in railway carriages, scribbles on window panes' suffered him only 'to ride on a buffer, on Parliamentary trains'.

Run-up to a Mania

The third class Parliamentary trains were the most notable result of an Act* which, when originally presented as a bill, had included far-reaching proposals for, for instance, state purchase of railways, but which were too strong for Parliament to accept. This bill had in turn arisen out of the reports – no less than six of them – of a select committee, which had been appointed at the proposal of W. E. Gladstone as President of the Board of Trade, during the 1844 session of Parliament to consider standing orders relating to railway companies: for railway promoters were on the move again, and Parliament at the beginning of the session had found no less than sixty-six railway bills before it, for the construction of some 900 miles of route.

What had happened was that the trade depression had bottomed out just at the time when the first generation of main lines had been in operation long enough to demonstrate that they were both profitable and generally beneficial. We saw above how Dickens describes the effect on North London of construction of the London & Birmingham Railway: here, from a later page of *Dombey and Son*, is how he describes the effect of its completion:

---

* This Act is variously referred to as the Railway Regulation Act 1844, the Cheap Trains Act, or simply as Gladstone's Act – possibly because (for the record) its full title is 'An Act to attach certain Conditions to the construction of future Railways authorised by any Act of the present or succeeding sessions of Parliament; and for other Purposes in relation to Railways'.

Where the old rotten summer-houses once had stood, palaces now reared their heads, and granite columns of gigantic girth opened a vista to the railway world beyond. The miserable waste ground . . . was swallowed up and gone, and in its frowsy stead were tiers of warehouses, crammed with rich goods and costly merchandise. The old by-streets now swarmed with passengers and vehicles of every kind: the new streets . . . formed towns within themselves. . . . Bridges that had led to nothing, led to villas, gardens, churches, healthy public walks.

As to the neighbourhood which had hesitated to acknowledge the railroad in its straggling days, that . . . now boasted of its powerful and prosperous relation. . . . There were railway hotels, office-houses, lodging-houses, boarding houses; railway plans, maps, views, wrappers, bottles, sandwich-boxes, and time-tables; railway hackney-coach and cab-stands; railway omnibuses, railway streets and buildings. . . .

To and from the heart of this great change [that is to say from London itself] . . . crowds of people and mountains of goods, departing and arriving scores upon scores of times in every four-and-twenty hours, produced a fermentation in the place that was always in action. . . . Members of Parliament, who, little more than twenty years before had made themselves merry with the wild railroad theories of engineers, and given them the liveliest of rubs in cross-examination, went down into the north with their watches in their hands, and sent on messages before by the electric telegraph, to say that they were coming. Night and day the conquering engines rumbled at their distant work . . .

The first-generation main lines had largely been financed by northern industrialists and commercial men, such as the Liverpool party, who had experienced for themselves the earlier successes of the Liverpool & Manchester and Stockton & Darlington Railways. Now in turn, with great main lines running into London, City financiers and stockbrokers, and after them the public at large, woke up to the possibilities of railways as a medium for speculation. There were, after all, many parts of Britain still to be served by rail, many direct routes to be built between important places where existing routes seemed too circuitous. . . .

The immediate outcome of this was that in 1844 forty-eight of the sixty-six railway bills were passed, and authorised construction of some 810 miles of new railways. They included the Lancaster & Carlisle as part of the route to Scotland, with several miles of 1 in 75 at Shap; the Chester & Holyhead, as far as Bangor and through Anglesey – to link these sections, a new bridge over the Menai was favoured though not as yet authorised; the North British from Edinburgh to the Border at Berwick; the South Devon from Exeter to Plymouth; and many lesser lines.

But more and more railways were being proposed. 'Is then no nook of English ground secure / From rash assault? . . .' queried Wordsworth in 1844, in his sonnet *On the Projected Kendal & Windermere Railway.* Lord Cockburn, the noted Scottish judge, was more crusty. On circuit in April 1845, at which date there was no existing railway further north than local lines in the Dundee area, he commented in his journal: 'From Edinburgh to Inverness the whole people are mad about railways. The country is an asylum of railway lunatics. The Inverness patients, not content with a railway to their hospital from Aberdeen, insist on having one by the Highland road from Perth. They admit that there are no towns, or even villages, no population, and no chance of many passengers. But then they will despatch such flocks of sheep, and such droves of nowt! And in furtherance of this shares are actually up for a railway through Killiecrankie, and by Dalwhinnie and Aviemore!'

In fact, by comparison with some schemes which were shortly to bedazzle the investing public, this one was by no means unsound, for among its promoters was Joseph Mitchell, veteran engineer of Highland roads, who knew the country. It was to be another two decades, however, before a railway was actually built over the route.

While some railways which were now proposed were in effect extensions of established lines, others threatened to provide alternative and in some instances shorter routes between places already served by rail. The consequence was to put established lines on the defensive, to protect their own interests by supporting proposals which would feed traffic to them and by opposing others, and indeed by promoting their own schemes to rival competing proposals. Although such competitiveness was originally forced upon the existing lines, promoters such as George Hudson and managers such as Mark Huish, who had been headhunted (to use a modern term) by the Grand Junction in 1841, seem to have taken to the situation with relish.

But the government too was concerned. Gladstone was authorised by the House of Commons, following one of the select committee's reports, to enlarge the Board of Trade's Railway Department to form a new Railway Board under the chairmanship of Lord Dalhousie. The board was empowered to examine railway proposals to be brought before Parliament. This it commenced to do, comprehensively and conscientiously, taking into account the promoters' bona fides, the advantages both national and local of the proposed lines, their engineering circumstances, and the estimates of construction costs, traffic, and working expenses, so that the likelihood of the line's being completed and efficiently worked might be judged.

Thus equipped, Parliament commenced the task of considering the 220 railway bills deposited before it in the autumn of 1844 for the session of 1845.

1845

The Dalhousie board did its work well. It tended to favour extensions to existing lines – such as Cambridge to York rather than a direct line from London to York – but this was not so obstructive as it may appear. The total capital required to complete all railways then proposed (the number of bills is said eventually to have reached 240) was around £100 million which could not have been raised without what Grote Lewin describes in *The Railway Mania and its Aftermath* as 'serious financial derangement'; furthermore, the supply of qualified engineers and labour for construction was limited.

Nevertheless, Parliament did find itself overloaded and was unable to consider all the bills that session. There were passed, however, some ninety-one railway acts, authorising construction of 2,170 miles of railway in Great Britain (including 423 in Scotland) and 645 in Ireland. (Parliament had not taken up the recommendations for Ireland of the 1836 commissioners, so that railway promotion there had suffered from a sort of planning blight ever since.) There was also passed in this session the Railway Clauses Consolidation Act. Its 165 clauses specified certain standardised powers and obligations of railway companies, so that subsequent railway bills could be both shortened and simplified by their omission.

The measured and sensible progress being made under Dalhousie's board did not, however, please everybody – particularly those whose railway schemes when scrutinised were reported upon unfavourably. From 10 July 1845 the Board of Trade decided to cease investigating new proposals: Grote Lewin attributes this to powerful interests and private jealousies. The way was open for wild speculation in railway proposals over the next few months, and in the long term for construction of the nation's railway system on principles of laissez-faire. These, though they would eventually produce a system which would serve its purpose, would do so at the expense of large amounts of capital wasted on futile Parliamentary contests, and on construction of duplicate and uneconomic routes; and subsequently of inter-company competition for traffic which would in some instances pass far beyond the point at which the public benefited from cheap fares to that at which services suffered because the companies concerned were beggaring themselves. The consequences of all this affect the railway map adversely to the present day.

In the summer and early autumn of 1845, however, all was optimism. The bubble of financial speculation that was called the Railway Mania was inflating wildly. It was much helped by the activities of men such as George Hudson. By now he was in control of all the railways which formed the route from Rugby to Gateshead; he chaired the company formed to continue the line to Berwick, and when the North British was unable, for lack of capital, to go to Parliament for its line from Berwick to Edinburgh, Hudson's York & North Midland subscribed for £50,000 worth of shares.

The Y&NM was then steadily paying a dividend of 10 per cent per annum, a rate equalled only by the London & Birmingham, Grand Junction and Liverpool & Manchester companies. More typical were the Great Western with 8 per cent and the Edinburgh & Glasgow with 6. The Eastern Counties, which could manage only 2 per cent per annum for the first half-year in 1845, suddenly jumped to 6 for the second: but then Hudson became chairman in October of that year.

For a railway company promoter, a judiciously spread rumour that Hudson 'The Railway King' was interested could send the price of shares soaring. Railway promotion, originally a matter for routes where the need was evident and the engineering practicable, had spread first to routes where demand was doubtful and the engineering full of problems, and from early concern to achieve the most level route the pendulum had swung to the opposite extreme – now no terrain seemed too rugged for a railway, hence a profusion of 'Direct Such and Such' railways at this time. But then promotion had spread still further. People could subscribe for shares in new companies, pay perhaps £1 in every £10 for which they had put their names down, and be confident that railway 'scrip' would rise in price so much that by selling only a small part of their holding they would raise enough cash to pay the balance they owed. With the public clamouring for railway shares, companies now were being formed solely so that promoters might in due course unload their shares at a premium, leaving others to hold their unlikely babies. When *The Times* printed a list of all proposed railways registered to 31 October, it included such improbable undertakings as the Direct Independent London & Manchester Railway, the Great North Eastern & South Western Connecting Railway, and the Grand Hibernian Central Junction Railway.

The Satirists

Such activities were too blatant to go uncommented upon. The October 1845 issue of *Blackwood's Edinburgh Magazine* contains the (fictional) account of 'How we Got Up the Glenmutchkin Railway, And how we Got Out of it'. A pair of hard-up young Glasgow gentlemen see in promoting a railway company the way out of their difficulties, and over a cask of malt whisky sit down to prepare the prospectus. Where is the railway to be, when England is out of the question and there is hardly a spot in the Lowlands not occupied already? Why not the Highlands? There must be lots of traffic there in sheep, grouse and Cockney tourists. Glenmutchkin's the place, on the West Coast – 'There's a distillery there, you know, and a fishing village at the foot; at least there used to be six years ago. . . . There may be some bother with the population, though, the last laird shipped every mother's son . . . to America; . . .'

So the prospectus for the Direct Glenmutchkin Railway is drawn up, with a provisional committee headed by

> Sir Polloxfen Tremens, Bart. of Toddymains
> Tavish M'Tavish of Invertavish
> (*both of these worthies being figments of the promoters' imagination*)
>   The M'Closkie
> ('We must have a real Highlander in the list' – 'You're devilish

CUTTING THE FIRST SOD OF THE SHEFFIELD AND LINCOLNSHIRE RAILWAY.

11 Extending the railway network – 1. With the line surveyed, the Act obtained and some at least of the money raised, cutting the first sod of a new railway was a matter of ceremony.
(*Mary Evans Picture Library*)

12 Extending the railway network – 2. Constructing the works – this is Ballochmyle Viaduct on what became the Glasgow & South Western Railway route from Glasgow to Carlisle.
(*Mary Evans Picture Library*)

THE EVESHAM STATION.

13 Extending the railway network – 3. The works completed, opening a line was cause for further and greater ceremony. Evesham station is seen during opening day celebrations of the Oxford, Worcester & Wolverhampton Railway. (*Mary Evans Picture Library*)

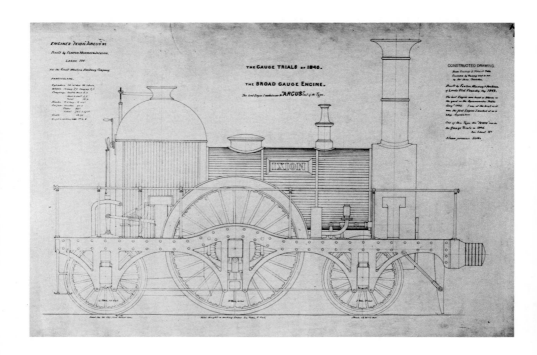

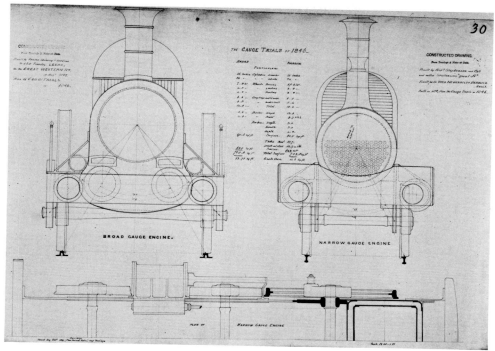

14 *(below opposite)*, **15, 16** Drawings prepared by the noted Victorian engineer
David Joy, illustrate the principal contending locomotives in the gauge trials of
1845–6. Side elevation of the 'Great A' is contemporary, that of *Ixion* and the
comparative front views of the two locomotives were prepared in the 1890s from
notes and tracings made fifty years earlier. Joy had personal experience of
locomotives of both types.
(The Institution of Mechanical Engineers)

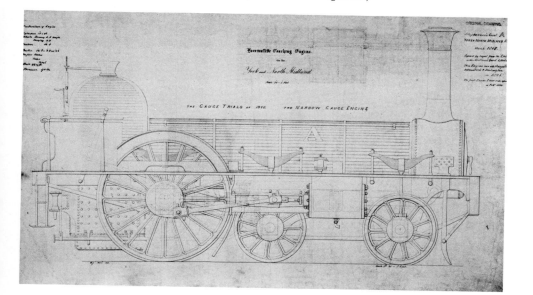

17 *Above* At the dawn of the railway era, c.1837, Post Office mail coaches provided a swift and efficient national transport network: but Post Office pay was low and it was from passenger fares that they could keep that mail coach contractors derived their profits. Here, while the Dover mail passes a village post office without stopping, the mail guard has dropped off a letter bag and is about to pick up another – it was from this practice that railway mail bag exchange apparatus evolved shortly afterwards.
(*The Post Office*)

18 *Right* Top hat has given way to cap, but when this Post Office mail guard, employed on railway duties, posed for his photograph in the early 1860s his uniform was still closely derived from that of his predecessors on road mail coaches.
(*The Post Office*)

scrupulous, Gus' – 'I don't know a single Celt in Glasgow, except old M'Closkie, the drunken porter at the corner of Jamaica Street . . .')

and so on through such figures as

    Samuel Sawley Esq., Merchant

('Old Sam Sawley, the coffinmaker')

    The Captain of M'Alcohol

    Factor for Glentumblers

down to

    Engineer – Walter Solder Esq.

(We must announce an engineer – 'there's Watty Solder, the gasfitter, who failed the other day. He's a sort of civil engineer by trade' . . .)

'The necessity of a direct line of Railway communication through the fertile and populous district known as the VALLEY OF GLENMUTCHKIN, has been long felt and universally acknowledged' announces the prospectus, and goes on to stress the two hundred thousand improvable acres close to the line, the four million cattle it is expected to convey annually. The population, it says, is extremely dense, the position on the West Coast has afforded the means of direct communication with America, 'of which for many years the inhabitants have actively availed themselves'. The railway will be twelve miles long and can be completed in six months after the Act, for 'there are no viaducts of any importance, and only four tunnels along the whole length of the line. The shortest of these does not exceed a mile and a half.'

Glenmutchkin shares are many times over-subscribed, of course, by people greedy for a quick profit, and our heroes successfully part with most of their own at a healthy premium.

All manner of people were involved in railway speculation. Not merely bankers and lawyers, but physicians, chemists, priests, Jews, Quakers, and Members of Parliament many of whom were deeply enough involved for it to affect their votes. Hardly a family in the land was not involved, directly or indirectly. It was against this background that Thackeray's *Diary of C. Jeames de la Pluche* appeared, with Pluche ascending the social ladder in consequence of his newly-acquired wealth. His first pair of horses he calls *Hull* and *Selby*, for they are purchased out of what he has made from transactions in that railway's shares;* and when he engages a 'vally de shamber' (Plush's – I beg your pardon, Pluche's – spelling is not his strong point) he calls 'this Vally my *Trent Vally*, for it was the prophit I got from that exlent line, which injuiced me to ingage him'. But from being a figure of fun, Pluche becomes one of pathos also, for as he mingles with the aristocracy he is acceptable to them only as a potential means to redeem their mortgaged estates – of this he is aware, and indeed proud, but he remains unconscious of the sniggers behind his back. And then, when he becomes engaged to Lord Bareacres's daughter Angelina, who should turn out to be her lady's maid but his dear Mary Ann Hoggins from whom, when she was in Flimsy's employ, he had borrowed his first £20?

With Jeames's wealth increasing daily by leaps and bounds – *he* does not intend to realise his scrip until the right moment – he plans an extravagent wedding. But the day before, he finds that Lady Angelina has eloped to Gretna Green with her true love, and with the assistance, it seems, of her lady's maid. . . . Too distraught to study share prices for three days, Pluche eventually returns to them – to read ruin in the railway share list, the Panic is in full operation and prices have collapsed. Unable to meet his commitments, he is imprisoned for debt. At last, after his release, we read that Lady Angelina (who has come into some money) 'has presented five hundred pounds to her faithful and affectionate servant, Mary Ann Hoggins, on her marriage with Mr James Plush, to whom her Ladyship also made a handsome present . . . the lease . . . of the Wheel of Fortune public-house, near Shepherd's Market, Mayfair: a house greatly frequented by all the nobility's footmen. . . .'

The Reality

This phase of the Railway Mania came to an abrupt halt on 16 October 1845. The Bank of England raised the bank rate (to 3%) and, as *The Times* remarked, 'The Railway share market was not buoyant this afternoon'. The report appeared the following day on a page full of details of bubble companies. *The Times* was already unsympathetic: 'The mania for railway speculation has reached that height at which all follies

---

* Jackman (*The Development of Transportation in Modern England*) notes that Hudson made a profit of over £3,000 in a shady deal in Hull & Selby shares: this does not seem to have been public knowledge until 1849, but one wonders if it was being rumoured at the date when Thackeray was writing.

. . . cease to be ludicrous . . .' thundered the editorial on 18 October. Wild speculation ceased, to be replaced by panic as prices of shares in speculative railway companies slumped, to be followed in turn by share prices of established railways and in other markets. Those who had got rich quick suddenly found themselves poor again; some who had previously enjoyed modest wealth now found themselves liable for sums far beyond their means. Families were broken up, many men were imprisoned for debt, some sadly committeed suicide.

But the juggernaut continued to roll. By no means all railway promotions were bubble flotations, and the task of surveying lines and preparing applications to Parliament had been continuing. Draughts-men, engravers, printers were overrun with work and could charge as they pleased. The last date for reception of railway plans by the Board of Trade was set at 30 November, and as that date approached representa-tives of more and more companies arrived with their parchment rolls of plans and sections. On the Great Western alone eight special trains were hired by company promoters to carry them to London. Such specials were not everywhere welcome: one established company refused a special to the promoters of a rival line, only to be outwitted when (according to the *Ilustrated London News*) the rival promoters hired an undertaker's hearse, placed plans, sections and a clerk inside, and despatched it by special train to London. We are into fact now, not fiction.

At the Board of Trade there were scenes of wild confusion as more and more last-minute arrivals drove up on that Sunday evening. The door was eventually closed at midnight: a quarter of an hour later (reported the *Illustrated London News* for 6 December 1845) a post-chaise which had got lost on the way drove up in hot haste with reeking horses. Its occupants (from Harwich) rang the doorbell, were refused admission, and so threw their vast rolls of plans in through the open doorway, knocking the lamp over and breaking it. The plans were thrown out into the street again. When the door was opened a second time, the process was repeated (apart from the lamp), and at 2 am, when the reporter left, the railway promoters from Harwich were still trying to gain admission.

Perhaps they were eventually successful, for the Harwich & Eastern Counties Junction Railway appears in the list of projected railways lodged with the Board of Trade which was published in the same issue of the *ILN*. This extends to some 650 titles, and though the wildest extravagances have disappeared (though the Great Hibernian Central

Junction was still there) there were still some unlikely undertakings – Manchester & Southampton, say, and Great West of England. It comes as a surprise to find in such company the name Great North of Scotland, and realise that it was to make it through to being a well-known and respected railway. But most of the titles did have an air of reality about them – Shrewsbury & Birmingham, for instance, and North Staffordshire.

1846

So great was the confusion that it is impossible now to get an accurate figure for the number of railway schemes before the public; but a report by a House of Commons select committee, which was considering the position, stated on 17 February 1846 that there had been 562 petitions for railway bills, 395 for England, 120 for Scotland and 47 for Ireland. They were considered – as they had been in the previous session – in geographical groups by committees of MPs, and a Royal Commission was set up to consider railway proposals for the London area. Its principal recommendations were that no railways should be extended into the central part of London, and that it would be desirable to have a railway encircling London, linking the railways approaching from the North and the South with each other and with the docks.

As the session progressed it became clear that the termination of the Dalhousie board in July 1845 had been premature, and Railway Commissioners were established to do a comparable task. As things turned out they proved superfluous, and were disbanded five years later, for already in 1845 it was evident that increasing difficulty in raising capital for construction was going to be far more effective in killing off railway schemes than any government board. Nevertheless, during the 1846 session of Parliament, 270 railway Acts were passed, authorising construction of 4,540 miles of railway at a cost of £131,713,206 (at 1846 values).

The following session, 1847, saw a further 189 railway Acts of Parliament, authorising construction of 1,414 miles of railway at a cost of £34,767,746. During the 1846 session, some schemes had been lost which were potentially useful, and in some instances these were backed by established railways to establish themselves in territory which might otherwise be served by competitors. Reintroduction of such schemes accounted for many of the lines authorised in 1847. But 1847 turned

out to be a year of financial crisis, following failure of the potato crop in
1846 and repeal of the corn laws, and the amount of capital being
swallowed up by railway construction became a matter of concern to the
government. Companies with bills before Parliament were allowed to
suspend them, for reintroduction in the next session; several did so.
But the financial crisis deepened, and when after an election Parliament
met in November 1847 for the 1848 session, there were proposals that
railway construction should be prohibited for a time. This parliament,
however, included 102 MPs connected with railways, Robert Stephenson, Joseph Locke and George Carr Glyn among them, and an Act
authorised railway companies to apply for extensions of the time allowed
for completing their lines. The mileage of new railways authorised fell
year by year until it reached a mere 6¾ miles in 1850. That was the
nadir: subsequently mileages authorised started to increase again.

The Railways that were Built

Nor were all railways that were authorised in fact constructed: the
money shortage saw to that. Grote Lewin states that by 1856, of 9,792
miles of railway authorised during 1844–50, only 5,597 miles had been
built. Even this, however, was an enormous mileage. The peak year was
1848 which alone saw completion of 2,893 miles. Macaulay's Railway
Map of Great Britain, published in 1852, depicts a recognisable railway
network with its extremities at Aberdeen, Yarmouth, Dover, Dorches-
ter, Plymouth, Swansea, Holyhead and Greenock. Almost all principal
lowland towns and cities are served: the main blanks on the map are
Cornwall and Herefordshire and West Wales – in all of which railways
are shown as under construction – central Wales, north Devon, the
north Pennines and the Highlands of Scotland. To attempt to detail all
the railways which were opened at this period would be to produce no
more than a very long list; besides, Leslie James's *A Chronology of the
Construction of Britain's Railways 1778–1855* does include both a
detailed chronology and a revealing series of maps showing which lines
were opened when.

Some account of the development of the most important routes is
desirable, however. On what became known as the West Coast Route
from London to Scotland, the Trent Valley line between Rugby and
Stafford, opened in 1847, enabled long-distance trains to avoid Birmingham. Promoted originally as the Trent Valley Railway, this had

been absorbed before its opening by the London & North Western Railway, the formation of which by amalgamation will be mentioned below. Further north the route was extended by the Lancaster & Carlisle Railway, opened in 1846, and the Caledonian, opened in 1847–8 from Carlisle over Beattock summit to a junction with earlier local railways in Lanarkshire. Their existing lines were used to give access to Glasgow, and a branch from Carstairs ran to Edinburgh. From 1848, both Glasgow and Edinburgh could be reached by train from London in 12 hours. The local railways, including a short segment of the pioneer Monkland & Kirkintilloch, were also used to commence extension of the route further north. New construction by the Caledonian, Scottish Central, Scottish Midland, and Aberdeen Railways then took the line forward by Perth and Forfar to Aberdeen, reached in 1850.

On the East Coast Route, provision of a direct railway northwards from London to York became in the mid-1840s a matter of extreme controversy. The London & Birmingham Railway favoured the existing route from Euston, the Dalhousie board favoured extension of the Eastern Counties from Cambridge, Hudson favoured anything which would keep the maximum amount of traffic upon the lines he controlled. The position was further complicated initially by two rival groups of promoters planning entirely new lines, the Direct Northern and the London & York. During the course of a prolonged parliamentary contest which commenced during the 1845 session and was continued during that of 1846, these two pooled their resources and eventually the Act was passed in 1846 for the Great Northern Railway, with 285 miles of line to be constructed at a cost approaching £7 million – both of them record sums, according to Grote Lewin.

The Great Northern's engineer was William Cubitt, who only a decade earlier had been completing Telford's Birmingham & Liverpool Junction Canal after the death of the latter, and had subsequently engineered the South Eastern Railway. Hudson attempted unsuccessfully to promote extensions of both the Eastern Counties and the Midland to extract traffic from the region where the Great Northern was building, and when the GN line was opened in 1850 from a temporary terminus at Maiden Lane near King's Cross, its trains ran to Doncaster and thence, over a branch of the Lancashire & Yorkshire Railway to Knottingley, on to a recently-built connection to the York & North Midland Railway. This conveyed them to York itself. Against the interests of two of his largest companies, the Midland and the Eastern

Counties, Hudson had thus salvaged the main East Coast traffic for a third, his original YNMR: but by the time the new route came into operation Hudson, as we shall see, was no longer in charge. It was to be many years before a direct line from Doncaster to York was built, and then not by the GN, but in 1852 the GN opened its London terminus at King's Cross and a direct line from Peterborough to Retford – earlier trains had used the loop via Lincoln which had been opened first. (The complexities of the order in which the various sections of the Great Northern were opened might have been designed to baffle the railway historian!)

From York northwards, however, Hudson's efforts had met with greater success, resulting in lasting achievement. Rail communication through to Edinburgh was open by 1848 when temporary bridges came into use over the Tyne at Newcastle and the Tweed at Berwick, to be replaced the following year by the High Level Bridge and the Royal Border Bridge respectively, Robert Stephenson being engineer for both. Formal opening of the Royal Border Bridge by Queen Victoria in 1850 was taken as symbolising completion of the East Coast Route to Edinburgh.

Further north the Firths of Forth and Tay presented what were at that date unbridgeable obstacles to an extended East Coast Route. Across the Forth, however, from Granton to Burntisland in 1850, the Edinburgh, Perth & Dundee Railway instituted a train ferry – generally said to be the world's first, and although there had been earlier instances of chaldron and similar waggons carried on boats, there seems no doubt that it was the first to form part of a steam railway trunk route. Goods vehicles only were normally carried, passenger coaches on rare occasions. A similar ferry was intituted across the Tay; the designer, of these and the loading ramps on shore, was the railway's engineer Thomas Bouch, who would doubtless have gone down in history with a modest claim to fame as the originator of the train ferry had he not subsequently attempted to build a replacement bridge across the Tay with less happy results. The train ferries across the Forth continued in operation for forty years.

On the Chester & Holyhead Railway, Robert Stephenson's plan for a tubular bridge across the Menai Strait had been approved, and an Act to close the gap in the authorised line was obtained in 1845. Even so, the immense engineering difficulties involved meant that the Act did not immediately discourage promoters of lines to Porthdinllaen, who continued to be active for some years. Funds subscribed for the North Wales Railway Company, which obtained an Act in 1845 to build from Bangor (on the C&H) to Porthdinllaen, were abstracted by a dubious financier, during the capital shortage which followed the mania, to build the Richmond Railway near London. Stephenson's Britannia tubular bridge over the Menai Strait was eventually completed in 1850, and with it the Chester & Holyhead Railway. So Holyhead was re-established as the port for Ireland: despite continuing efforts, no railway was ever built to Porthdinllaen, although powers were obtained as late as 1913. The remarkable story of the alternating fortunes of successive proposals for both routes is well told in M. Elis-Williams's book *Packet to Ireland*.

For railways in Ireland itself, capital was even more difficult to raise after the mania than for railways in Britain. From 1845 to 1848 Ireland was in a state of famine, the potato crop failing from disease. It was the start of a process which was eventually, with emigration, sadly to halve the population, at a period when that of Britain continued rapidly to increase, and so to alter radically the balance of economic importance between the two islands. The immediate effect was that construction of the authorised railways was largely held up, not only by lack of investment, but also by hopes of government finance to alleviate distress. This was eventually forthcoming, though it appears only on a limited scale to assist companies, which had already raised substantial private capital, to complete their lines. In this way Dublin was eventually linked to Cork in 1849, to Galway in 1851 and to Belfast in 1855. Completion of the latter route had been delayed by the need to build a large bridge across the River Boyne at Drogheda – and also by the gauge question, for it was in Ireland that controversy over the gauge of railways first became of national importance.

The Irish Gauge

Since the Irish Railway Commissioners of 1836 had set the track gauge for Irish railways at 6 ft 2 in. this is at first sight surprising. But when after some delay work commenced on building the Dublin & Drogheda Railway, its engineer John MacNeill, despite the recommendation and having been himself one of the commission's engineers, decided to adopt a gauge of 5 ft 2 in. As to why he did so, a possible explanation appears below.

Meanwhile the 6 ft 2 in. gauge Ulster Railway was being opened in sections from Belfast to Portadown, reached in September 1842. Since it was clear that the two lines would ultimately be linked to form a through route from Dublin to Belfast, a dispute about the gauge arose between the two companies, and early in 1843 they asked the Board of Trade to adjudicate. The board referred the matter to its chief inspector, Maj. Gen. C. W. Pasley, and what Pasley did is best described in his own words, given in evidence to the Gauge Commissioners (whom we shall meet shortly) in December 1845:

I accordingly wrote a circular letter to a number of the most eminent locomotive engine-makers and railway engineers, to request that they would give an opinion, supposing that no railways existed in England, what, from their experience of the working of the Great Western, and of the London and Birming-ham, and other existing railways, they would recommend as being the best gauge for general use. I did not apply to Mr. Brunel, because I considered him pledged to the 7 feet gauge, and I thought therefore that it would be indelicate to put the question to him. I also considered Mr. Stephenson and Mr. Robert Stephen-son, who first introduced the narrow gauge of 4 feet 8½ inches on passenger railways in England, to be pledged in the same manner to that gauge; so that it was not my intention at first to have applied to them for their opinion. But having ascertained after-wards that those gentlemen had expressed a regret that they had adopted so narrow a gauge as 4 feet 8½, I wrote to them also, and they replied that they considered that gauge to be the best, although they admitted that they had at one time been of opinion that a wider gauge would have been desirable; but they stated that the great improvements in the construction of locomotive engines had been such as to render a gauge of 4 feet 8½ not only perfectly convenient, but preferable to any other. All the other engineers wrote, that they considered 5 feet to be the narrowest, and 5 feet 6 to be the widest gauge, that was required either for the con-venience of the machinery of the locomotive engine or for speed or safety. Several of them said that they considered some intermediate gauge, such as 5 feet 3 inches, to be the best . . . I made my report . . . dated the 10th of March 1843, in which I recommended that the gauge of 5 feet 3 inches should be sanctioned for the Dublin &

Drogheda Railway, and that all future railways in Ireland should be required to adopt this gauge, and that as the Dublin and Kingstown Railway, and the Ulster Railway, the only ones then made in Ireland, were of very limited length, the Directors of those railways should be required to change their gauge to 5 feet 3 inches, when they became connected with other railways, which would not be attended with any great inconvenience or expense, especially as the Ulster Railway had only one line of rails.

Clearly MacNeill's choice of gauge had been closely in line with current engineering thinking.

Pasley's report was accepted. The standard gauge for Ireland became 5 ft 3 in., the Dublin & Drogheda was laid to this gauge and opened in 1844. The Ulster Railway laid a second track to 5 ft 3 in. gauge, completed early in 1847; later the same year the original track was narrowed to match. The Dublin & Kingstown also was converted.

Break of Gauge at Gloucester

That most engineers, in 1843, favoured a gauge wider than 4 ft 8½ in. is particularly interesting in view of what was about to happen in Britain. Here, in 1844 for the first time, a broad gauge railway met a standard gauge one and the resultant difficulties, previously considered only in theory, became physical fact. The place was Gloucester on the route between Birmingham and Bristol, and the problems were enhanced not only because this was, then as now, probably the most important cross-country railway route, but also because it lay in the no-man's-land between the main lines of the Great Western and the London & Birmingham into which both companies would soon be seeking to expand.

At Gloucester the standard gauge Birmingham & Gloucester Railway, opened in 1840, met two broad gauge railways, the Bristol & Gloucester, opened in 1844, and the Great Western from Swindon, completed the following year. So at Gloucester all through traffic had to change between broad and standard gauge trains. For passengers, this meant no more than the inconvenience of changing trains, as at a junction, on what would otherwise have been a through route. Goods, however, had to be unloaded from wagons of one gauge and re-loaded into wagons of the other, with risk of damage and pilferage, and when livestock, cattle and horses, were released from one wagon they were often so nervous that it was difficult to persuade them to enter another at all. This was, as it soon became known, the 'evil of break of gauge'. The Railway Clearing House later estimated that the cost of transhipment between the gauges was equivalent to twenty miles of extra carriage.

This was also the start of the 'Battle of the Gauges' or the 'Gauge War'. Before considering how this spread further afield, however, it is best to see how things turned out at Gloucester. Despite their differing gauges, the boards of the Birmingham & Gloucester and Bristol & Gloucester companies were on friendly terms, and from 1 January 1845 arranged for their traffic to be worked by one management, until the companies could be amalgamated. The Great Western then approached the Birmingham & Gloucester to extend the broad gauge to Birmingham, and started negotiations to take over both Gloucester companies. They stood out, however, for better terms than those at first offered by the GWR: and at this point there appeared what present-day readers of the financial pages know as a 'white knight', in the form of the Midland Railway, and in particular its deputy chairman, John Ellis.

Now many of the places served by the Midland imported and exported goods through Bristol, so the Midland had a strong interest not only in the absence of a break of gauge en route but also in a line on the same gauge as its own, the standard gauge, throughout between its system and Bristol. When the directors of the Gloucester companies who were negotiating with the GWR were told that it would not raise its offer, they went immediately to Ellis and agreed terms for their lines to be taken over by the Midland. Agreement was reached in February 1845 and ratified by Act of Parliament the following year. Even so it was not until 1854 that the Midland completed the works necessary for standard gauge trains to reach Bristol.

The Gauge War Widens

The Midland takeover of the Birmingham–Bristol route was no more than a matter of first round to the standard gauge companies. In 1844 the Great Western opened its branch from Didcot to Oxford, and then lent its strong support to two proposals to extend the broad gauge further – the Oxford & Rugby Railway, and the Oxford, Worcester & Wolverhampton Railway. The London & Birmingham countered with a proposal for a standard gauge line to leave its main line at Tring and run via Banbury and Worcester to Dudley and Wolverhampton, with branches from Bicester to Oxford and Banbury to Rugby. This the Dalhousie board supported, pointing out that break of gauge would be more convenient at Bristol and Oxford than Wolverhampton and Rugby. Nevertheless, after an extremely tough battle before Parliamentary committee (which heard all about the evil of break of gauge at Gloucester) in 1845 the two Great Western offshoots were authorised, with the proviso that over much of them the gauge should be mixed, either from the start or if required later by the Board of Trade.

By now the Grand Junction Railway was taking a hand. In dispute with the London & Birmingham, for reasons to be described below, it had promoted the Birmingham & Oxford Junction Railway, a broad gauge line to link the GJR at Birmingham with the Oxford & Rugby at Fenny Compton north of Banbury. Furthermore Huish announced that the Grand Junction had investigated the desirability and practicability of 'adding the broad gauge on the Grand Junction' – i.e., introducing mixed gauge – and found it to be practicable, at reasonable cost. The effect – probably the desired effect – of this vision of broad gauge from Paddington to Liverpool and Manchester was to bring the London & Birmingham into negotiation with the Grand Junction: the following year the two were amalgamated. But with strong local support linked with that of the GWR, the Birmingham & Oxford Junction scheme went ahead nonetheless, with a separate terminus in Birmingham at Snow Hill, and was authorised in 1846.

The Gauge Commission

The Gauge War therefore was not at first concerned so much with the intrinsic merits of broad and standard gauges, as with their effects on the extension of the railway system. This was accentuated by the supercharged speculative atmosphere of the Railway Mania, then at its height. By mid-1845, however, Parliament had become sufficiently concerned about the question for a royal commission to be appointed to enquire whether in future railway Acts 'provision ought to be made for securing an uniform gauge, and whether it would be expedient and practicable to take measures to bring the Railways already constructed, or in process of construction, in Great Britain, into uniformity of gauge, and to enquire whether any other mode could be adopted of obviating or mitigating the evil apprehended as likely to arise from the break that will occur in Railway communications from the want of an uniform gauge'.

The 'Gauge Commissioners' were Sir Frederick Smith, Professor Barlow, and Mr G. B. Airy, Astronomer Royal. Their terms of reference related to the technical aspects of the two gauges as much as the geographical ones, and during the autumn of 1845 they examined the principal figures of the day connected with railways, both on the engineering and the traffic sides; their eventual report, with minutes of evidence given verbatim, runs to some 850 pages and gives a remarkable insight into the practices, understandings and concerns of the day.

By 1845 the Eastern Counties Railway had, the previous year, reduced the gauge of its lines from London to Chelmsford and Cambridge from 5 ft to 4 ft 8½ in., as a preliminary to linking with other railways, and certain short lines in Scotland which had been built on the 5 ft 6 in. and 4 ft 6 in. gauges had either converted their lines to the 4 ft 8½ in. gauge or planned to do so. So the position in Great Britain in July 1845 when the commissioners were appointed was that there were in operation 1,925 miles of railways of 4 ft 8½ in. gauge (or for which conversion to this gauge was planned), and 274 miles of 7 ft gauge. But already sanctioned by Parliament or, it seemed likely to the commissioners, to be sanctioned during the current session, were a further 2,230 miles of 4 ft 8½ in. gauge and 651 miles of 7 ft. The only break-of-gauge point already in existence was at Gloucester, but construction of these additional railways would introduce many more – notably at Rugby where it was expected that coal from the Midlands en route for Banbury and Oxford would have to be transhipped.

Of what was actually happening at Gloucester, the commissioners obtained evidence, probably as near to being unbiassed as any, from Mr William Bass. Bass was Pickford's district agent, and his district extended from Coalbrookdale to Plymouth. To him, the change of gauge at Gloucester interfered with his business 'very materially indeed'. Goods trains from Birmingham 'may probably contain 20 or 30 trucks, some of ours, some belonging to the Railway Company, some belonging to other carriers'. The 11.45 am train brought Pickford's trucks from Manchester, Yorkshire, Leicester and Birmingham: but they were not necessarily together, and to get them together and into the transfer shed allocated to Pickford and two other carriers took time. Then: 'The goods upon the narrow-gauge truck, if they are light packages, furniture, or bulky packages, are always put upon the top of

99

the truck, and are necessarily taken off to get at the heavy loading, to put the heavier loading at the bottom of the broad gauge truck.' In other words, light and fragile goods had to be stacked on the platform while heavy goods were transferred. Bass estimated the delay due to tranship-ment at four to six hours, and needed five men to attend to it.

Transhipment was inconvenient, though there seems no reason to suppose that goods were any more likely to be damaged than they were during transfer to road or water at either end of a rail journey: but the fairly orderly scene described by Bass could be, and was, exaggerated into scenes of disorder bordering on chaos by protagonists of the standard gauge who were anxious to prevent broad gauge expansion. Even then, perhaps they were seen to overstate their case: certainly Thackeray found another adventure for Jeames in what that worthy describes as 'that nashnal cuss, the Broken Gage'.* In the confusion of transferring himself, Mary Hann and twenty-three pieces of fragile lug-gage from one gauge to another at Gloucester he finds, once they settle down into the darkened second class carriage, that they have left behind on the platform . . . their baby. 'It all came of the break of gage.'

Comparative Trials

In retrospect, of course, it is the evidence given to the commission by I. K. Brunel which is the most intriguing. The first few questions he answers in monosyllables; then, warming to the task, he soon answers provocatively to a question whether it was injudicious to widen the Great Western's gauge to 7 ft: 'I should rather be above than under 7 ft now, if I had to reconstruct the lines.' Increasing traffic and increasing speeds merited it. His evidence about specialized rolling stock which could have mitigated break-of-gauge problems makes interesting read-ing and is quoted in chapter eight. It was also Brunel who suggested practical comparative trials on the two gauges to test the accuracy of the opinions given before the commissioners: 'I believe that . . . if experi-ments are made, it will be found that speed and economy, and safety, are attained to a much greater extent on the wide gauge than on the narrow. . . . ' Certainly the Gauge War had the effect of increasing train speeds, on both broad gauge and standard, and encouraging design of increasingly powerful standard gauge locomotives to haul them.

When the trials were held, they convincingly demonstrated the

---

* *Punch: Jeames on the Gauge Question* and *Mr Jeames Again.*

better performance of the broad gauge. On trial between Paddington and Didcot in December 1845, the broad gauge locomotive *Ixion*, already four years old, achieved a maximum speed of 60 mph with an 80-ton train, and averaged 50 mph with a train of 60 tons. The standard gauge trials were held between York and Darlington, but the best that could be achieved by a brand-new 4–2–0 numbered 'A' was 55¾ mph with 50 tons, and another locomotive came off the track during a trial and turned over.

The Gauge Commissioners were impressed. 'The public are mainly indebted', they observed in their eventual report, 'for the present rate of speed, and the increased accommodation of the Railway carriages, to the genius of Mr Brunel, and the liberality of the Great Western Railway Company.' But that handsome compliment was about all the broad gauge party got out of the report, although it was comprehensive and generally fair. The greater mileage of standard gauge, the greater ease of converting broad gauge to standard rather than standard to broad, these carried the day. The commissioners recommended that the 4 ft 8½ in. gauge should be used on all public railways then under construction, or constructed later; that a standard gauge link should be made via Oxford and Reading between the northern and southern standard gauge lines; and that broad gauge lines should be narrowed, or some other course adopted to allow standard gauge carriages to pass along broad gauge lines.

These recommendations were reflected in the Gauge of Railways Act, 1846, which states: 'It shall not be lawful (except as herein-after excepted) to construct any Railway for the Conveyance of Passengers on any Gauge other than Four Feet Eight Inches and Half an Inch in *Great Britain*, and Five Feet Three Inches in *Ireland*.' The qualification 'passengers' is remarkable, seeing that it was goods traffic that was mainly affected; the exceptions were for the most part lines already authorised, or about to be authorised, which extended existing broad gauge routes, and lines built in the future with special Acts to define their gauge.

So, although this was the end for ambitious broad gauge schemes such as the Worcester & Porthdinllaen, for a few years broad gauge lines continued to be built. But as early as 1846 the Great Western pledged itself to complete a standard gauge link between Basingstoke and Oxford, and only by so doing successfully opposed another company's application to Parliament to build the link. The expedient most used to reduce the evil of break of gauge was addition of a third rail to broad gauge track to allow standard gauge trains to use it also. Curiously this possibility, of mixed gauge track, had been little regarded by the Gauge Commissioners, partly because they equated it with the evident dangers of running trains which contained vehicles of both gauges, although there is a hint of it in their final recommendation. One suspects that at that time neither the broad nor the standard gauge parties really wanted it, so it was little promoted.

The Oxford, Worcester & Wolverhampton Railway, promotion of which had done much to inflame the Gauge War, was eventually built largely as a standard gauge line, the additional rail for broad gauge trains being omitted from part of the route. It was completion of this line which eventually prompted provision of a mixed gauge track from Oxford to Paddington, reached in 1861. The Oxford & Rugby Railway fared even more strangely: sufficient of it was built only to make an end-on junction with the Birmingham & Oxford Junction, and the line to Rugby was never completed, though earthworks for it can be seen at Fenny Compton. Midlands coal continued to be conveyed to Banbury and Oxford by canal. It was 1900 before a railway link between Banbury and Rugby was provided, by the Great Central Railway, and even then this did not connect with the rest of the railway system at Rugby but pursued its independent way northwards to Nottingham.

Intermingling of broad and standard gauge vehicles in the same train on mixed gauge track was very rare indeed, though occasionally a broad gauge pilot locomotive might double-head a standard gauge train, and Acworth in *The Railways of England* (1889) records operation in West Cornwall of slow-moving goods trains containing both standard and broad gauge vehicles, marshalled in separate portions and linked by a match truck with special couplings and buffers. By then, the broad gauge era was almost over anyway: the Great Western converted its last remaining broad gauge sections to standard in 1892. But much earlier than that, when the gauge for the first railways in India was decided in 1849, a gauge of 5 ft 6 in. was chosen in accordance with the best preferences of the day. Lord Dalhousie was Governor-General.

Power from the Atmosphere

So the Battle of the Gauges was to some extent a red herring at the time of the Railway Mania: but a far greater one was atmospheric propulsion.

However, although the Battle of the Gauges did have some long-term, useful effect on the development of the railway system, atmospheric propulsion had almost none, and so need detain us for far less space. Besides, although the lines for which atmospheric propulsion was proposed were many, the lines upon which it was actually tried were few – apart from the two already mentioned above, in the British Isles only two more: the London & Croydon Railway (engineer, William Cubitt) and the South Devon (engineer, Isambard Brunel).

By 1845 the Dalkey line had been operating successfully for a year and a half. Extension of the Croydon Railway to Epsom was proposed, with atmospheric traction, and since the Croydon's existing line, which was now being used also by trains of the London & Brighton and South Eastern Railways, was becoming congested, the company decided to lay an additional track for its own local traffic and to work this atmospherically. The line was built between Forest Hill and Croydon, five miles, and, following trials during the autumn of 1845, came into use in January 1846. Apart from its type of motive power, this line incorporated a further novelty in the form of the first flying junction or railway flyover, built so that it might cross from one side to the other of the original lines. North of Forest Hill locomotives continued to be used.

The Croydon atmospheric line was not so successful as that at Dalkey. Trouble was experienced with the stationary pumping engines and, more seriously, with the longitudinal flap valve which proved difficult to keep airtight. Meanwhile the South Devon Railway, authorised in 1844, was under construction, with atmospheric power and eight pumping stations between Exeter and Newton Abbot. But when the line was opened as far as Teignmouth in May 1846, and to Newton Abbot later in the year, locomotives provided the power. Not only were there difficulties in obtaining and installing the equipment for atmospheric traction, but the company was watching progress on the Croydon line. Progress there was not in fact very happy, with trains assisted by locomotives and atmospheric working suspended for repairs for six weeks in the summer of 1846; in May 1847 its use was discontinued.

On the South Devon, however, after experiments in the early part of that year, atmospheric trains started to operate the service between Exeter and Teignmouth in September 1847, and were extended to Newton Abbot the following January. The trains were fast, averaging

35 mph, and sometimes made up time lost on steam-worked sections earlier in their journeys. But the Achilles heel of the system was the longitudinal valve. L. T. C. Rolt states in his biography of Brunel that if this became unseated by only one-thousandth of an inch over a mile of pipe, the opening was equivalent to that of a pipe fifteen inches in diameter. Successively on the Croydon and South Devon Railways, sealing compositions based on beeswax, tallow, soap, and cod-oil proved equally ineffective; in the summer the compositions melted, in winter the leather froze hard, for its natural oils had been drawn out of it. Leaks meant that South Devon pumping engines had to work harder, and since the electric telegraph was not yet installed, for longer periods than anticipated, so that the costs were far greater. In June 1848 the best oxhide leather of the South Devon's continuous valve, installed at great expense a couple of years earlier, was found to be rotting throughout its length.

That was the end: Brunel called a halt to further experiment (where a lesser man, as Rolt points out, might have continued into total fiasco). Steam locomotives replaced atmospheric power on the South Devon, toiling up the steap gradients laid out in anticipation of easy atmospheric passage. On the Dalkey line, atmospheric traction continued until 1855, and on a 5½-mile line in France it lasted until 1860. So nearly successful, atmospheric traction turned out to be the great might-have-been in Victorian railway engineering.

Amalgamations – the North Western

To return from the practical to the political, the remaining notable feature of railways during the second half of the 1840s was amalgamation. Indeed, amalgamations between two or more companies, either by full merger or by lease (often against a guaranteed dividend) became a continuing feature of the railway scene. 'End-on' amalgamations which brought together components of a through route were viewed much more favourably by Parliament than those which brought together companies serving the same region, although the latter were not totally disallowed. Indeed the first substantial amalgamation, that forming the Midland Railway, had contained elements of both.

Undoubtedly the most important of all amalgamations at this period, which has already been hinted at, was that which formed the London &

North Western Railway. Yet although amalgamation of the London & Birmingham with the Grand Junction, as parts of a continuous through route, seems obvious on the map, and although the two companies did initially co-operate, eventual amalgamation was achieved only after many years of strained relations between them. These seem to have originated partly from antipathies between the boards of the London-dominated London & Birmingham and the Liverpool-financed Grand Junction. Their opposite attitudes towards the use of their lines by carriers, described in chapter ten, cannot have made for harmony, especially where through traffic was concerned. A more substantial cause, however, was that both companies faced paying the penalties of being pioneers: completion and successful operation of their railways immediately encouraged promotion of competing lines, yet a line which would be wholly unacceptable to one of them as a competitor might well seem desirable to the other as a feeder of traffic. The Grand Junction was particularly vulnerable because it achieved its goals of Liverpool and Manchester by making a junction with the Liverpool & Manchester Railway at approximately its mid-point, and was therefore open to competition by construction of more direct lines from the South to these places; its position was accentuated by the fact that important London–Dublin traffic, which had previously gone by road via Holyhead, was diverted to rail via Liverpool as soon as the line from London was complete.

Having spent a lot of its shareholders' money on building its own line, the GJR had then no great interest in furthering the cause of proposals which would be expensive to construct and would divert traffic from it, such as Vignoles's proposal of 1836 for a line to Porthdinllaen from Stafford. It was not the Grand Junction but the little Chester & Crewe company which responded in 1838 by getting George Stephenson to make a preliminary survey between Chester and Holyhead. Although the Grand Junction absorbed the Chester & Crewe shortly before its line was opened in 1840, and agreed with the London & Birmingham that both companies would contribute substantial finance to the Chester & Holyhead, the GJR suddenly withdrew before application for this line was made to Parliament. The Chester & Holyhead was therefore built largely with London & Birmingham money (for its construction was certainly in that line's interest) and with finance from other sources.

To the east of the Grand Junction main line, there were constant proposals for a direct line from Manchester to the South dating even from before the GJR was opened. Eventually the Grand Junction succeeded in getting these modified into the Manchester & Birmingham, which in fact ran from Manchester to Crewe (the GJR delayed opening of the connection until 1842) and the Trent Valley from Stafford to Rugby; but in the meantime many of the proposals were supported by the London & Birmingham which saw in them, as relations with the GJR deteriorated, a line direct from Rugby or thereabouts to Manchester which would cut out the GJR altogether. It was against this background that the Grand Junction became interested in links with the Great Western via Wolverhampton, Birmingham and Oxford, and in adding broad gauge to its own line, to give it a route to London independent of the London & Birmingham.

Even this rather wordy account is a simplified, if not over-simplified, version of a complex sequence of events which also included controversy over the rail links to – among other places – Birkenhead and, particularly, Shrewsbury. In *The Archaeology of the Transport Revolution* I described how the Birmingham Canal Navigations got swept up into it, coming under railway control in return for providing the London & Birmingham with the route for a railway alongside the canal from Birmingham to Wolverhampton, competitive with the Grand Junction Railway route: yet by the time this line (today the main line between Birmingham and Wolverhampton) was completed, the Grand Junction's broad gauge proposals had done their work and the London & Birmingham had agreed to amalgamate with it to form the London & North Western. This was late in 1845. Earlier in the year the Grand Junction had already amalgamated with the Liverpool & Manchester; the Manchester & Birmingham had just agreed terms for a merger with the London & Birmingham in anticipation of a direct line to link the two which Parliament in fact disallowed, and so came into the greater amalgamation. When the London & North Western Railway Company was authorised by Act of Parliament in 1846 it owned over 400 miles of route. Glyn of the London & Birmingham was chairman, Huish of the Grand Junction general manager, Booth of the Liverpool & Manchester secretary jointly with Richard Creed of the L&B; by 1851 the LNWR was working 800 miles and was both the most important railway and, with capital of more than £25 million, by far the largest joint stock company in the United Kingdom.

Amalgamations – the Rest

Though the London & North Western amalgamation was the most important of its sort, it was nevertheless but one of many. Other company names which were to become familiar appeared in this way at this time – notably the London, Brighton & South Coast Railway, formed by amalgamation of the London & Brighton and London & Croydon, and the Lancashire & Yorkshire Railway, which title was adopted in 1847 by the Manchester & Leeds after absorption of various lesser lines. Grote Lewin lists forty-five instances during 1846 of consolidation between railway companies by amalgamation, lease or other means.

In 1848, during the slump which followed the mania, talks started for an amalgamation on the grand scale between London & North Western, Great Western and London & South Western companies: but whether Parliament would have sanctioned this was never put to the test, for the companies themselves were unable to agree terms. Such an amalgamation would have altered dramatically the subsequent course of railway history, for to this day the lines of these three companies remain for the most part in separate regions of British Rail. However, two later amalgamations were to produce companies with near-monopolies of rail services in their areas. One of these formed the North Eastern Railway out of the York & North Midland, York, Newcastle & Berwick and Leeds Northern Railways in 1854 – the companies had been working their traffic jointly for a year previously and were able to demonstrate the general benefit of this. The other, in 1862, produced the Great Eastern Railway from an amalgamation of the Eastern Counties with several smaller lines in East Anglia.

Stephenson, Hudson and Huish

Rapid expansion of the railway system during the mid-1840s produced a shortage of new locomotives. The Grand Junction Railway started to build its own locomotives at its new works at Crewe in 1845, with Francis Trevithick, son of pioneer Richard Trevithick, in charge. The Great Western followed suit at Swindon in 1846. Although the slump which followed the railway mania was soon to mean that locomotive builders had excess capacity, construction of locomotives in their own works became a continuing and unusual feature of railways in Britain.

The year 1848, the peak year for opening of new railways, saw also the death, in August, of George Stephenson. During his life of sixty-seven years, by no means an exceptionally long one, he had seen the wooden waggonways of Tyneside develop into a national steam railway system. Despite controversy over the precise extent to which the 'Father of Railways' contributed to this – he seems, unfortunately, to have been reluctant to give credit elsewhere where due – there is no doubt that he had done more than any other individual to bring that metamorphosis about. He was outlived by his son Robert by only eleven years, for Robert died in 1859 aged fifty-five. The colossal workload born by engineers of that generation tended to lead to regrettably short lives: Brunel too died in 1859 aged fifty-three, and Locke in 1860 at fifty-five. Vignoles, on the other hand, survived to become a grand old man of the engineering profession before he eventually died at the age of eighty-two in 1875.

George Hudson too survived to reach old age, dying in 1871. But his last years were spent in obscurity and disgrace. Having flown high during the mania, he fell hard afterwards. In agreeing that Great Northern trains should enter York over the York & North Midland, Hudson the Railway King gave his assent to a route from London to York twenty-nine miles shorter than via Rugby and the Midland Railway. That cost him his chairmanship of the Midland, in April 1849. But worse was already happening. Increasingly poor financial results of railways during the slump were encouraging shareholders to investigate their companies' affairs and examine the accounts. Investigation into Hudson's companies produced more and more evidence of irregularities. For example, rails manufactured at Hudson's personal financial risk had been sold by him to his companies at considerable profit. He had bought shares in his old Great North of England Railway and then sold these at a substantial profit to his York, Newcastle & Berwick when the latter was in process of taking over the former. Company accounts had been 'arranged' to make things 'pleasant'. Revenue items had been charged to capital, those lovely dividends paid out of it.

Generally, Hudson's practices seem to have benefited the companies concerned as well as lining his own pockets: as long as he was making everyone richer and richer, shareholders would no doubt have been happy to overlook them. By 1849 the slump was in full swing and they turned upon him in fury. By the middle of the year he had resigned all his railway chairmanships, and subsequently he repaid large sums to some of his former companies. While Hudson spent much of the rest of his life abroad, some of the companies he had originated, notably the

Midland and the North Eastern (formed, as mentioned, by an amalgamation which included many of his lines in North East England) went on eventually to become prosperous and powerful concerns.

In considering Hudson's manipulation of company accounts it must not be forgotten that the sheer size of railway undertakings was as much a novelty as their equipment, and there was as little experience in or precedent for administering the companies as there was for operating their locomotives and rolling stock. Errors of procedure were as likely to result from inexperience as from ill-intent, problems had to be solved as they arose. Huish, as befitted the general manager of the largest railway company of all, was a pioneer of good management, and his personal contribution to management accounting practice (according to T. R. Gourvish: *Mark Huish and the London & North Western Railway*) was outstanding. This applied particularly to correct treatment of depreciation and renewals. The results of his thinking were published for the benefit of the railway industry generally.

Yet at the same time Huish, probably after the fall of Hudson the most prominent figure in that industry, was acquiring something like his notoriety. For within a few years of the formation of the LNWR he found himself again having to defend his railway's London–Manchester traffic: the new Great Northern Railway was to link with the Manchester, Sheffield & Lincolnshire (the old Sheffield, Ashton-under-Lyne & Manchester enlarged) at Retford to produce a London–Manchester route little longer than that of the LNWR. Then there were the constant threat of Great Western extensions on the opposite side of the LNW main line, and the very Anglo-Scottish traffic itself to be defended against the shortened East Coast Route. Huish's principal method was establishment of traffic agreements with other companies: agreements that, in effect, they would route their traffic on to the LNWR rather than lose the substantial traffic that the LNWR sent to them. Such agreements may well in some instances have been against the public interest, let alone that of the smaller companies' shareholders; carried to excess they rendered both the LNWR and Huish himself extremely unpopular. In 1858 Huish, by then isolated, resigned.

Railways Settle Down

By the mid-1850s the country, and the railways, had largely recovered from the violent financial fluctuations of the mania/slump period, and trade was proceeding normally. Some but by no means all railways were prosperous: of fifty-nine companies in England and Wales in 1854, ten paid dividends between five and ten per cent, but fifteen paid no dividend at all. Train speeds, after the spurt at the time of the Gauge War, had shown little tendency to increase further. The system was expanding steadily rather than spectacularly: some 7,100 miles open in 1852 increased to 9,800 in 1859. Most of this expansion had taken place in areas previously served inadequately – the West Country, South East England, North East Scotland (from Aberdeen to Inverness). In 1857, however, the Midland eventually reacted to being bypassed as a through route to the North by opening its line from Leicester to Hitchin, whence the Great Northern took its trains to London. It was the start of a process which would eventually give the Midland its own routes to London and (for Scotland) Carlisle, in 1868 and 1876 respectively.

This process of steady expansion continued over succeeding decades. Railways were constructed by new companies over many of the routes for which they had been authorised during the mania but remained unbuilt because of the slump. Gaps in the railway map were filled in, London termini were built (Charing Cross and Cannon Street in 1864 and 1866 respectively, Liverpool Street in 1874), railways were built in the mountainous regions of mid-Wales and the Scottish Highlands during the 1860s and 70s. The long-proposed direct line to Liverpool, crossing the Mersey at Runcorn, was opened in 1869. Amalgamations continued: the pioneer Stockton & Darlington Railway, and the Newcastle & Carlisle, were amalgamated with the North Eastern in 1861, and in the mid-1860s a series of amalgamations took most of the lowland railways in Scotland into either the North British, the Caledonian or the Glasgow & South Western.

The urban underground railway was born in 1863 with the opening of the Metropolitan Railway (authorised in 1859) from Paddington to Farringdon Street. It was of mixed gauge and, of course, steam-worked. The same year the practicability of steam locomotives on a gauge much narrower than previously known was demonstrated when steam traction was introduced on to the 1 ft 11½ in. gauge Festiniog Railway. The obvious economies to be derived from building railways to a narrower-than-standard gauge resulted in another mild gauge war: but the results of this were seen not so much in Britain (where memories of the Battle of the Gauges were too green) as elsewhere – for instance in construction of secondary lines of 3 ft gauge in broad gauge Ireland, and 1 metre gauge or less in broad gauge India. From favouring a broad gauge, objective engineering opinion was reversed to favouring a narrow one — few countries under British influence into which railways were subsequently introduced for the first time adopted a gauge as wide as 4 ft 8½ in. But here the author is being lured away from the present subject into a specific enthusiasm. Having outlined the general development of railways down to the 1860s, let us now consider the development of their principal features.

5 : The Post Office and the Railways

Mail by Rail

One of the most important influences on railway operation, at the start of the main line era, was the Post Office. Perhaps it was the most important. The Post Office at that time was not merely the national communications undertaking – it was also, with its mail coach system, the national passenger transport undertaking. Its services extended throughout the length and breadth of the British Isles. It was effective, efficient, essential, influential, and powerful. The methods by which it achieved this, involving frugality in the national interest allied with strict but not inhuman discipline, have been outlined in chapter one. Yet the new railways held within themselves the power to cause its collapse, and in 1837 this likelihood became a matter of national concern.

In the early 1830s that possibility had been far from evident. The mail coaches were feeling the competition from fast day coaches which had been introduced, following widespread road improvements, between London and towns up to 100 miles distant, but the system was still functioning well. Indeed without the easy mobility which effective mail and stage coach networks gave to engineers, lawyers and financiers, the railway system could never have been built as quickly as it was.

The suggestion that the Stockton & Darlington Railway might be used to carry the mails had been made to Francis Freeling, Secretary to the Post Office, in 1827, but not at that time taken up. The Post Office was, however, prompt to make use of the Liverpool & Manchester Railway. Using it to carry the mails was being considered during October 1830, and on 11 November, less than two months after the opening of the line, the mails were first conveyed by train. On 15 November, Freeling reported to the Postmaster General that 'the new arrangement for conveying the Mail Bags between Liverpool and Manchester by the Railway has commenced and succeeded well for the first two days'.* Now, stage coaches had adopted the term *guard* from mail coaches, and railways in turn adopted it from stage coaches for the man in charge of a train. But so far as the mails were concerned, it continued to be a Post Office mail guard who was in charge of them: he was supplied from and acted under the mail coach department. Only his conveyance was changed. The usual mail coach of the roads was replaced by one of the railway mail coaches described in chapter eight. According to Bury (*Coloured Views on the Liverpool & Manchester Railway*) three to four hours were saved in the time of writing and receiving an answer between the two towns. On arrival at Liverpool, at certain times, the mail guard had to walk with the bags to the post office; at others they were conveyed by horse.

The GPO proposed to seek insertion of clauses for compulsory carriage of mails into the Acts for the London & Birmingham and Grand Junction Railways, but withdrew them on the understanding that the respective companies would enter into agreements. In April 1835, however, it entered into a contract with the Dublin & Kingstown Railway, opened a few months earlier, for that company to carry the mails. The Dublin & Kingstown, though only six miles long, formed part of the grand line of communication between England and Ireland: a special train was kept available at Kingstown from 5.30 am, waiting to convey the Holyhead mails onward to Dublin as soon as the steamer arrived. Other mails were carried by ordinary trains, the mail guard and the mails travelling in a compartment of an ordinary coach. The London & Greenwich Railway was in due course used to carry local post.

In May 1837 Lt Col. Maberly, who had succeeded Freeling, and George Louis, Surveyor and Superintendent of Mail Coaches, inspected the Grand Junction line as it neared completion, and agreement was reached with the company in time for the GJR to carry mails from its opening day. On the evening of 3 July 1837, George Louis set out from London accompanying the Liverpool mails, by coach at the usual time of 8 pm. But the coach ran to Birmingham, arriving there in the early morning in time, it appears, for the mails, and the superintendent, to be transferred to the very first train from Birmingham to Liverpool.

So far, so good. The average speed of Grand Junction trains at first

---

* Post Office Archives ref. POST 11/16 item 2.

was about 21.6 mph, more than double that of mail coaches on the roads. But it was not merely the wish of the Post Office to take advantage of the accelerated means of transport that had caused it to transfer the mails to the railway: the change was forced on it in any event because the mail coach contractors, aware that they would no longer get the passengers essential to their operations once the faster railway was open parallel to their routes, gave notice to quit. Four mail coach routes were discontinued once the Grand Junction was open, and at least one other was diverted to run through towns further away from it.

However, although the superiority of the railway was clear to the mail coach contractors, to the directors of the Grand Junction the full capabilities of their railway – the first long-distance trunk line – were as yet far from clear, and so were the costs likely to be involved in running it. They soon found that the Post Office had driven a hard bargain over the carriage of mails, while the early morning and late evening trains needed for them were unpopular with passengers, sometimes carrying only seven or eight people. The Grand Junction considered that it was losing £10 a day from carrying the mails: in the autumn of 1837 it gave the Post Office notice to quit from 5 February following.

Now the Post Office was just as inexperienced as the Grand Junction directors in knowing what level of service it might reasonably demand from a long-distance railway, and what it should cost. But one thing was uncomfortably clear: whereas the Post Office had been able to impose its own stringent conditions on the mail coach contractors, it itself was going to be entirely at the mercy of the railway companies, which had the power to exact what terms and conditions they pleased, unless something was done. What was in fact done was that in November 1837 a select committee of the House of Commons was appointed to consider the subject, and legislation followed.

In the meantime the Post Office had to conclude a new agreement with the Grand Junction. After detailed negotiation between George Louis and John Moss (GJR chairman), an agreement was reached, the gist of which was that the railway would convey the mails by trains at agreed departure times; it was to last until the London & Birmingham Railway was opened, at which point the times would have to be revised. The Post Office was to pay the railway a certain amount per trip, paying more for the morning and evening trips to make up for the lack of passengers. This agreement, John Moss announced, increased revenue considerably without exacting from the Post Office unreasonable conditions. On the other hand, Postmaster General Lord Lichfield considered that the Grand Junction terms were exorbitant: they would triple annual expense to the Post Office, but he had no alternative but to agree.

Select Committee and Act of Parliament

The Select Committee on Communications by Railroads was appointed at the end of November 1837. Witnesses before it included Post Office administrators such as Lt Col. Maberly and George Louis, coach contractors such as William Chaplin and Benjamin Horne, railway administrators such as John Moss, railway engineers such as Robert Stephenson and Joseph Locke, and mail guard Philip Salt who was working the Birmingham–Manchester route. The latter's near-monosyllabic replies, compared with the loquaciousness of other witnesses recorded in the evidence, are suggestive of some embarrassment in such exalted company! Generally, the evidence given before the committee provides a window opening on to the concerns and conditions of the time, and much of what is written here is derived from it.

The select committee reported on 28 March 1838. Its first resolution was 'that it appears to this Committee that Companies which are the Proprietors of Railways have it in their power practically to prevent the due transmission of the Correspondence of the Country by the means of the Post-office, as well as to impose upon the Public whatever terms they think fit for its conveyance'. The legislature, it resolved, should take steps to ensure regular and speedy transmission of this correspondence by railways on terms affording their proprietors just and reasonable remuneration. This meant a bill before Parliament to compel railway companies to perform all such services as might be required from them by the Postmaster General; if the Post Office and the Companies were unable to agree upon the price to be paid, then they should go to arbitration. One arbitrator each was to be appointed by each of the contracting parties, who between them would name a third, and their decision was to be final. All this seems very reasonable, indeed a good example of the ability of the legislature of the period to get quickly to the heart of a problem when it was essential to do so.

Much more surprising to modern eyes is the committee's final resolution, that it appeared 'expedient that a power should be given to the Post-office to run their own engines upon any Railway, with a train containing a limited number of passengers and weight of luggage, if they shall so think fit, without the payment of any Tolls; subject, however, to a payment . . . for any services and accommodation which may be required from the Company by the Post-office'. But of course this was largely the mail-coach concept transferred to rails: it was not yet then fully understood that the specialised nature of a railway track meant that it was not going to be just another form of public highway. Nevertheless the idea of the Post Office running its own trains hauled by its own locomotives up and down the railways of Britain is an intriguing one.

It did not come to that, of course, although the bill as published was a draconian measure which would have given the Post Office far-reaching powers over the railway companies; these in turn petitioned against it with some success. What eventually passed into law on 14 August 1838 was *An Act to provide for the Conveyance of the Mails by Railways*. This enabled the Postmaster General to require railway companies to carry mails over railways already made, under construction or built subsequently. The mails were to be conveyed by ordinary or special trains at such hours as the Postmaster General might direct, together with mail guards and other officers of the Post Office. If required by the Postmaster General the companies were to provide carriages fitted up for sorting letters – of this, the travelling post office, more below. Railways were obliged to carry mail coaches or carts on carriage trucks. All this was to be done against reasonable remuneration by the Postmaster General, the amount to be determined by arbitration in event of difference of opinion. On carriages provided for the service of the Post Office there were to be painted the royal arms. This Act was eventually repealed in 1953, but it provided the foundation upon which present-day arrangements for carrying mails by rail continue, so far as I am aware, to be based. Upon today's travelling post office carriages is still to be seen the royal coat of arms.

While the select committee was considering, and legislation was working its way through Parliament, the London & Birmingham Railway was approaching completion. The mail coach contractors affected gave notice to quit upon its opening, and the GPO had to make arrangements for temporary continuance of the coaches. Short sections of the line had been opened in 1837, and it was open from Euston to Denbigh Hall, and from Rugby to Birmingham, early in April 1838. On 19 May the Postmaster General and the railway company reached agreement in principle over the arrangements for carriage of mails by train. The financial terms were agreed later in the month by arbitrators – one gets the impression that the Post Office and the railway company were endeavouring to follow the select committee's proposal, although the railway in appointing its engineer Robert Stephenson to act on its behalf seems to have made a curious but not unsuccessful choice. The terms were based on the premise that the Post Office should reward the railway company for running the trains which carried the mails, but not for building the railway, this being considered analogous to the way in which the Post Office paid the mail coach contractors, but was exempt from payment of tolls to turnpike trusts. The agreements were reproduced in full by H. S. Wilson in *T.P.O. A History of the Travelling Post Offices of Great Britain*, Part 1.

Mail Coaches on Carriage Trucks

With the L&BR open from London to Denbigh Hall, the Holyhead mail was transferred to rail between those points – that is to say, the mail coach was conveyed complete on a carriage truck, and resumed its usual journey down the Holyhead Road from the railway's temporary terminus. The agreement contained provision for passengers by such mail coaches to pay the proper fares to the railway. But this particular arrangement probably did not last long. Certainly, from early in 1839 the mails for Dublin were taken by train to Liverpool and thence by steamer. Telford, between 1815 and 1830, had carried out his very extensive series of improvements to the Holyhead Road, culminating with construction of his great suspension bridge to carry it across the Menai Strait; now, a mere nine years later, the Holyhead mail coach was withdrawn and the road lost the most important part of the traffic for which it had been made.

That was perhaps the most dramatic of the many changes from road to rail conveyance for mails during the period of transition which had commenced with the opening of the Grand Junction Railway. As soon as the main railway lines were opened, the mails were transferred to them. In some cases the mail coaches were, as initially on the London & Birmingham, taken on carriage trucks as far as the railway went, to complete their journeys by road. In others, mail guard and mails were carried on railway mail coaches, as on the Liverpool & Manchester and the Grand Junction. In others again, the mails were carried in travelling post offices. The first had come into use on the Grand Junction early in

1838. And, of course, as the railway system spread, so the mail coaches on roads parallel to the new railways were withdrawn; and mail coaches to and from places as yet unserved by rail had their timings altered so as to connect with London trains at the nearest convenient railheads.

In May 1838 not only the Holyhead mail coach but also mail coaches for Liverpool, Manchester and Carlisle were being carried by rail between Euston and Denbigh Hall. Once the London & Southampton Railway was open as far as Basingstoke, in June 1839, it was used to carry the *Quicksilver* mail coach – the Devonport mail coach which had been famous as the fastest of them all – between London and Basingstoke. From December 1839 mail coaches were carried on the Great Western, at that date open as far as Twyford. A late instance of transfer of a mail coach complete to carriage by rail came in December 1845 when, following completion of the London & Birmingham Railway's branch to Peterborough, the London to Louth mail coach was carried by rail as far as Peterborough.

Railway Mail Coaches

By then many railways were carrying the mail, in carriages provided by the companies and bearing, in accordance with the Act of Parliament, the royal coat of arms. Grand Junction Railway mail coaches were similar to those of the Liverpool & Manchester, described in chapter eight; on the Grand Junction at least, some of the mail bags went in the boxes on the roof, others, for intermediate stations, went on the roof without further protection apart from the surveillance of the mail guard on his outside seat. In August 1837 slides and ladders were provided at Birmingham and Warrington to facilitate loading and unloading the bags. There were at that date four trains each way daily carrying mails over the GJR, and this meant not only the mails between Birmingham and Liverpool and Manchester, but also, for a section of their journeys, the mails from London to those places, to intermediate towns on or near the railway, to Carlisle, Glasgow and Edinburgh and part of the mails from London to Ireland, the other part still going via Holyhead.

Indeed, while the Post Office found the speed of Grand Junction trains welcome, it did also find that their punctuality and reliability were initially much inferior to the standards it was accustomed to achieve with its own highly disciplined mail coach system. Arrivals between half an hour and two hours late were all too common, and could

19 The 1938 replica of an 1838 sorting carriage was on view at Crewe in 1987 for the 150th anniversary celebrations of the Grand Junction Railway.
(*Author*)

20 The Post Office mail guard supervises loading of bags onto an early travelling post office. Bag exchange apparatus is clearly shown.
(*The Post Office*)

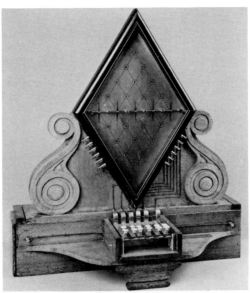

21 On Cooke & Wheatstone's five-needle telegraph instrument of 1837, the keyboard was used to deflect any two galvanometer needles simultaneously and in opposite directions, pointing out the letter to be transmitted: twenty indications in total could be made. Instruments of this type were used on the Great Western installation between Paddington and West Drayton, and had probably first been used on the trials between Euston and Camden Town.
(*Trustees of the Science Museum, London*)

THE BLACKWALL RAILWAY.

22 The Blackwall Railway, with its cable drums and, on the left, a telegraph instrument. The man on the right with his back to the artist appears to be operating another telegraph instrument with his right hand, and using his left to work a lever controlling a winding drum.
(*Trustees of the Science Museum, London*)

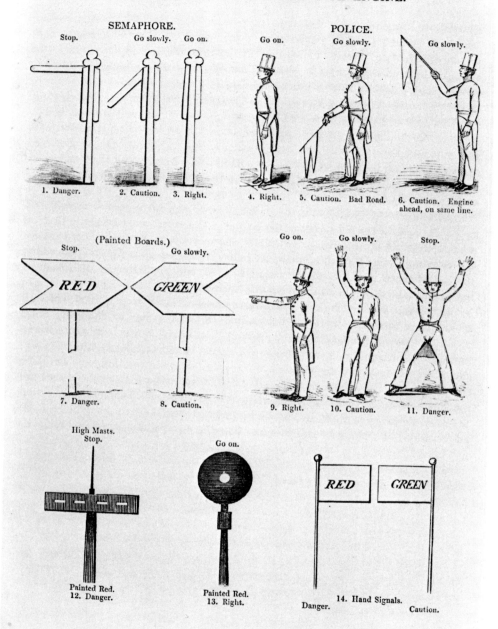

23 Signals by hand, flag, semaphore, and disc & crossbar were illustrated in Tredgold's *Principles and Practice of Locomotive Engines*, 1850. (*Trustees of the National Library of Scotland*)

24 The first railway upon which the telegraph was used to control trains on the block system was the single-track Norwich & Yarmouth Railway, opened in 1844. Cooke's principles were adopted. Similar instruments were installed at each station: in the illustration, the Norwich telegraphist has moved his handle to the left, indicating that he has a down train ready to leave, and this indication has been repeated on all the other instruments; telegraphists at Brandon Junction and Brundall have moved their levers so that the needles for those stations indicate acceptance of the train. A two-needle telegraph for general communication is mounted above the train-control instruments. (*Trustees of the Science Museum, London*)

25 This is how the *Illustrated London News* depicted the scene in the Nine Elms telegraph office in 1845 when a game of chess was played over the London & South Western Railway's electric telegraph, between players in London and Gosport. Wheatstone was probably present, and is perhaps the bespectacled figure on the left. (*Mary Evans Picture Library*)

dislocate connections as far afield as Edinburgh. But transfer of mails from road to rail went on inexorably. Probably the introduction of penny postage in 1840, which greatly increased the volume of mails, would have been impossible otherwise.

In 1841 the Post Office reported to the House of Commons the railway routes upon which mail guards were employed, and as an indicator of the extent of mail carriage by rail in that year the list is worth reproducing in full:

London – Bristol	Leeds – Hull
London – Lancaster	Liverpool – Manchester
London – Rugby	Liverpool – Warrington
London – Southampton	Manchester – Leeds
Birmingham – Derby	Manchester – Warrington
Birmingham – Gloucester	Masborough (Rotherham) – Sheffield
Birmingham – Liverpool	Rugby – Leeds
Carlisle – Newcastle	Stockton – Darlington
Crewe – Birkenhead	Wakefield – Darlington
Derby – Nottingham	Dublin – Kingstown

It also mentioned five railway routes over which the mails were sent without mail guards:

Arbroath – Forfar	
Glasgow – Ayr	Glasgow – Paisley
Glasgow – Greenock	Kilwinning – Ardrossan

The mails were first carried by rail between London and Brighton later in 1841, and between Edinburgh and Glasgow by 1845. In 1848, with the Chester & Holyhead Railway open as far as Bangor and in Anglesey, the mails for Dublin reverted to the Holyhead route and the *Irish Mail* train was introduced. For two years, until Robert Stephenson's Britannia Tubular Bridge was ready, the mails once again crossed the Menai Strait by Telford's road bridge; but in 1850 the railway was complete through to Holyhead.

The last horse-drawn mail coach to operate out of London was that to Norwich via Newmarket. It was withdrawn in January 1846. In the provinces, however, coaches continued to run, often in connection with trains. At this period, for instance, the mails from London to Glasgow were conveyed by train as far as the railhead at Lancaster, and thence by road coach. Because withdrawal of mail coaches on the roads was a mirror image of expansion of the railway system, mail coaches lasted longest in those areas which railways were slow to reach. They were still running in Cornwall, Mid-Wales, and through the Peak District from Derby to Manchester during the 1850s, and in the far North of Scotland in the 1870s. In some remote parts of Scotland through which railways never were built, horse-drawn coaches continued to carry the mails into the present century – between Kingussie and Fort William for instance. They were eventually replaced by motor vehicles.

Railway Mail Guards

On the roads, the Post Office mail guards on the mail coaches had built up a formidable esprit de corps, and they were popular men. As the transfer of the mails from coach to train proceeded, mail guards often found continuing Post Office employment as mail guards on trains. As early as 1840, says J. G. Hendy in his *History of the Travelling Post Office*, out of 337 mail guards, 67 were employed on railway duties. One effect of this was to increase greatly the cost to the Post Office of employing them. The guards on mail coaches received their weekly wage of 10s 6d on the understanding that this would be supplemented by tips from passengers; on railways they were no longer in a position to receive these. The Post Office seems to have appreciated the position as soon as mail guards started to travel on the Liverpool & Manchester Railway in 1830, for these guards received an allowance of one guinea a week, though whether this was in addition to or instead of their usual wage is not clear. In 1837 the Post Office established a scale of pay for railway mail guards which ranged from £70 a year for those with under three years' service to £130 a year for those with more than fifteen. In consequence the cost to the Post Office of the mail guards establishment increased from £10,513 in 1836 to £24,598 in 1840.

On the roads, should a mail coach be immobilised by accident, snowdrift or flood, the mail guard's responsibility was to get the mails forward as best and as quickly as he could – on foot, on horseback, or perhaps by hiring a post-chaise. At least one mail guard died from exposure in the snow in the attempt. The unreliability of early trains gave mail guards continuing cause to exercise their primary responsibility to get the mails forward in event of trouble. Here is an extract from the mail guard's report on a journey from Liverpool to Birmingham which commenced at 6.15 pm on 24 August 1837 – that is, during the Grand Junction Railway's second month of operation:

> While proceeding from Liverpool and between Whitmore and Stafford about four miles from Whitmore the Axletree of the Engine broke at 9.0 pm. [I] was obliged to wait on the line until another Engine arrived from Birmingham which Engine did not arrive till 7. am next morning – after starting it was found that something was the matter with this Engine and that it could proceed no further than Stafford from whence I took a chaise and four to Birmingham arriving there at 11.13 am Twelve Hours beyond my proper time. (Post Office Archives ref. Post 10/66)

H. S. Wilson records that on 4 September 1840 the North Midland Railway's down mail was delayed south of Masborough by an accident to the previous train. On this occasion the mail guard carried the bags three miles to Masborough where a special train was arranged.

Tragedy came to mail guard Thomas Dougall following his transfer from road to rail. Dougall had been guard on the mail coaches by road between Carlisle, Hawick and Edinburgh, and in 1840 had been a mail guard for twenty-nine years. By then, however, he was mail guard on the Newcastle & Carlisle Railway. On 6 March he was in charge of the mails on a train from Newcastle to Carlisle: about twelve miles short of the latter place, the mail coach was derailed and thrown down an embankment: Dougall was killed. A long rake of loaded coal wagons had been attached to the rear of the mail coach, and it was thought that the train had stopped too suddenly at a station so that the great weight of these had pushed the mail coach off the rails. Dougall left a widow with ten children destitute: she petitioned the Treasury for a pension with the support both of local notables – for Dougall had been well known and popular in the locality – and also Post Office officials, despite the absence of a precedent. Unfortunately, Post Office Archives file Post 10/121, from which these particulars are extracted, does not record whether she was successful.

It seems particularly sad that this accident should have occurred on a railway which generally treated mail guards well, protecting them from the weather by providing a compartment in which they travelled. The

N&CR's 'mails', says Whishaw, conveyed the bags and the guard only, the former in the body which was four feet high and the guard in his taller compartment at one end. The wheelbase was only 4 ft 7 in.; the evident small size of the vehicle may be relevant to the cause of the accident. Otherwise, although the position of the mail guard outside on a road mail coach was exposed enough in winter, his position high up outside a railway coach among the smoke and smuts and travelling at twice the speed was much more so. The Postmaster General authorised purchase of spectacles, or goggles, for railway mail guards, and from about 1841 more and more mail guards were travelling with the mail bags in ordinary compartments. In 1848 the Post Office made further arrangements with railway companies for the mails on some routes to be carried in charge of the railways' own guards; the importance of Post Office mail guards was reduced, although in 1854 there were 200 employed, and they remained in service for many years thereafter.

The Travelling Post Office

Two of the earliest new developments in transport made possible by railways were the travelling post office and, closely associated with it, the mail bag exchange apparatus. The history of these is fascinating, and has been little described in print. Post Office Archives hold two unpublished typscripts, *History of the Travelling Post Office* and *History of Mail Bag Exchanging Apparatus*, which were compiled in 1905 from official records by J. G. Hendy, who was curator of the Post Office record room at that time. Two recent publications, H. S. Wilson's three-part *T.P.O. A History of the Travelling Post Offices of Great Britain* and Peter Johnson's *The British Travelling Post Office* are most valuable additions to knowledge of the subjects.

Let us take the travelling post office first, although both TPO and mail bag exchange apparatus developed contemporaneously, as indeed they did also with the general expansion of mail services by railway described above. Even during the era of mail coaches on the roads there had been thoughts of constructing a vehicle within which letters could be sorted on the move, but practical difficulties had evidently prevented its adoption. Mail coaches had continued to make halts at 'forwarding offices' in principal towns no more than one hundred miles apart, so that letters could be sorted and passengers refresh themselves. The proposal that a railway vehicle could be used as a post office, in which letters could be sorted while travelling, was made by a Post Office surveyor called Karstadt and adopted by the Post Office – on the recommendation of the mail coach superintendent – during the winter of 1837–8. The advantage was not merely that halts while letters were sorted at forwarding offices would be eliminated, but that the task of post offices at intermediate places would be very much simplified, for instead of making up separate bags of letters for each of the places served by rail they would make up a single bag addressed to the travelling post office. It was considered that the number of bags to be made up daily at Walsall, for instance, on the Grand Junction Railway, would be reduced from nineteen to three.

The first travelling post office commenced operations, as an experiment, on the Grand Junction Railway between Birmingham and Liverpool towards the end of January 1838: H. S. Wilson suggests 24 January as the most likely date. The actual sorting carriage was converted from a horsebox by the GJR; presumably a horsebox had the headroom necessary for the sorting clerks to stand up and move around, which an ordinary passenger coach of the period lacked, as will be explained in chapter eight. The clerks themselves – 'active and well disposed persons' – included Mr Karstadt's son (not previously a Post Office employee). The experiment was a success.

Soon after the London & Birmingham Railway had been opened from London as far as Denbigh Hall, a travelling post office was instituted, probably on 22 May 1838. Shortly after that, the Grand Junction Railway was asked by the Post Office to build a permanent sorting carriage. Four such vehicles were in use before the end of the year. Francis Whishaw, in his *The Railways of Great Britain and Ireland*, published in 1840, describes a London & Birmingham Post Office carriage. It was fitted up in two compartments. One was a sorting room, with mahogany counter and drawers and above them several tiers of shelves with vertical divisions for sorting letters and newspapers according to destination; the other was chiefly for the letter bags distributed and collected at various places. The bag exchange apparatus described below was fitted. Whishaw had accompanied one of the Post Office clerks on a journey and, while generally admiring, was forcibly struck by the need to warm the carriage which during the winter was 'miserably cold'. The coach was 18 ft 6 in. long overall with a body 6 ft 6 in. high.

A replica of a sorting carriage of this time was built in 1938 by the

London Midland & Scottish Railway for the celebrations of the centenary of the service. It now forms part of the collection of the National Railway Museum. Small though it appears to us, the London & Birmingham company considered the original uncomfortably large and broad, and likely to delay trains from its wind resistance. The same company was reluctant to meet the Post Office demand for mail trains to run at night, for fear of accidents in the dark.

However, completion of the London & Birmingham Railway in September 1838 enabled the L&BR and GJR TPO services to be combined, and then the opening of the North Union Railway at the end of October enabled the service to operate between London and Preston, 218 miles. This was the service known to the Post Office as the 'Grand Northern Railway Post Office'. Early travelling post offices were called railway post offices, but the term 'travelling post-office' appears as early as February 1838 in Col. Maberly's evidence to the Select Committee on Railroads. Since 'travelling post office' is the term which has survived to become familiar I shall continue to use it here, to indicate a postal sorting office housed in one or more railway carriages travelling a particular route, in which mails are sorted while travelling.

As well as clerks to sort the letters, the first travelling post offices had a staff of mail guards who were otherwise responsible for the letter bags, their receipt and dispatch. The original converted horsebox was no longer used for sorting, but continued in Post Office use as a 'bag tender': Whishaw explains that this was for conveyance of through letters and newspapers. In 1840 the TPO was extended further north over the newly-opened line to Lancaster, and although lack of traffic over this section meant that from early in 1841 the TPO terminated again at Preston and bags for further north were taken by a mail guard in an ordinary compartment, from 1844 the Lancaster terminal was reinstated. By 1846, according to P. Johnson, there were eleven postal vehicles in use on the London & North Western Railway, and more were built during the 1850s; meanwhile, in 1847 the service was re-named the North Western Travelling Post Office; by this date it was running to Carlisle.

The second travelling post office to be instituted was the service between Rugby and Newcastle upon Tyne in 1845; the two sorting carriages used were similar to those on the London & Birmingham Railway. Two more carriages were added in 1850 and two more again in 1852, the latter being owned jointly by the Midland and other companies on the route, which practice was to continue, with their successors, until nationalisation in 1948. Hendy lists the following services as operating in April 1852:

London–Perth (Night Mail)   Gloucester–Tamworth
London–Perth (Day Mail)   Rugby–Newcastle
Bristol–Exeter

Holyhead got a TPO later the same year. About the same time the Rugby–Newcastle service was altered to start from Tamworth, the point at which the West Coast Route intersected that between the South West and the North East, and combined with the Gloucester–Tamworth service; in 1855 it was extended still further south so as to run between Bristol and Newcastle, becoming known as the Midland TPO. Meanwhile a day TPO between Rugby and Leeds had commenced in 1852.

The Great Northern Railway completed its main line in 1852 and in 1853 a fast overnight train was instituted over the East Coast Route between King's Cross and Edinburgh, almost certainly in an attempt to get the mail contract. It was unsuccessful: the positions of the West Coast Route, and the Midland, were entrenched, and it was to be almost twenty years before a night mail service started between London and York, and that used bag tenders in which the mail bags travelled in the charge of mail guards; a night TPO did not commence on the East Coast Route until 1910. A day mail, using bag tenders, did commence in 1853 between King's Cross and York and eventually became a TPO in 1891. Back in 1853, the principal effect of the introduction of the fast night train over the East Coast Route was to cause the West Coast night mail to be accelerated so that Perth was reached from London in 15 hours instead of 17 hours 43 minutes. Mail trains from Rugby to Edinburgh via York were accelerated similarly.

On the Great Western, mails had been carried by bag tender since the line was opened to Bristol, but it was not until 1855 that a TPO was introduced. When it did appear this proved to be not merely a TPO but for the first time a Special Mail, a train exclusively for Post Office use. When it commenced to run between Paddington and Bristol in February of that year it comprised a Fire Fly class locomotive, hauling two sorting carriages and a van.

The first travelling post office in Ireland started to run between

Dublin and Cork at the beginning of 1855. A TPO was introduced between London and Brighton in 1859, and between London and Dover, for accelerated mails to France, in 1860. Hendy lists some eleven routes over which TPOs or district sorting carriages operated in this year; staffing arrangements were altered and mail guards were no longer employed in sorting carriages, which were staffed by clerks and sorters (to which latter grade many mail guards transferred). The whole was now under direct supervision of the Inspector-General of Mails.

On the West Coast Route, the three companies concerned – at this date the LNW, the Lancaster & Carlisle and the Caledonian – agreed after much negotiation to a Post Office proposal that passenger and parcel traffic on the night mail trains should be strictly limited in quantity. This meant both that the trains could be accelerated and that they were more punctual. The trains became called the 'Limited Mails'; they were to become special mails exclusively for Post Office use in 1885, and subsequently gained the names *Up Special TPO* and *Down Special TPO* by which they are still known.

The Mail Bag Apparatus

Before railways, mail coaches on the roads were tightly timed, and it was the practice, when one passed the post office in a village where it did not stop, for the mail guard to drop the letter bag off, while the postmaster held the outgoing bag aloft on a forked stick for the mail guard to catch. This activity is shown in the illustration number 17. Attempts were made to do the same with railway trains, but meant that the trains had to slow down to eight or ten mph. On the Grand Junction, trains slackened speed at certain stations for the mail bags to be thrown down, and the Great Western was asked in 1840 for its night mail trains to slow down at West Drayton, Slough and certain other stations for bags to be dropped. But in 1837, even before the first travelling post office was introduced, it had occurred to Nathaniel Worsdell (whose earlier coach building activities are described in chapter eight) that an apparatus could be devised to enable mail bags to be exchanged. This would enable the exchange to be done at speed and in safety.

Worsdell by 1837 was carriage superintendent of the Grand Junction Railway; following experiments during that year he was granted a patent for his apparatus early in 1838. Drawings which accompanied his patent application show an arrangement of spikes and prongs at the end of an arm projecting from a GJR mail coach, so as to collect a bag from, or deliver it to, a lineside standard; on the coach the apparatus is positioned high up, to be worked by the mail guard from his elevated outside seat. These drawings are reproduced in Johnson's *The British Travelling Post Office*. Col. Maberly enquired Worsdell's terms for use of the patent, at which Worsdell asked £3,500 for its outright purchase: the Post Office responded by offering £500 for its use. Worsdell suggested £1 per mile per year and then, when that was refused, £1,500 for the use of the patent. This in turn was refused by the Post Office on 28 May, and Worsdell had lost his chance.

While Worsdell had been haggling, John Ramsey, a senior clerk in the office of the Secretary of the Post Office, had invented a different apparatus. This comprised an iron frame supporting a net, fixed to the side of a railway vehicle and arranged to open out to receive a mailbag suspended from a lineside standard, and another arrangement for dropping a bag on to the ground beside the line, where guard boards were to be fixed to prevent it going under the wheels. The whole apparatus was demonstrated satisfactorily on 30 May at Boxmoor, London & Birmingham Railway. In considering the development of the two types of apparatus, it is worth bearing in mind not only that the Post Office knew how to drive a hard bargain (in the national interest), but also that Ramsey's apparatus was the better suited for fitting to TPO vehicles – presumably it was designed with this in mind – while at this period the Post Office was locked in combat with the Grand Junction over the rates and conditions under which the mails would be carried, so that anything originating from Grand Junction sources is unlikely to have been particularly welcome!

The TPO vehicles were equipped with Ramsey's apparatus and lineside equipment was erected also at Berkhamsted and Leighton Buzzard. These came into experimental operation on 27 October 1838, and again were so satisfactory that the Postmaster General authorised erection of further sets of lineside equipment at six more places between London and Liverpool. On 5 March 1839 Ramsey's apparatus was accepted by the Post Office and came into general use: Ramsey himself, the following month, received a payment of £500 on the understanding he would take out no patent.

Operation of the bag exchange apparatus, on a TPO, was the responsibility of a mail guard. It was a task not without difficulties, as a sad little clip of correspondence in Post Office archives (ref. Post 10/113) bears out. On 17 November 1839 it was reported to Col. Maberly, by the postmaster at Northampton, that the 'down Railway Bag' had been brought back from Blisworth by the driver of the mail cart, who stated that though the bags (sic) were hung up on the standard the net was not out to receive them.

Simultaneously a report arrived, on a printed form headed 'GRAND NORTHERN Rail Way Post Office REPORT of INCIDENTS and FAILURE of BAGS', to the effect that the 'Day Mail Down' had not caught the bags at Blisworth on account of the net not being down in time, although the bags had been dropped. Mail guard J. Peters's defence, which Maberly forwarded to the Postmaster General on 19 November, is worth quoting in full:

> London November 18th 1839
>
> Hon'd Sir
>
> I [am] extremely sorry to inform you that on going down with Train yesterday I had the Missfortune to Miss the bags at Blissworth in consequence of not letting the Net down time enough it being a fog and the Steam escaping from the Engine prevented me from distinctly seeing the station the Engine also being a new one and of greater power was going much faster than the Ordinary One I was just in the act of putting the bag out at the time [illegible] thinking I was at least a mile from the Station. Hon'd Sir I am sorry that such a misstake should occur through my Neglect and this being the first that has Occurred with me I hope and trust you will Excuse
>
> > I Remain
> > Hon'd Sir
> > Your Obedient
> > Humble Servant
> > J. Peters

Pity poor mail guard Peters in his scarlet uniform, newly transferred perhaps from proud position aloft on a mail coach on the Holyhead Road, now struggling with bags and nets within the chilly confines of the sorting carriage as it rumbles northwards through the fog and escaping steam! But he was a man of good character: so the incident only cost him two days' pay.

More serious than human errors were mechanical failures of the bag exchange apparatus. Despite the initial satisfaction which it had given on trial, it was soon found that failures constantly occurred, from causes such as sinkage of the rails, high speed, oscillation of carriages, high wind and loose tarpaulins (on the Grand Junction, loaded goods wagons ran in the same trains as the mail). The Post Office appointed John Dicker, formerly an inspector of mail coaches, as an inspector specifically to supervise the working of the apparatus, and to get defects repaired. It appears that lineside apparatus was both erected and maintained at the expense of the Post Office. After long experiment, Dicker eventually produced an improved apparatus; the Postmaster General approved full scale trials in 1848.

Principal features of Dicker's apparatus included, for the first time, leather pouches in which were enclosed the letter bags to be exchanged, lineside nets in which the bags were caught, a winged carriage net with a line across its mouth to detach the pouch from the lineside standard, and the 'traductor', a hinged arm which extended outwards from the side of the carriage and from which bags for delivery were suspended.

Dicker's apparatus was first tried out at Croydon for use by South Eastern Railway trains. It had recently been decided to install bag exchange apparatus on that line. At that period there was no TPO on the SER: the apparatus was mounted upon an ordinary second class carriage. It worked well, further installations were made at New Cross and Edenbridge, and it came into general use on the SER in September 1848. But it was feared that it might infringe Worsdell's patent: further installations were deferred until after expiry of the patent early in 1852. It was then brought into use generally, and by September 1852 Dicker's apparatus had superseded Ramsey's at all installations. That meant it was installed at three places on the South Eastern railway, twenty-six between London and Perth, and thirteen between Rugby and Edinburgh via York. As for vehicles, it was fitted to sixteen travelling post office carriages and six bag tenders. Installation of Dicker's apparatus was an important factor in the acceleration of the mail trains to Scotland which took place in 1853.

The Post Office then wished to accelerate carriage of mails to the South West by installing bag exchange apparatus at several stations between London and Plymouth. In this proposal, however, it encountered the opposition of the engineer to the Great Western, Bristol & Exeter and South Devon Railways – Mr Brunel, no less. Brunel's objection boiled down to what we would now call tight clearances, between trains and lineside structures, which would not permit the necessary projection from the carriages; as for extending the apparatus from carriages when required and then withdrawing it, he considered this would be attended with much danger, because the high speed of broad gauge trains resulted in short intervals of time between passing lineside structures which the apparatus would foul. (All the same, Brunel was such an enthusiast for mechanical novelty that one cannot help but wonder if there might have been an element of 'didn't think of it first' in his objections!)

Eventually, in 1858, the Post Office secured a general mail contract with the GW and B&E Railways which allowed limited use of the apparatus. Hendy quotes the relevant clause:

> The Company to allow the Postmaster-General to employ the Bag exchanging apparatus and to affix it, at the cost of the Post Office, to the mail carriages of the Company, and along the lines of railway, in all cases in which the Company are unable to shew to the satisfaction of an umpire – to be named in the case of difference with the Post Office – that the employment of such apparatus will be attended with greater danger than applies to its use on other lines on which it is now employed.

Bag exchange apparatus was then installed at six stations between Paddington and Bristol, and accelerated mail trains introduced from the beginning of 1859. The London & South Western Railway directors, however, were adamant against its installation between London and Southampton.

Mail bag exchange apparatus of the same basic pattern remained in use on British Rail until 1971: by that date internal combustion had had the dual effects both of increasing the use of road transport for local collection and distribution of mails, and of enabling trains hauled by diesel locomotives, with good acceleration, to make longer and more frequent stops than were practicable with steam. The Post Office subsequently made sets of apparatus available to railway preservation societies, and sets have been installed and are demonstrated by the Great Western Society, Didcot, and the Great Central Railway, Loughborough.

Travelling Post Offices, however, despite the impacts of road and air transport, remain a basic ingredient of mail distribution; and the name by which one service is still known – *Great Western TPO* – continues to be a direct link not merely with the pre-grouping companies but with the earliest era of main line railways.

6 : The Electric Telegraph and Railway Signalling

The Great Coincidence

In the last chapter we saw how existing traditions and practices of the Post Office, strongly established during the mail coach era, persisted into the new age of railways. In this one, by contrast, we are concerned with the effect of sudden development of a new technology, which was perhaps in the long run to be of even greater importance than steam traction. That is the electric telegraph, the first practical application of electricity.

It must be one of the most remarkable coincidences of history that the electric telegraph was brought to usable form just at the period when the first main line railways were being built. Each, to realise its full potential, desperately needed the other. Only railways could provide the continuous strips of property running the length and breadth of the land that were needed for electric telegraphs, private property where the wires would be protected from harm. Only the electric telegraph could provide the railways with the means to operate their lines in safety. Yet William Fothergill Cooke and Charles Wheatstone, from working, originally, quite independently of the railway pioneers, obtained their first patent for an electric telegraph on 12 June 1837, just three weeks before the Grand Junction Railway was opened for traffic.

Today on railways, 'signals and telegraphs' seem indissolubly linked. It was not so in the beginning. Let us here first trace the origin of the electric telegraph, then consider how the early railways were signalled and operated, and then see how the two combined.

Now the early main lines, as I have pointed out, increased the speed of travel from the 10 mph of stage coaches to 20, 30 or even 40 mph, and this at the time was remarkable enough. Yet the electric telegraph did far more – it increased the speed of communications from the coaches' 10 mph to the point at which it became in effect instantaneous. But that last point needs to be qualified. There had been earlier attempts at swift communication over long distances, and some of these, from beacon fires onwards, had been effective. In 1791 the French engineer Claude Chappe invented a system of visual telegraphy: it comprised a series of towers, each within telescope sight of the next, and each having mounted on it dials upon which rotating pointers similar to clock hands indicated characters. Shortly afterwards Chappe developed his system into the semaphore telegraph: instead of pointers, hinged arms at various inclinations and in various combinations were used to pass coded messages. In England, during the Napoleonic wars, the Admiralty installed a telegraph between London and Portsmouth. Such devices could of course only be used in daylight and clear weather, and they were expensive to maintain and operate. For that reason lines which had also been built from London to Plymouth, Yarmouth and Deal were abandoned in 1816, though the Portsmouth line was maintained. In 1832 the Stockton & Darlington Railway considered establishing a telegraph between Middlesbrough and the collieries, the better to control the progress of laden and empty waggons, so that they might arrive at port and collieries as and when they were needed, without congestion or shortage. Three intermediate signalling stations would have been needed, and the scheme seems to have fallen through because of objections by landowners to the siting of these.

During the late eighteenth and early nineteenth centuries men of science were investigating the possibility of using the effects of static electricity to send messages over a distance, and after batteries to produce electric current became available the Danish scientist H. C. Örsted observed that a compass needle was deflected by electric current flowing through a wire nearby. This demonstrated, for the first time, the link between electricity and magnetism. In 1821 J. S. C. Schweigger formed the wire into a coil near a pivoted magnetic needle to increase the effect and produce the galvanometer.

Wheatstone

In May 1823 Örsted visited London; one of the people he encountered there was a young man called Charles Wheatstone, and a long-lasting friendship developed. Wheatstone's father was a London musical instrument maker and music teacher. Charles Wheatstone (1802–1875) himself developed when young an interest in science coupled with an ability to construct complex mechanisms; in particular, his musical instrument background led to investigations into the properties of sound and the transmission of sound. He made his mark among the scientific establishment in London – becoming friends with Michael Faraday, for instance, about 1825. Continued investigations into sound and light led to invention of the concertina, which Wheatstone patented in 1829, and appointment in 1834 as Professor of Experimental Philosophy (i.e., practical physics) at the newly established King's College, London. Extreme shyness in public meant that the number of lectures he was to give was very limited, though he retained the chair until he died.

At that time also Wheatstone was engaged in experiments to measure the speed of electricity, both as a spark across a gap and through a conductor. Part of the apparatus was a circuit of four miles of copper wire installed in the college basement. He had also long been interested in communication over a distance and turned his attention to electricity as the communicating agent. An essential preliminary was to establish how fast electricity travelled through a wire – whether, as some scientists of the day thought, it was but a few miles a second which would be of little use, or whether, as Wheatstone had eventually established, it was so fast as to be for practical purposes almost instantaneous. Using the four-mile circuit of copper wire he showed that the familiar effects of electricity could be made to take place at a distance – magnetic needles could be deflected, sparks produced and so on, and in June 1836 he pointed out to students how his apparatus could be converted into a telegraph.

He produced a 'permutating keyboard' in which buttons connected to battery terminals could be depressed to contact bars connected to wires leading to galvanometers, in various permutations to enable a few wires to be used successively for several different circuits. Wheatstone also had a better understanding that anyone else in Britain of Ohm's law and his work on the mathematics of electric circuits – which had been published in German in 1827 but was not available in English until published at Wheatstone's instance in 1841 – and this too was an essential prerequisite for the design of electric telegraph circuits. He later claimed to have discussed with a Mr Fox, engineer on the London & Birmingham Railway, the establishment of an electric telegraph along its line; but Fox was a junior engineer and this discussion, if it was serious, had no consequence. Wheatstone's inclination was leading his career more and more into academic research: by early 1837 he had both the knowledge and the equipment to make a practical electric telegraph, but this might have remained indefinitely a scientific curiosity in a college basement had not a stranger called on 27 February of that year. The visitor was William Fothergill Cooke.

Cooke

Cooke's father had been a surgeon at Ealing, but later moved to Durham. W. F. Cooke (1806–1879) himself went to school at Durham, and then to Edinburgh University. After a spell in the East India Company's army he returned to England in 1833 because of ill-health. He then developed a remunerative skill at making models of anatomical dissections in coloured wax, went to Paris to study anatomy, and subsequently to Heidelberg. There, on 6 March 1836, he witnessed a demonstration by Professor Muncke of an electric telegraph.

The apparatus that Muncke demonstrated had been developed from Örsted's and Schweigger's work by Baron Schilling von Canstatt. It linked one room with another: in each room was an instrument, and a battery. The instrument was a galvanometer in which the magnetic needle was suspended horizontally within the coil by a silk thread. Above the needle was s small disc of card with a cross marked on one side and a straight line on the other: as the needle swung in one direction or the other, according to the direction of the current, so either the cross or the line was exhibited. There were no switches or buttons to press: the ends of the coil wire were connected to cups of mercury, into which the ends of the line wires were dipped, presumably when a message was expected. The message was transmitted by holding the other ends of the line wires against the appropriate plates of the battery.

The demonstration had a most marked effect on Cooke. In his own words: 'I was so much struck with the wonderful power of electricity, and so strongly impressed with its applicability to the practical transmission of telegraphic intelligence, that from that day I abandoned my former pursuits and devoted myself thenceforth . . . to the practical realisation of the electric telegraph.' The conversion of St Paul on the way to Damascus was scarcely more unexpected, or more complete.

Three weeks later Cooke had completed his first telegraph. Its two instruments each had three needles, and six wires were used to give three distinct circuits. Since each needle could be deflected in either direction to exhibit either side of a card disc, or remain static to show its edges, the indications possible totalled 27. Each battery comprised one copper and one zinc plate separated by a damp porous membrane and mounted axially on a shaft; each plate was circular with on either side a projecting arm. Keys enabled the shaft to be rotated a little one way or the other: this dipped the two arms on one or other side into mercury cups to connect up the battery, the cups being wired so that the current flowed in the direction desired. Indications were shown on the instruments at both receiving and transmitting ends. So that the sender could attract the attention of the recipient, Cooke devised an 'alarum' operated by clockwork which was set in motion when an electro-magnet withdrew a catch from it.

This gave him the idea that he could avoid having a multiplicity of circuits by using a similar arrangement to start or stop a clockwork mechanism, of the type used in musical boxes, so as to indicate letters on a dial. This he called the 'mechanical telegraph' and then wasted a lot of time attempting to perfect such a device, failing at this stage because it proved almost impossible to synchronise the sender's and the receiver's clockwork mechanisms. By then he had returned to England, in April 1836.

Cooke attempted to promote his electric telegraph for communication of government orders and commercial news. He envisaged that long-distance telegraph lines might be laid alongside turnpike roads or the railways then being built. He discovered that railways had to keep extra locomotives available to assist trains up steep gradients, and suggested they install the electric telegraph to get advance warning of trains needing assistance. The first particular application for which he attempted to have the electric telegraph adopted was related to this, though not identical. Through a friend of his father he obtained an introduction to Henry Booth and proposed that the Liverpool & Manchester Railway should install it on the line between Edge Hill and Liverpool Lime Street, opened on 15 August 1836 to provide a passenger terminus more convenient than the original one at Crown Street. It was an inclined plane through a tunnel over a mile long: down the plane to Lime Street, trains ran by gravity, and up it they were hauled by cable from a stationary engine at Edge Hill.

Signalling for Inclined Planes

On all inclined planes there was of course a vital need for instant communication, between engine man or winding drum operator at the top and train crew or other staff at the bottom, to ensure that the cable did not move until the train was properly connected to it and all was ready; but how Cooke came to know of this does not appear to be recorded. However, an upbringing at Durham in the early 1820s meant that he was better-placed than most to be aware of the inclined planes with cable haulage which were a feature of the coal-carrying railways of the area.

W. W. Tomlinson in *The North Eastern Railway* tells us that both audible and visible signals were used to communicate between bottom and top of such inclines. The former comprised a bell at the bank head operated by a wire from the bank foot. The latter, on the Stockton & Darlington Railway, comprised a white disc on a 20-ft high pole at the foot of the incline which was turned edge-on to the engine house to indicate when it was safe to start hauling. On the Stanhope & Tyne there were two poles, one at the foot and the other at the top of the incline, connected by a wire – pulling over the lower post raised the one at the top. Such systems were not immune from problems, such as cows getting their legs caught in the wire and giving false signals.

The need for effective communication between Lime Street and Edge Hill was the more pressing because here trains carrying passengers were to be cable-hauled through a tunnel which meant that the engine house at the top of the plane was out of sight of the station at its foot. On at least one occasion there was a fatal accident: a porter at Lime Street was still stowing luggage on top of a coach when the train started. Had he lain down and kept still he would probably have been safe – instead he attempted to get off and was killed.

In January 1837 W. F. Cooke showed the Liverpool & Manchester directors 'mechanical' telegraph instruments, capable of giving sixty signals. The directors thought them too complex; Cooke, back in London, designed simpler instruments to give fewer signals. The L&M, however, decided upon a less revolutionary solution to their problem – a pneumatic telegraph, which was an air tube with a compressed air supply at one end and a whistle at the other by which a signal could be given. This was ready by March 1837, and although Booth still anticipated no objection to Cooke's making trials with his electric telegraph, this particular project seems to have died a natural death. By then, in any event, Cooke had other preoccupations.

Cooke and Wheatstone

W. F. Cooke's problem during the autumn of 1836 had been that he could not tell over what length of wire the 'galvanic fluid' would operate the electro-magnets essential to his 'mechanical telegraph'. He obtained an introduction to Faraday, who was unable to be of much help; he carried out experiments with a mile of wire installed around his solicitor's chambers in Lincoln's Inn with unsatisfactory results. Eventually, when he was on the point of giving up, P. M. Roget (of the *Thesaurus*), secretary of the Royal Society, advised him to approach Charles Wheatstone.

In Wheatstone, when he visited him in February 1837, Cooke found the one person who had the knowledge that he sought, and more. But although both men were deeply interested in the prospect of an electric telegraph, their approaches could not have been more different. Wheatstone was an academic; when his researches were complete, he intended that they should be published for anyone to use. Cooke by contrast was a man in search of his fortune: he planned to take out a patent. The upshot of the meeting was that in March they agreed to form a partnership and take out a patent jointly. On Wheatstone's side at least there seems in this to have been an element of 'if you can't beat 'em, join 'em'. When the partnership was eventually finalised in the autumn, Cooke was business manager, and had the sole right to contract to install telegraph lines. As business manager he was entitled to ten per cent of the profits; the remainder were divided equally.

In the spring however the partners had experimented together; they petitioned for a patent in May, which was granted, and sealed on 12 June after which it could be made public. (It was finally enrolled in December.) Laid aside for the moment was Cooke's 'mechanical telegraph'. What they developed was a galvanometer-based instrument, with, for the first time, vertical needles. This was Wheatstone's idea. A row of four or five needles on horizontal axes were positioned in line across a vertical plate or dial, which was diamond-shaped and marked with a grid. Such an instrument appears in illustration 21. Each needle was in fact one of two on a common axis, the other one being concealed behind the plate within a coil. The two needles were weighted to hang vertically when no current was passing, and formed an astatic pair, that is to say the north magnetic pole of one was uppermost and the south pole of the other. This had the dual result of increasing their response to the magnetic field of the coil (because one needle was within the coil and the other outside it) and reducing the effect on them of the earth's magnetic field.

Movement of the needles when deflected was limited by brass pins which aligned them with the lines of the grid. These passed through the axes of the needles; wherever else two lines intersected was a letter of the alphabet. To pass a message, any letter could be indicated by deflecting two needles simultaneously to point to it. Electrical connections were made and broken by Wheatstone's permutating keyboard: there were no more cups of mercury. Indications were given simultaneously on the sender's and the recipient's dial: the circuit ran from the sender's battery to one of his needles, to the corresponding needle on the recipient's dial, to another needle on his dial, back to the corresponding needle on the sender's dial and so back to the battery. This meant that as many wires were needed as there were needles on each instrument.

Experiments at Euston

The opportunity now arose to try such instruments out much nearer home than Liverpool. The London & Birmingham Railway was almost complete, and the approach to its London terminus at Euston was very similar to the approach to Lime Street: an inclined plane nearly a mile long from Camden Town, down which arriving trains ran by gravity, and up which departing trains were to be hauled by cable from stationary steam engines at the top. Cooke obtained an introduction to the chairman and secretary of the company, who passed him on to Robert Stephenson, their engineer.

Now Cooke and Stephenson had both been brought up in North East England, and had already a common acquaintance in J. W. R. Hoppner, who had originally invited Cooke to attend Muncke's lecture, but was now on Stephenson's staff. Furthermore R. M. Birse states (*Engineering at Edinburgh University*) that Cooke was at Edinburgh University 'about 1823' and Robert Stephenson for the session 1822–3, so it is possible that they came into contact at this time. No doubt in any case the shared experience helped to bring the two men together. At any rate Stephenson was sufficiently impressed to put men, materials and a large building at Cooke's disposal for trials. The building was probably the coach shed. Within it Cooke eventually laid out some fifty-five miles of wire, which could be divided into a 13 ¾-mile line of four wires for four-needle instruments.

On 4 July 1837 a demonstration was held before the railway directors. Cooke, fortunately, was in the habit of describing the progress of his work in letters to his mother which have survived, and here is how he described the demonstration:

> . . . I worked till 10 at night [on 3 July], and commenced again at 4 this morning. All my wire ends were brought to a table at one end of the room, and neatly arranged over-night; but I would try no experiments till the morning, dreading lest some of my contacts should prove imperfect, and make me fidgetty. Burton Lane [his solicitor] was with me by 6 this morning, when I applied my battery, and tried a length of two miles first — all right; then two more with the last — all right; then six miles — all right; then 8, 10, 12, 13 with the same result. . . .
>
> I . . . went home . . . and got back by 10 o'clock, the hour appointed. About 20 of the Directors were soon assembled. Mr. Wheatstone could not be present [this reads as though he had been overcome by his notorious shyness before an audience]; so I commenced my explanations . . . I . . . did not offer the experiments as a sample of what my Telegraphs were to do, but simply to show that the current of fluid would pass through miles of wire instantaneously, &c. I commenced by putting my Heidelberg instruments in motion, which excited great interest. I then rung a bell, &c., &c., and finally displayed the gradual decrease of galvanic energy in lengthened circuits by transmitting the current first through two miles, and so on to the thirteenth. . . . Mr. Stevenson (sic) was present, and played with the instruments more than anyone else. . . .

Cooke's experimental installation was evidently incomplete at the time of the demonstration described above, which was carried out at the request of directors who delayed their departure from London for a day to see it — perhaps they wanted to find out what he was up to in their carriage shed. By the end of July, however, he had a line installed between Euston and Camden Town, and was able to demonstrate this to Robert Stephenson. It appears that four-needle instruments were used, with the wires carried within a hemp rope. Insulation seems to have been inadequate, and the line was re-laid with the wires sealed into slots in lengths of wood. A short length survives to be exhibited in the Science Museum with some other relics of the period. Further trials, probably with five-needle instruments, took place over some 14 miles of wires on 8 September, without mistakes or blunders over an hour of constant working. Robert Stephenson had become enthusiastic: he recommended to his directors that they should adopt Cooke & Wheatstone's electric telegraph.

Despite this, the directors remained unconvinced. A pneumatic telegraph, with whistles, was installed on Camden Bank. As Osborne's *London & Birmingham Railway Guide* put it, after describing the pneumatic arrangement:

Electricity was thought of as a quicker signal agent, and some successful experiments were tried with it, but experience has proved that the whistle is more advantageous and suitable in every respect.

When Cooke and Wheatstone's patent, 'Improvements in giving signals and sounding alarums in distant places by means of electric currents transmitted through metallic circuits', was eventually enrolled in December it included the instrument described, the method of insulating and supporting the wires in lengths of wood, Cooke's method of sounding a clockwork alarum, a relay to sound an alarum electrically, and means to locate damage to the wires.

The Electric Telegraph on the Great Western

Towards the end of September 1837, Cooke had received a letter from I. K. Brunel, from a Great Western address, requesting a meeting. During the winter the two men became friends and Cooke negotiated with the Great Western Railway Company. The eventual outcome was very much more satisfactory than that of the negotiations with the London & Birmingham. On 3 April 1838 Cooke was able to write to his mother that he had that day concluded an agreement with the GWR. There was to be a trial of the electric telegraph between Paddington and

West Drayton, and if approved it was to be extended to Maidenhead, with an option, on the GWR's part, of extending it much further.

The installation to West Drayton was made by Cooke as contractor at the GWR's expense. There were instruments at Paddington and West Drayton, and intermediately at Hanwell. Five-needle instruments were used, and described by Wheatstone to the House of Commons Select Committee on Railway Communications in February 1840. Instruments first installed at Euston and Camden Town may have been re-used: authorities differ on this. Cooke in his book *Telegraphic Railways*, published in 1842, includes an illustration of a pair of four-needle instruments 'employed on the Great Western Railway', but does not state at which stations they were used, or on what date they were introduced. The wires, six of them, were insulated by a mixture of cotton and india-rubber and then drawn though iron pipes, a method suggested by Brunel. At first these pipes were buried, but there was so much trouble from penetration by damp that in some places they were subsequently raised above ground.

The GWR's electric telegraph was working as far as Hanwell by April 1839, and was completed and came into full use in July. It was the first electric telegraph to be used on a regular, rather than experimental, basis: and with it, electricity ceased to be just a curious phenomenon of the laboratory, and became an practical agent in the service of man.

The Great Western's first electric telegraph was not there to control trains. Its purpose was to pass all sorts of messages and to enable its capabilities to be assessed. After it had been in use for about seven months, Charles Saunders, company secretary of the GWR, described the uses made of it to the Select Committee on Railway Communications. He said that for two months the times at which trains passed West Drayton and Hanwell had been telegraphed to Paddington: this had been done to establish the reliability of the telegraph in constant use, which it had done, 'admirably'. Subsequently it was used to pass any message of importance, ranging from summoning a spare engine in the event of breakdown, to arranging for horses to be available at Paddington for passengers who required them on arrival. He foresaw that a more extensive installation would simplify the working of the railway, reduce the quantity of locomotives and carriages required, ensure punctuality, and enable accidental damage to be put right quickly. Specifically he considered it would be most useful at junctions where trains were due to connect – telegraphed messages of their punctuality would enable useless delays to be avoided; and he agreed, in answer to questions, that the telegraph would be useful in avoiding collisions.

The benefits of the telegraph were therefore mostly intangible, while the cost of installing it, though small in relation to the total cost of the railway, was substantial. It was not until 1843 that Cooke, with the benefit of a new agreement, succeeded in extending the line, as far as Slough. Here, for the first time, the wires were suspended from insulators mounted on posts. The latter were made of cast iron. The number of wires was reduced because the five-needle instruments were removed — one of them can now be seen in the Science Museum — and new ones installed: these had only two needles. The needles could be deflected together or separately, parallel with one another or not, and two or three times successively: in this way sufficient permutations were obtained to make more than fifty different signals — letters, numerals, codes. Operating them became a skilled task.

The new agreement enabled Cooke to run the telegraph over railway property at a peppercorn rent; railway messages were transmitted free of charge and public messages could be taken. So as well as railway messages, the telegraph was used to order chickens or fish, to trace lost property, to announce the birth of a son to the Queen at Windsor, and (this really brought it to the attention of the public) to report early in 1845 the presence on a train of a suspicious character seen boarding it at Slough — in consequence of which John Tawell was followed by the police from his arrival at Paddington, arrested the following day and subsequently hanged for the murder of his mistress.

During the 1830s other inventors had been active in attempting to develop a practical electric telegraph. The most notable was Samuel Morse in the USA, who started work on it in 1832, demonstrated one in 1837 and obtained a US patent, was refused a British patent in 1838 and brought his first commercial installation, between Washington and Baltimore, into use in 1844. Meanwhile another British application of the electric telegraph, which at first sight appears specialised, was to have far-reaching effects on railways. This was the installation on the London & Blackwall Railway.

The London & Blackwall Railway Telegraph

The London & Blackwall Railway was built between 1836 and 1841 to carry passengers between the City of London, residential areas, and

Blackwall where trains were to connect with steamers on the River Thames: its engineers were George and Robert Stephenson and G. P. Bidder. Bidder, like Robert Stephenson, had been a contemporary of Cooke at Edinburgh University, though whether they were acquainted at that time is uncertain. Later, though, as an associate of Robert Stephenson he must have been well aware of the electric telegraph experiments at Euston. The Blackwall line was three and a half miles long and there were initially five intermediate stations, with later additions. The stations were therefore very close together, only a few hundred yards apart. Intensive traffic was anticipated and it was probably in order to carry this safely, and also speedily and economically, that it was decided to operate the railway not by steam locomotives but by reciprocating cable haulage.

The railway was opened between Blackwall and Minories in 1840 and extended for a short distance to Fenchurch Street the following year. There was double track, of 5 ft gauge, and a stationary engine close to each terminus. As trains were hauled towards one terminus, the tail rope was paid out from a winding drum at the other, the tension closely controlled by a brakesman. Trains did not call at intermediate stations: rather, coaches were slipped to terminate there, and later re-attached to the stationary cable by grips before it was set in motion to take them back to their starting point. Passengers travelling between intermediate stations had to go via one terminus or the other. Good communications between stations, brakesmen and engine houses were imperative, but the line appears to have been considered too long for a pneumatic telegraph to be installed. Here at last Cooke had his opportunity to install an electric telegraph to control operations over a cable-worked line: he was asked to do so by Robert Stephenson in the autumn of 1839.

What he provided was a series of single-needle telegraphs between intermediate stations and the termini; the wires were within pipes as on the Great Western. Instruments at the termini were combined into a common frame, and the one which was at Blackwall is in the Science Museum. Bells worked electrically attracted the attention of staff when a message was about to be transmitted. Needles could indicate either 'ready' or 'stop'. The telegraph was used like this: suppose there is a train at Blackwall, and individual carriages at several intermediate stations; as the carriages at the intermediate stations are attached to the cable, staff telegraph the winding drum brakesman that they are 'ready' and, when they are all ready and he is too, he telegraphs 'ready' to the winding engine at Minories to start the cable. When carriages are being slipped from the cable at intermediate stations, staff there telegraph 'stop' as they arrive. In this way the London & Blackwall Railway safely operated a half-hourly service from each terminus on each line; cable traction lasted until 1849, when locomotives were introduced.

Operating the First Main Lines

Long before 1849, however, the system he had introduced on the London & Blackwall had set Cooke thinking about how it could be adapted to ordinary steam-worked railways, and so both reduce costs and greatly improve safety. Before considering this, however, it is necessary to consider how railways generally were signalled and operated at this period: and that takes us back straight away from the age of electricity to that of the horse and carriage and the open road, on which safety depended upon the driver's sight, and his ability to pull up clear of obstructions.

Horse railways, whether wooden waggonways or iron tramroads, were generally if possible laid with double track, one track being reserved for traffic in each direction; though many, for economy, were not, and had single track with sidings or passing places. The Stockton & Darlington Railway, being very long by the standards of its time, was laid as single track with a passing place every quarter of a mile or so. At these, a complex set of priorities involved locomotives and horse-drawn trains, laden and empty waggons and passenger coaches, up and down trains, and crossing and overtaking trains. It gave ample scope for altercation between drivers, no doubt brought to an end only when the line was doubled during 1831–2. A lighted candle placed in the window of a station house indicated by night the presence of passengers wishing to be picked up.

The Liverpool & Manchester Railway was built with double track. The company maintained a 'police establishment', according to *The Railway Companion* (1833), and had policemen stationed every mile or so along the road. Their duties were to guard the road, to prevent or give notice of any obstruction, and to render assistance in the event of accident. When a train approached, the policeman signified a clear road to the driver by 'assuming an erect posture with his arm outstretched': an obstruction was indicated by the position 'stand at ease'. When a passenger was waiting to join a train, a red flag was hoisted by day, and a swinging light shown by night. Initially, Liverpool & Manchester passenger trains ran at an average speed of about 17 mph, with 20 mph the maximum allowed. Passenger trains departed from the termini at fixed times, but goods trains did not: when a passenger train caught up a goods train, the latter had to be shunted into a siding for the passenger train to overtake it. Points were worked by local levers and the speeds of trains much reduced while passing over them. Subsequently, on open line, passenger train speeds were increased, though not very much. The practice known as time-interval operation grew up: policemen allowed one train to follow another only after an interval of five minutes had elapsed.

In 1833 the L&MR started to put up flag poles at junctions and crossings, to the top of which in the event of obstruction a policeman could hoist a flag to warn an approaching train to stop. From about 1834 red or white lamps were put at the top of lamp posts to signal to trains. In 1837 vertically pivoted boards, mounted at the tops of posts, were introduced on the Grand Junction Railway from its opening, and on the Liverpool & Manchester Railway at about the same time. They were the first fixed signals. The board – on the Grand Junction Railway it was a semicircular disc, the curved side uppermost, and with holes to reduce wind resistance – was presented at right angles to the track to indicate the presence of an obstruction for which the train must stop. When there was no warning to be given, it was turned parallel to the track, and therefore edge-on and almost invisible to the driver of an approaching train. Red and white lights gave the equivalent indications by night.

Signalling arrangements – hand signals, flag signals (the flags being held by hand or mounted on posts), and fixed signals of various types, all in various combinations and supplemented by lamps at night – were introduced by the other railways as they were opened. On some railways point indicators preceded fixed signals proper. In 1839 the Great Western had a point lever at Maidenhead fitted with a 'target' to indicate its position, and in the same year brought capstans into use to operate points, with a disc or target fitted to the upper part of the shaft to indicate how the points were set. By 1840 the Newcastle & Carlisle Railway had 4 ft diameter red-painted disc signals at stations: showing the signal indicated danger on both lines, and if a train was in the station a train approaching on the other line had to stop clear of the station and wait until the first had left.

Double track was usual on railways built after the Liverpool &

Manchester, with each track reserved for trains in one direction – although it was quite common in the early days, when a train was late and suspected of having broken down, for a locomotive to be sent to look for it, travelling towards it on the line upon which it was due. Should the rescue locomotive meet the delayed train in motion, a hasty reversal was necessary. This procedure was not quite so hair-raising as it sounds today, for speeds were low, curves gentle and visibility generally good. Locomotives carried white lamps in front, so that their approach might be seen in the dark (green lamps on the Great Western), and at the tail of each train a red lamp was placed. Trains followed one another on the time-interval system, so that safey was very much dependent upon enginemen keeping a good lookout. On some railways the time-interval system was developed so that as well as the 'stop' and 'clear' signals, a 'caution' signal was given to indicate that the preceding train had passed the policeman or signal only a few minutes earlier.

Following two conferences held during the winter of 1840–1 and attended by representatives of ten or more railways as widely separated as the London & Croydon and the Newcastle & Carlisle, the signalling and operating practices of the Liverpool & Manchester Railway were adopted wholly or in part by many other companies. Even so there was little standardisation of signals, but underlying almost all of them was a common principle that the function of a signal was to warn of danger when an obstruction was known to be present, and that its normal position was clear. This consideration had given rise to the use of a white light at night for clear – it was the normal colour of lights. In 1840 the Great Western had an exception in the form of a signal, installed at the approach to Reading and possibly elsewhere, in which a ball or lamp was hauled to the top of a mast to indicate that the line was clear for a train to enter the station. In general, however, it was another forty years or so before it became accepted that the normal indication for a signal should be danger, and it should show clear only when the line was known to be so.

Junctions were controlled by hand and flag signals until 1839 when for the first time, it is believed, a fixed signal was installed to control one. This was Corbett's Lane junction, where the London & Croydon Railway, opened that year, diverged as a branch from the London & Greenwich. Here a disc signal operated by the pointsman was put edge-on or showed a white light when the points were set for Greenwich: with the disc or a red light showing, the points were set for

Croydon. The Greenwich trains ran every fifteen minutes, the Croydon trains hourly.

Another development which was to be of long-lasting significance took place on this system in 1841 when C. H. Gregory, engineer of the London & Croydon Railway, erected at New Cross a signal based on the semaphore visual telegraph apparatus. An arm was mounted on a horizontal pivot at the top of the post, to indicate 'danger' when horizontal, 'caution' when inclined downwards at 45 degrees and 'clear' when vertical in which position the arm disappeared within a slot in the post. A second arm could be added at the other side of the post so that the signal could be used for trains in either direction, and such signals were installed throughout the length of the London & Brighton Railway completed the same year. The arms were operated by handles at the foot of their post and separate lamps gave indications by night.

Such were the forerunners of the semaphore signals later to be common throughout British railways: but their spread was gradual rather than immediate. At the same period (authorities differ about the precise date) the Great Western introduced an improved form of disc signal which was to last to the turn of the century. These were probably the first fixed signals to give positive indications of both 'danger' and 'clear', and replaced the ball signals. At the top of the mast were mounted at right angles to one another a disc and below it a horizontal crossbar. The masts themselves were 40–60 ft high, and pivoted at the foot so that they could be turned through 90 degrees by a lever. When the disc was showing the bar was edge-on: this was the 'clear' position – discs were usually painted red but the colour was of no significance beyond enhancing visibility. When the disc was turned edgeways the crossbar showed to indicate 'stop'. Crossbars were subsequently modified so that a plain crossbar applied to the up line, a crossbar with downward projections at the ends applied to the down line, and one with both upward and downward projections, like a flattened H, applied to both lines. White and red lamps were used at night.

This type of signal could not show a 'caution' indication, and for this purpose a subsidiary signal on a lower post was provided: green and red flags were suspended by rings from a bar forming part of a fan-shaped frame at the top of the post, and were unfurled or furled to give the indication required. The flags were not proof against West Country gales, and these signals were soon replaced by what became another distinctive Great Western signal: it comprised a pivoted horizontal crossbar with one end pointed like an arrow and the other with a recess of similar shape. One side was red, the other green: the signal was held at red, for stop, for three minutes after a train had passed, and then at green for a further seven minutes. In this state another train might pass the signal slowly, the driver understanding that there was another train ahead which he might catch up. These signals inherited the name 'fan-tail' from the earlier flag signals.

Visual signals of any sort were of little value during fog and in 1841 the detonating fog signal or detonator was invented by E. A. Cowper. A case of thin metal containing explosive had thin metal ears which could be bent down to fasten it to the head of a rail, to be exploded by the weight of a train. Gregory allowed experiments on the Croydon railway; soon afterwards detonators were adopted by the London & Birmingham and their use spread rapidly.

Despite the gradual introduction of fixed signals, hand signalling remained important. *The Illustrated London News* for 28 December 1844 describes Great Western signalling with fixed signals at stations, tunnels and junctions, and 'line signals' given by the railway's police-men or servants. They indicated 'All right' by holding the right arm horizontal, pointing across the track upon which a train was running. To indicate 'Caution' or 'slacken speed' the policeman faced the train, one arm held straight up, and 'Stop' was shown by his facing the train with his feet apart and both arms held above his head. On the London & Birmingham Railway the policeman indicated 'all clear' by standing upright with his flag furled and held beside his body. To indicate that a train must go slowly because another had preceded it within five minutes, he held out a green flag, the staff pointing upwards at about forty-five degrees; to indicate caution because of defective track, the green flag was held with its staff pointing downwards. 'Stop' was shown by waving a red flag. Other companies had similar arrangements. At night, lights took the place of flags or hand signals – red for stop, green for caution, white for clear. As the mnemonic put it:

> White is right, red is wrong;
> Green means gently go along.

Accidents

On the face of it, it seems surprising that railways operated in such an untroubled manner did not immediately have a succession of ghastly accidents. But that, once again, is to apply the standards of today to the conditions of a century and a half ago. By later standards trains then were infrequent, light in weight and slow, and in these respects inherently less dangerous than those of later periods. Nevertheless, the conditions under which they were operated were more restricting than anything known previously, and railway operators were at first inexperienced: they began the uncomfortable process, which continues to the present day, of learning from their mistakes.

At Rainhill on the Liverpool & Manchester Railway, for instance, on a foggy day in 1832, one train ran into the back of another which was stationary. Several people were killed. The directors decided that in future, when a train stopped at a station in fog, the policeman or gateman must immediately run 300 yards behind it to warn any oncoming engine. Away from stations, platelayers, other staff or in their absence the fireman were to do the same thing. Other accidents were caused on the L&MR by points being left wrongly set, and by trains running into wagons left on the line. Occasionally – and only occasionally – one train would run into another because the enginemen had not kept a proper lookout.

As the railway system spread rapidly at the end of the 1830s, an inevitable shortage of experienced staff led to accidents. 1840 was a bad year. Between 7 August 1840 and 25 January 1841 the Railway Department of the Board of Trade recorded thirty-five railway accidents involving personal injury, of which seventeen were the result of what may be called operating causes. Trains ran into vehicles left on the line, they collided with one another, they ran into the backs of preceding trains. For instance, on the Midland Counties Railway on 8 January 1841, a mail train ran into the back of a 'luggage train' which had been stopped by the freezing of a pipe on the engine. Two people were killed, two or three more injured. Earlier, on 11 November 1840, on the York & North Midland, a luggage train had run into the back of a passenger train at a station. Here too, two people had been killed, and two injured.

By 1845 the Board of Trade was attributing accidents to inefficient or absent signalling apparatus. However the Gauge Commissioners, in their report of 1846, summed up the causes of railway accidents thus: 'collisions, obstructions on the road, points wrongly placed, slips in cuttings, subsidence of embankments, a defective state of the permanent way, loss of gauge, broken or loose chairs, fractures of wheels or

26, 27 Where the line to
Bricklayer's Arms diverged
from that to London
Bridge, the South Eastern
Railway installed a lever
frame to work the points
with an additional
arrangement of stirrups and
chains to work the
associated semaphore
signals. Stirrups were linked
together to prevent
conflicting signal
indications.
(*Mary Evans Picture
Library*)

28 Edward Bury's bar-framed *Liverpool*, as rebuilt in 1831 with a multi-tubular boiler, was the fore-runner of many locomotives of this type built by Bury. (*Trustees of the Science Museum, London*)

29 Stephenson Planet-type locomotive is seen here with a train at Parkside, Liverpool & Manchester Railway. (*Trustees of the Science Museum, London*)

30 In 1837 the Liverpool & Manchester Railway had two 0–4–2 'luggage engines' built by Todd, Kitson & Laird of Leeds. One of them, called *Lion*, has survived to become the oldest workable locomotive in Britain, and is seen here in action 150 years later at the Crewe Heritage Festival in July 1987.

(*Author*)

31, 32 Period detail to be found beneath *Lion*: her eccentric rods terminate in gabs to operate her valves – they are seen here (31) in mid-gear position; her driving axle supports four springs, two outside the frames and two inside – one of the latter is seen here (32) – presumably a precaution against crank axle breakage. (*Author*)

axles, &c; and, lastly, from engines running off the line through some other cause'. A further problem was arising, however: as a result of the Battle of the Gauges, standard gauge companies had accelerated some of their trains to run at 'express speed', which caused difficulties. The first was 'The difficulty of arranging the trains, where the traffic is frequent, so that the fast trains shall be entirely protected from the chance of interfering with or coming into collision with the slower trains, or those that stop at numerous stations', and the second 'The difficulty of seeing signals, especially in foggy weather, in time to enable the engine driver to stop the fast trains'.

Telegraphic Railways

That collisions and similar accidents could be prevented by the electric telegraph was clear. Use of the electric telegraph to operate a loco-motive-worked railway was to be a technical innovation second in importance only to the steam locomotive itself. Yet, remarkably, the date and location at which this was first done are open to considerable doubt.

A strong contender is Clay Cross tunnel on the North Midland Railway, opened on 11 May 1840. According to Clement Stretton in *The History of the Midland Railway*, George Stephenson who was engineer to the North Midland was met by Cooke and Wheatstone in 1839, while the tunnel was under construction, and they explained to him the importance of the electric telegraph for controlling the working of trains. Stephenson then had an electric telegraph installed through the tunnel, and arranged for the arrival and departure of each train to be reported. If a second train arrived at either end before the previous one was telegraphed as 'arrived', it was detained until such message was received. In 1841, continues Stretton, Cooke and Wheatstone further introduced at Clay Cross electric instruments or dials to show at a glance whether the line was clear or blocked.

George Stephenson, one may reasonably assume, had been kept informed by his son of the progress of the electric telegraph since the Euston experiments of 1837, and the 1,760-yard tunnel at Clay Cross would have been an ideal opportunity for them to try it out. Yet, although Stretton must have got his information from somewhere, I have been unable to trace the story further back than his book, which was published in 1901. F. S. Williams does not appear to have mentioned it in his *The Midland Railway, Its Rise and Progress* of 1876, although he makes much of Stephenson's discovery of coal during construction of Clay Cross tunnel. Nor does Smiles mention it in his sycophantic biography of the Stephensons, though he could scarcely have resisted crediting them with so important a development had he been aware of it. W. F. Cooke made no reference to Clay Cross tunnel in his book *Telegraphic Railways* (1842), which is mentioned below – although he included an installation made on the Edinburgh & Glasgow Railway in 1842. George Stephenson himself was called before the Select Committee on Railways of 1841 – and though the principal task of that committee was to consider what powers should be given to the Board of Trade to prevent railway accidents, it spent much time hearing about practical means of doing so. Yet Stephenson, in his evidence, given on 29 March 1841, was concerned with the need for 'self-acting' (or, as we would now say, 'automatic') brakes – in appreciating the need for which he was decades ahead of his time – and in development of self-acting signals in which a locomotive, by coming into contact with something, would wind up a weight, to provide an indication to the next train how much time had elapsed since it passed. He made no mention of the electric telegraph, or of control by intervals of space instead of time.

L. T. C. Rolt, in *Red for Danger*, states that the first installation of an electric telegraph for block or space interval working through a tunnel was made in 1841 at Clayton Tunnel, London, Brighton & South Coast Railway – (although at that date the railway company was the London & Brighton). Here again, there appears to be no mention of such an installation where one would expect to find it, in Dendy Marshall's *A History of the Southern Railway* (1936), although Marshall mentions the early installations on the London & Southampton and South Eastern Railways. There was certainly an electric telegraph installation through Clayton Tunnel later, for misunderstandings in its use led largely to a disastrous accident in 1861, the context in which Rolt mentions it. It was in the aftermath of that accident that the Institution of Civil Engineers turned its attention to the subject of railway electric telegraphs, with a paper by W. H. Preece which is mentioned below. In it Preece gives an indication of the possible date of the installation, for he says, 'The Clayton Tunnel telegraph worked satisfactorily for ten years, but it failed at last.'

At any rate, some time in the early 1840s, it seems, the electric telegraph first came to be used to control the passage of trains through tunnels. Of its course of development on a more extensive scale we can be much more clear. In 1842 W. F. Cooke set out his ideas in *Telegraphic Railways*. He starts with a detailed exposition of how a stage coach was safe because it could swerve or stop, while a train could not do the first and was slow to do the second: blindingly obvious it seems to us, but still by no means familiar fact to his original readers. What the engine driver needed was a bird's-eye view of the line before him, particularly considering rapidly increasing traffic, and an increasingly large number of junctions between one railway and another.

What Cooke advocated was that railways should be divided into 'grand divisions', the terminal stations of each division mutually controlling several 'shorter stages' into which it was subdivided. That this is a development of the way in which the London & Blackwall Railway was operated is obvious. Cooke wrote that the policemen (sic) at each station would communicate by telegraphs developed from those of the Blackwall railway to indicate that a train is about to start if the line is clear, to confirm that the line is clear, to advise that the train is on line, and that it has passed such and such a station. Instruments at every station in a division would indicate the position at all the other stations.

This was the origin of the block system, of separating trains by intervals of space rather than intervals of time, which was to become the accepted means of controlling railway trains.

What Cooke foresaw at the time, however, was not only the safety which would result from telegraphic operation, but also that it would enable railways to be built with a single track. On the few existing single track railways traffic had to be limited for safety. With the electric telegraph, this limitation would disappear, and railways could be built with a single track and a corresponding reduction in the cost of engineering works.

These ideas were put into practice almost at once. The Norwich & Yarmouth Railway was incorporated in June 1842, with George Stephenson as chairman and Robert Stephenson as engineer. G. P. Bidder seems to have been in charge of construction, and had earlier recommended telegraphic operation to Robert Stephenson. The line was built with a single track, and equipped with block signalling by Cooke & Wheatstone's electric telegraph almost exactly as Cooke had proposed – the whole line corresponding to one 'grand division'. The railway was opened at the end of April 1844. The same system was used on the Norwich & Brandon Railway, which amalgamated with the

Norwich & Yarmouth to become the Norfolk Railway before its opening in July 1845. One of the Norwich & Brandon instruments, originally at Norwich Trowse, is now an exhibit in the Science Museum. While the Norwich & Yarmouth was under construction, Parliament had insisted, in 1843, in the Act for the London & Birmingham Railway's Blisworth–Peterborough branch, that it should have the electric telegraph. Here also Robert Stephenson was engineer, with Bidder under him. This line too was built as a single line and opened as such in June 1845. Heavy traffic, however, led to its being doubled within eighteen months. Earlier, the South Eastern Railway branch from Tonbridge to Maidstone had been built with a single track, equipped with the electric telegraph, and opened in September 1844.

Meanwhile other railways were installing electric telegraphs for general use. Whereas in 1843 the Board of Trade reported that only the Blackwall and Great Western Railways had the electric telegraph, in 1846 both the South Eastern Railway and the London & South Western Railway had been equipped with it throughout, and it was being installed on the London & Birmingham, Midland and other lines. The powers of the LSWR installation were impressively demonstrated in April 1845 when a game of chess was played between noted contestants situated in the telegraph rooms at its termini, Nine Elms (London) and Gosport. After about nine hours the game was eventually abandoned, but as a demonstration of the electric telegraph it was a success. Other messages were passed over the telegraph during the course of the game. According to *The Illustrated London News*, which reported the game on 12 April, the electric telegraph was normally used to 'telegraph trains, and to convey messages to and from the servants of the company'. It was also available to the public on payment. The telegraph extended from London to Gosport and Southampton, and separate wires were provided for the use of the Admiralty, which had in 1844 entered into a contract with Cooke for an electric telegraph between London and Portsmouth.

By 1845, however, not only were increasingly large amounts of capital being required for construction of more and more electric telegraph lines, but the long-simmering row between Wheatstone and Cooke was coming to a head. The partnership between two such disparate characters had never been a happy one, and a rift had been evident since about 1841. Each man tended to claim more than his due, each probably genuinely believed that the greater part of the invention and development of the electric telegraph was his own. In 1845 Cooke sought financial backing for a company to raise the capital needed. G. P. Bidder introduced him to financier J. L. Ricardo, promoter of the North Staffordshire Railway for which Bidder was engineer. Together they formed the Electric Telegraph Company with Ricardo as chairman, Bidder and Cooke as directors, the latter effectively managing director. Robert Stephenson became a substantial shareholder and, later, chairman. The patents were assigned to the company in 1846 and most of Wheatstone's rights were purchased for a lump sum of £30,000. Wheatstone himself may have been appointed scientific adviser to the company and subsequently resigned, or the intention to appoint him may never have been completed: controversy once again was to rumble on for years. Cooke and Wheatstone were never again associated, though distinguished but independent later careers culminated in knighthoods for both.

Railway Telegraph Progress

That first Great Western installation of the electric telegraph does seem however, after the initial novelty had worn off, to have been little used. In 1848 the Electric Telegraph Co, was telling the Great Western that unless the railway met part of the cost it would take the line down. Then in 1849 one of the cast iron posts fell and damaged a locomotive, and the railway company claimed compensation: following this incident, the telegraph line was dismantled.

By then, however, the Great Western had already late in 1847 installed a block telegraph through Box Tunnel. According to Mac-Dermot the instruments were driven by clockwork actuated by electricity, so presumably one of the 'mechanical' telegraph designs was adopted. The Great Western's next block telegraph installation was made in 1852 on part of the Swindon–Gloucester line, which included steep gradients and Sapperton Tunnel, following an accident the previous year which could have been avoided by use of the telegraph. Meanwhile in 1850 the railway had contracted with the Electric Telegraph Co. to install a telegraph for general use between Oxford and Banbury, and installation throughout the system commenced the following year.

Tomlinson records that constituents of the future North Eastern Railway – York & North Midland, York & Newcastle, Newcastle &

Berwick, Leeds Northern, Newcastle & Carlisle – all installed electric telegraphs between 1846 and 1853. These appear to have been for general railway use, hindered to some extent by the inexperience of staff in using the instruments. This was a not uncommon problem. Elsewhere Edward Tyer, whom we shall encounter shortly, was sent for a round journey of 200 miles to examine an instrument which he had installed two days earlier, and which was supposedly out of order, only to discover a tin box had been placed on top of it and was short-circuiting the terminals.

The South Eastern Railway's telegraph system by 1850 extended from London to Rochester, Maidstone, Ramsgate, Deal, Dover and Tunbridge Wells. Along the main line from London to Dover, a pair of wires linked the termini and otherwise had instruments only at the important stations of Tonbridge, Ashford and Folkestone. A second pair of wires was interrupted at Reigate (now called Redhill), Tonbridge, Ashford and Folkestone, each section having intermediate instruments to serve local stations. Similar arrangements were made on other parts of the system; single and double needle instruments were used, and alarum bells. We know all this because the company's telegraph engineer C. V. Walker described it in his book *Electric Telegraph Manipulation* published in 1850. Based on this book, and an illustration which appears in it, the Science Museum has recreated the SER's Tonbridge telegraph office, complete with two life-size waxwork clerks. Instruments exhibited include two Cooke & Wheatstone double-needle instruments of 1843 and a Cooke single-needle instrument of 1845.

The South Eastern Railway used its telegraph system extensively for what we would now call traffic control. Walker records that between 1 August and 31 October 1848 the Tonbridge office dealt with over four thousand messages, which he classified as: concerning ordinary trains, 1,468; special trains, 429; carriages, trucks, goods, sheets etc., 795; company's servants, 607; engines, 150; miscellaneous, 162; and messages forwarded to other stations, 499. The SER's telegraph system was also much used by the public: Cooke had sold exclusive telegraph rights in Kent to the railway company.

Block Signalling by Bells

During 1851 Walker was asked by the manager of the South Eastern to provide a telegraph link between Spa Road, 820 yards short of the terminus at London Bridge, and the terminus itself, so that the Spa Road signalman could tell the pointsman at the terminus what sort of train was coming. What Walker did was to provide a telegraph giving its indications entirely by bells: one blow on the bell to indicate a Croydon train, two a Brighton and three a South Eastern. From this was developed a block signalling system installed throughout most of the SER over the next decade, in which messages were passed from signalman to signalman, over the electric telegraph, by bell codes. To ask if he might send an up train from station A to station B, the signalman at A sent one blow on the bell to his counterpart at B, or two successively where a down train was involved. The signalman at B returned the same number of blows of the bell to A to say 'yes, you may'. When the train arrived at B, the signalman there sent three blows of the bell to A to say that it had arrived, which A repeated to show that he had understood. All bell signals, and the time at which they were sent, were entered in a book at each station. Here is the origin of inter-signal box communication by bell codes which is still in everyday use, though with more complex codes. The system spread slowly to other railways; the National Railway Museum exhibits a Stockton & Darlington Railway block bell of Walker's design dating from 1852, and the system was subsequently used on the London, Chatham & Dover and North Eastern Railways.

While Walker was installing his bell telegraphs, Edward Tyer was working on a block telegraph which would combine both needle indicators and bell signals. Tyer (1830–1912) was perhaps the greatest of railway telegraph engineers: according to L. T. C. Rolt (*Red for Danger*) no other man made a greater practical contribution to railway safety. His greatest contribution, made to single-line operation in the 1870s, is mentioned below. But the instruments he designed in the 1850s for double lines – he had set up a business making electrical apparatus for railways in 1851–are important enough. He appears to have started to develop them in 1853, and they were in use on some of the busiest sections of the South Eastern by about 1856. Separate needles for up and down lines, coloured red and black respectively, could give the indication 'Train on Line' or 'Line Clear'; sound signals were given by a bell for one line and a gong for the other. Plungers or 'piston rods' enabled the signalman to ring bells and alter needle indicators.

Tyer in 1863 described the method of operation thus to members of the Institution of Civil Engineers: 'Supposing a down train had left station A for station B, the signalman at A called B, by pressing in one of the piston rods twice. The signalman at B immediately knew that a train had left A; he then pressed in the left hand piston rod, which caused his red indicator to pass over to "train on line", and made the index at A coincide with it. A could not alter the needle on his instrument; and his instructions were to keep the ordinary semaphores raised, till, on the train arriving at B, the needle was released, by the signalman at B, which A acknowledged by one beat in reply.'

At this stage of development therefore the line was normally considered to be clear, and bell signals were not given until a train was entering a section. This is of course at variance with later and modern practice, but Tyer's system was a good one by the standards of its time and was well thought of by the Board of Trade. Other railways upon which it was used included the North London, the Great North of Scotland and the Furness.

The London & North Western Railway, from 1855 onwards, installed on its main line a telegraph system developed from Cooke's ideas by Edwin Clark. This was in one respect better than Tyer's system, and in another worse. For the first time, the needles gave three possible indications – not only 'line clear' and 'train on line' but also, when no current was passing, 'line blocked', in which position the needle was vertical. It seems to have been the intention, however, to give the latter indication only in event of the telegraph's being out of order, or of accident or obstruction. Drivers were instructed to disconnect the telegraph wires if their train broke down and blocked the line. Clark's system was worse than Tyer's in the manner of its use: the railway between London and Rugby was divided into sections of about two miles, and on to each line in these sections (except through tunnels) two, three or even four trains were permitted simultaneously. The 'train on line' signal meant only that caution was required. Huish seems to have considered the electric telegraph more as a means to increase the capacity of the line without laying additional tracks than as an aid to safety. One of Clark's instruments is exhibited in the Science Museum, in the signal box to be found in the railway gallery.

Preece's Paper

In January 1863 W. H. Preece of the London & South Western Railway read a paper *On Railway Telegraphs* . . . before the Institution of Civil

Engineers, which with subsequent discussion is a valuable record of practice up to that date (much of the material here is derived from it). Members present included most prominent railway telegraph engineers of the day and discussion occupied the whole of two succeeding meetings. (During it Captain Tyler RE of the Board of Trade addressed the meeting in tones of firm politeness, or polite firmness, which are instantly familiar to anyone who has heard his present-day successor, Major Olver of the Railway Inspectorate, address meetings of the Association of Railway Preservation Societies!)

Besides the telegraph systems described above, others were in use. The Great Northern used a curious system similar to Clark's, but in which distinct needles were used for passenger and goods trains rather than for up and down lines: indications were given in code by momentary deflections and recorded in books. On the busiest length of the London, Brighton & South Coast a system developed by a Mr Bartholomew was used, which was not dissimilar to Tyer's. Preece himself advocated a system in which, for ease of comprehension, indications were given by miniature semaphores worked by electro-magnets: it was installed on the steep incline between Queen Street and St Davids stations, Exeter, in 1862. Block instruments designed by Charles Spagnoletti, telegraph superintendent of the GWR, had been installed on the Metropolitan Railway, just opened: red or white discs appeared bearing the legend 'Train on Line' or 'Line Clear' as appropriate. Captain Tyler considered that greater uniformity was desirable. On double lines certain principles should always be observed: distinct needles for each line to be used solely for the line to which they applied, with separate 'speaking instruments' (as they were then often called) to enable signalmen to communicate with one another without being tempted to use the train instruments. Needles should be kept 'blocked over' and only become vertical when something was out of order.

Despite all this there were still divergences of opinion, not only among railway managements but even among their telegraph engineers, about the extent to which a full block system, of separating trains by space instead of time, was wholly desirable on a double track railway. Should not the telegraph simply be used as an auxiliary aid to safety? The telegraph was still imperfect, said its detractors, and likely to be damaged by lightning. More important, there was a strong feeling that anything which tended to decrease the vigilance and caution incumbent on engine drivers was likely to increase danger rather than diminish it. (The same argument was used a century later against the automatic warning system.) Busy lines were still being worked without the electric telegraph – they included the LSWR's branch to Richmond, and the Liverpool & Manchester itself, now part of the LNWR. Accidents certainly resulted from the absence of the electric telegraph: they also, sadly, resulted from its presence – notably a particularly bad rear-end accident in 1861 at Clayton Tunnel, LB&SCR, due to bungled operation of flag signals and the telegraph, which was the installation mentioned above.

Single-Track Railways

For single-track railways the advantages of the block system were indisputable. The single line of the Shrewsbury & Hereford Railway (opened in 1852) was worked by telegraph, and so was the single track Middlesbrough & Guisborough Railway, opened for goods late in 1853 and passengers early the following year, and operated by the Stockton & Darlington. On the Great Western, until 1855 single-track lines were worked by one engine only; the first to be worked by telegraph, in that year, was from Grange Court (near Gloucester) to Hereford. Long single-track lines opened in Wiltshire and Somerset during 1856–7 were also worked by the telegraph. So were West Country lines of the London & South Western Railway, commencing with the Yeovil & Exeter opened in 1860. Preece described the arrangements in his paper: they were almost identical to Cooke's ideas, with each single line divided up into districts of about fifty miles in length. These were controlled by superintendents with the power to send telegraph messages to alter crossing places, for instance, when a train was running late. On the authority of these, station staff gave written train orders to drivers, using forms provided on paper of different colours according to purpose.

Such a system was safe enough as long as it was worked properly, but tended to become dangerous from misunderstandings of telegraph messages or simply from slack working. It was therefore to some extent mistrusted and another system of operating single lines had grown up, the train staff system. Preece described the train staff as 'a sort of truncheon, made of different sizes, forms, and colours; sometimes supplied to the guard, sometimes placed in a socket on the engine, or tender. Each section of line has one apportioned to it, different and distinct from every other. No train is allowed to travel over that section without its staff.'

The train staff system, though inherently safe, was inflexible, particularly where trains were required to follow one another through a section. On the LSWR Epsom and Leatherhead line, for instance, it frequently happened that a man had to be sent on horseback to the far end to obtain the staff. Preece mentioned the train staff & ticket system, but did not explain that the ticket was intended to reduce such inflexibility, by providing authorisation for a driver, who had seen the staff, to enter a section while leaving the staff for a succeeding train.

What Captain Tyler thought about it all was this, that the train staff 'answered admirably', and there had been no instance of an accident from trains meeting one another where it was employed; where telegraph instruments had been used without a train staff, there had been a number of accidents. 'The electric telegraph was not to be depended upon for the safety of traffic on single lines', the report of his remarks continues. 'It was an admirable auxiliary for convenience, and no single line ought to be unprovided with it; but for safety he considered the train staff alone ought to be trusted.' And there, for some years, the matter rested; although when the Inverness & Perth Junction Railway's single-track line from Dunkeld to Forres (soon to become the main line of the Highland Railway) was opened later in 1863, it was equipped with block signalling by electric telegraph controlled by a superintendent.

Signal Developments

While block instruments of various sorts were gradually finding their way into use, other developments were taking place with signals, points and their operation. In 1844 the South Eastern Railway had opened a new London terminus at Bricklayer's Arms, Old Kent Road, in what was to prove a largely ineffective attempt to gain a degree of independence from the original Greenwich Railway's terminus at London Bridge. However, to control the junction leading to it, which is shown in pictures 26 and 27. C. H. Gregory installed two double-armed semaphore signals and, at their foot, a frame in which the control apparatus for the points was brought together with that for the signals, for ease of operation by the signalman. While the points were operated by hand levers which still look familiar, the signals were operated by stirrups pressed down with the feet: and these stirrups were linked together to prevent conflicting indications from being shown by the signal arms. This was the first attempt at interlocking.

Another development took place on the North British Railway, opened in 1846. It formed a junction with the early Edinburgh & Dalkeith, which by 1849 had been extended to Hawick. At this junction, two crossbar signals were provided to protect the up and down lines respectively, and positioned about fifty yards on either side of the pointsman's box, in front of which were the point levers. The pointsman soon wearied of walking to and from his signals many times a day, and rigged up wires, with chairs as balance weights, so he could pull either signal to 'clear' from his box. Such an arrangement proved so convenient that soon afterwards a signal was put up near Edinburgh 250 yards in advance of the point of danger, and from this start the use of distant signals gradually spread. The Great Northern Railway was equipped from its opening with semaphore distant signals, probably the first of their kind. Early distant signals were not necessarily associated with fixed stop signals in the later manner: at Clayton Tunnel, for instance, at the time of the accident, the signalmen gave signals by flag, but one of the initial contributory causes of the accident was a distant signal which did not, as it was intended to, return to danger automatically when a train passed it.

Interlocking

In 1852 Atkinson, engineer of the Manchester, Sheffield & Lincolnshire Railway, installed at Retford a point detector in which a perforated plate attached to the points prevented an adjacent signal from being operated unless the perforation was opposite an extension of the signal rod. The following year C. F. Whitworth patented a point detector similar to that still in common use, in which a slide incorporated into a signal wire engages with a notch in a transverse slide attached to the point blades.

One of the drawbacks to Gregory's lever-and-stirrup arrangement was that the signals were still operated quite independently of the points. In 1856 John Saxby, then a foreman in the LB&SCR works, took out a patent for an arrangement in which points and signal arm were operated simultaneously by the same lever (it is remarkable how many improvements in signalling came from a railway which was nevertheless most reluctant to allow the block system to replace the time interval). Then in 1859 Col. Yolland, the Board of Trade's inspecting officer, refused to allow the LNWR's new line between Willesden Junction and the North London Railway at Kentish Town to be opened to passengers: he had found that although a stirrup-and-lever frame had been installed at Kentish Town Junction it was still possible to clear conflicting signals. Austin Chambers of the North London Railway then added locking gear based on the principles of the point detectors described above, and the Board of Trade allowed the line to be opened. This was the first application of interlocking to a lever frame: a lever movement, which depended upon another, could not be commenced until the first had been completed. Chambers patented his arrangement; subsequently it was purchased by Saxby & Farmer, Saxby having set up in business.

From this start interest in locking and interlocking devices spread rapidly, and some ninety patents for such devices were taken out during the period 1856 to 1874. This was a period of rapidly increasing traffic, and construction of stations with more and more extensive layouts which it became increasingly inconvenient, not to say unsafe, to work as hitherto by locally and independently operated points and signals. Often, at large stations, semaphore signals were mounted in groups above the signal box which controlled both signals and points: locating signals adjacent to the precise place which trains must not pass had yet to come. Development of safety devices continued apace during the 1860s and 70s: facing point locks and locking bars, to prevent points being moved under a train, both came into use at the end of the 1860s, and improved interlocking by tappets followed in the 1870s. W. H. Preece and an associate in 1870 first interlocked block telegraph apparatus with semaphore signals, using a bolt lifted by an electro-magnet to release a signal lever when the block instrument showed 'line clear'.

As the block system spread, so did use of semaphore signals giving only two indications, 'stop' and 'clear', instead of the 'stop-caution-clear' three-position signals of the time interval system. The old 'caution' position, with the arm inclined downwards at about 45 degrees was used for 'clear', and it was no longer necessary to mount signal arms in a slotted post. At night distinctive green lights for 'clear' replaced white. (Upper quadrant arms, and yellow lights for distant signals, were however twentieth-century developments.)

The author distinctly recollects seeing, when travelling on the Isle of Man Railway in 1961, a white flag displayed to the engine driver by a lady crossing keeper near Castletown as a sign of safety. It was interesting to learn from a recent conversation with Mr M. G. Warhurst, Assistant Operations Superindendent of the Isle of Man Railway, not merely that I was not mistaken, but that white or yellow is still used to indicate clear on that line. No doubt this practice dates from the opening of the first railway in the island in 1873, and has persisted because the Isle of Man, though a Crown possession, is not part of the United Kingdom and so its railways are affected neither by British legislation nor by the requirements of the Railway Inspectorate.

On single-track railways in the mid-1870s two horrific head-on collisions took place between passenger trains, with much loss of life. These, near Norwich and at Radstock, were both caused by slack and ill-disciplined operation of lines worked by telegraph and train order. The consequences were extreme public concern over the safety of single-track railways, and the invention by Edward Tyer of the electric tablet apparatus. The authority for a driver to enter a section was a metal tablet inscribed with its name, of which supplies were kept in instruments at each end of the section. These instruments were interlocked electrically so that once a tablet had been extracted from one of them, no more could be extracted from either until the first was replaced in one or other instrument. This meant that the direction in which successive trains passed through the section was almost immaterial. The system combined the safety of train staff & ticket working with the flexibility of telegraphic operation. Tyer patented his apparatus in 1878. Ten years later the electric train staff was introduced: it worked on the same principle but the tablet was replaced by a train staff of similar appearance to those already well known to railwaymen. On the Highland Railway, an extensive single-track system was still being operated by telegraph and train order in the 1890s, and safely too, but there as elsewhere tablet or electric train staff instruments were installed, becoming a familiar accompaniment to single-line travel into which radio control is only now starting to make inroads.

Back in the early 1880s, a multiplicity of block signalling bell codes had grown up, to cause confusion at junctions. A set of standard regulations for block signalling was formulated by the Railway Clearing House, and adopted by many companies, though many also in some respects clung to their own practices. Block signalling and interlocking, however, were eventually made compulsory by the Regulation of Railways Act 1889. Meanwhile the telephone had been introduced to Britain in 1876, and the electric telegraph as a means of general communication went into gradual but steady decline. Today, so far as I am aware, it is only for block signalling in the surviving un-modernised signal boxes of British Rail, and in the signal boxes of preserved railways, that it is possible to see galvanometer-type telegraph instruments at work.

7 : How Locomotives Developed

The Stephensons

There were, by 1830, three schools of thought among locomotive designers: that of the Stephensons, of Edward Bury, and of Timothy Hackworth. Of these, the most important and influential was that of the Stephensons. *Rocket* had shown how effective a multi-tubular boiler could be, but after Rainhill they continued rapidly to develop boiler design. *Rocket*'s boiler had twenty-four tubes of 3 in. diameter, but the boiler of *Dart*, the next locomotive built by Robert Stephenson & Co. for the L&MR and delivered early in 1830, had eighty of 2 in. diameter, and subsequent locomotives had still more. The cylinders were enlarged and, since *Rocket* tended to oscillate at speed, lowered to a position nearly horizontal. *Rocket* was altered to match and it is in this form that she is preserved in the Science Museum. The efficiency of the blastpipe as fitted to *Rocket* enabled coke to be burnt satisfactorily.

With *Invicta*, completed for the Canterbury & Whitstable Railway in April 1830, Stephenson & Co. produced for the first time a locomotive with cylinders towards the front, but they reverted to the steeply-inclined position, for *Invicta* was a 0–4–0 and cylinders had to clear the leading pair of wheels. *Invicta* had a multi-tubular boiler but evidently her proportions were wrong somewhere for she proved underpowered and unsatisfactory. In 1838 her boiler tubes were removed and replaced by a cylindrical furnace within the boiler and three large-diameter tubes leading forward to a smokebox. This seems to have rendered her almost useless, and she was retired in favour of horses. Fortunately she was not scrapped, but has survived to be preserved in Canterbury.

The first locomotive built with a smokebox at the front of the boiler, on which the chimney was mounted, was *Northumbrian*, which Stephenson & Co. delivered to the L&MR in July 1830. In *Northumbrian*, too, the firebox was for the first time made integral with the rear of the boiler, instead of being an appendage to the rear of it: the locomotive boiler had reached the form which remains conventional to the present day.

Mechanically, *Northumbrian* retained the 0–2–2 wheel arrangement with cylinders to the rear which had originated from *Rocket*. Shortly afterwards, however, three engineers – Robert Stephenson, Edward Bury and Timothy Hackworth – contemporaneously produced locomotives with the cylinders placed horizontally or almost so, between the frames and with the connecting rods driving a cranked axle. None of them, however, had originated this layout: it was pioneered in the mid-1820s by Goldsworthy Gurney in his steam road coaches.

Edward Bury

The first railway locomotive to incorporate horizontal cylinders and a crank axle was Edward Bury's *Liverpool*. Bury was a Liverpool sawmill proprietor turned engine manufacturer. He started work on his first locomotive in 1828; had she been ready in time she would have run for the prize at Rainhill. In fact this locomotive, the *Dreadnought*, was tried out on the L&MR in March 1830; she had a return flue boiler and, although carried on six wheels, proved too heavy for the track and was unsuccessful. However, construction of Bury's next locomotive *Liverpool* had already started, in October 1829. One deduces that he had made a close study of the Rainhill entrants. She was ready for trials on the L&M by the end of July 1830: a 0–4–0 with wheels of 6 ft diameter – the largest wheels so far. Dendy Marshall, in *A History of Railway Locomotives down to the End of the Year 1831*, states that the boiler was not tubular but contained several convoluted flues, and that the furnace was blown by bellows. In this form it is hardly surprising that she was unsatisfactory, but she was rebuilt with a multi-tubular boiler and was ready for further trials about a year later.

Liverpool now possessed two features which were to be typical of locomotives built by Bury over the next two decades: a large firebox resembling a vertical cylinder with a hemispherical top, but in fact D-shaped in plan, and main frames built up from iron bars. The latter were a feature of *Rocket*, but the Stephensons were shortly to abandon this form of construction.

E. L. Ahrons, in *The British Steam Railway Locomotive 1825–1925*, attributes the details of *Liverpool* to James Kennedy, Bury's works manager (and later partner) who had previously worked for R. Stephenson & Co. Nevertheless, I get the impression that Bury was as much influenced by Braithwaite and Ericsson as by the Stephensons; certainly Charles Vignoles was present during at least some of *Liverpool*'s trials. The crank axle had made its first appearance on a locomotive in *Novelty*, and *Novelty* also had bellows-driven blast for the fire. Furthermore, if one considers Braithwaite & Ericsson's boiler, as fitted to *Novelty* and *William the Fourth*, enlarges the diameter of its horizontal component (not very much) and makes it into a multi-tubular barrel with, of course, the smokebox and chimney at the front, then the vertical component becomes something very like Bury's firebox in shape, and the whole boiler takes on the form of *Liverpool*'s second boiler as shown in the illustration number 28.

Unfortunately *Liverpool* left the road and turned over during trials, killing driver and fireman; the accident was attributed to her large wheels (the L&MR then fixed on a maximum wheel diameter of 5 ft) though it seems likely that light track, already worn, was as much to blame. The *Manchester Guardian*, moving away from the contemporary understanding that a railway was a form of highway open for all, commented that the company directors ought to exercise their powers to prevent any engine from running on their line which their engineer thought at all unsafe. *Liverpool* subsequently worked on the Bolton & Leigh Railway; Bury built locomotives for various railways, including the L&MR in 1832, but his big break eventually came with construction of the London & Birmingham Railway. This is mentioned below.

Timothy Hackworth

In 1829 Timothy Hackworth had been asked to design a passenger locomotive for the Stockton & Darlington Railway. He had lately returned from the Rainhill Trials, where no doubt he had taken the opportunity to examine minutely the locomotives of the other competitors. Certainly the locomotive he designed, the *Globe*, not only included features which were developments of his own earlier practice, but also features which may be seen as derived or developed from the other Rainhill entrants. The boiler had a single furnace tube with, ahead of the grate, a series of small water tubes diametrically across it, and a large copper dome on top which is said to have given the locomotive her name. The four wheels were coupled, as on *Sans Pareil*, but their locomotive was carried on springs (*Novelty*) and a cranked axle (also *Novelty*) at the front was driven from cylinders positioned almost horizontally at the rear of the locomotive (*Rocket*, improved).

Globe was built by Robert Stephenson & Co. and entered service late in 1830. She is said to have given satisfaction, achieving speeds up to 50 mph, although the cross-tubes became clogged with sediment. The design, however, was not repeated. Passenger traffic on the S&DR was not of great importance – what mattered was the heavy coal traffic. For this Hackworth developed his earlier ideas to produce two types of heavy 0–6–0 in the early 1830s. The main difference between the two lay in the type of boiler: although both combined a cylindrical furnace tube with a multiplicity of small smoke tubes, in one type the smoke tubes extended forward from the furnace to a smoke box at the front, and in the other they returned parallel to the furnace from a chamber connected with it within the front of the boiler to a smoke box at the firedoor end. Both types reverted to vertical cylinders, which drove a crankshaft to which the wheels were coupled, and had two separate tenders, front and rear, for coal and water. These early attempts to produce a heavy freight locomotive proved well suited to their task, and the type was perpetuated, with minor modifications, during the ensuing two decades. A late example, the *Derwent* built in 1845, by which date Hackworth was positioning the cylinders diagonally with direct drive to the wheels, is preserved in Darlington Railway Museum. Locomotives of this type remained in service throughout the period covered by this book – *Derwent*, for instance, was not withdrawn until 1869 and was then sold for further service on a private line – but they saw little use away from the area in which they were developed.

Planet

Both *Liverpool* and *Globe* had inside frames, between the wheels. The consequence was that if the crank axle broke there was likely to be a bad accident. Manufacturing techniques of the period could not yet be depended upon to produce reliable crank axles, and Robert Stephenson took this into account in the design of *Planet*. *Planet* was delivered to the Liverpool & Manchester Railway early in October 1830 and had horizontal cylinders beneath the smokebox driving a rear crank axle; her main frames were outside the wheels, but four additional frames running between smokebox and firebox had bearings on the crank axle either side of each crank. The axle would still be supported even if it broke, and consequences of breakage would be inconvenient rather than disastrous.

Planet was a 2–2–0. Her main frames were made as a sandwich of timber between iron plates, and her cylinders were steam jacketed. Positioning the cylinders, and with them the valves, at the front of the locomotive meant that four separate sets of rods and links had to run from the footplate to the front of the locomotive so that she could be reversed – two to lift the ends of the eccentric rods, two to move the levers which altered valve positions. Robert Stephenson & Co. appear to have started construction of *Planet* after starting on *Globe*, but to have finished her first; at any rate it was in *Planet* that the steam locomotive reached its definitive form. More examples of the type were built, and early in 1831 the first of a 0–4–0 version was completed for the L&MR.

No Planet-type locomotives survived to be preserved, and in their absence *Planet* in physical form became the missing link in locomotive development: all the better, then, to learn during preparation of this book that the Planet Project has been set up by the Friends of Greater Manchester Museum of Science & Industry to build a full-size working replica. The museum is established at the Liverpool & Manchester Railway's original Manchester terminus, and the intention is that the replica *Planet* will eventually haul replica coaches in which visitors to the museum will ride.

Bogies and Vertical Cylinders

Not that the superiority of *Planet* was instantly recognised by all. When Isaac Dodds, who had trained at Killingworth, designed a locomotive for the Monkland & Kirkintilloch Railway he used the tried and tested Killingworth pattern, although a multi-tubular boiler was incorporated. The first of these locomotives was built by Murdoch, Aitken & Co. in Glasgow (the first locomotive built in Scotland) and completed in May 1831; others followed. When the Garnkirk & Glasgow Railway, on the other hand, acquired its first locomotives later the same year, it obtained Planet-type locomotives from Robert Stephenson & Co., the first being a 2–2–0, the second a 0–4–0.

Other engineers besides Hackworth and Dodds were as yet reluctant to move away from cylinders positioned vertically – this had, after all, been the usual position for stationary-engine cylinders for over a century. Galloway of Manchester built a vertical-cylindered locomotive for the Liverpool & Manchester Railway in 1832, Sharp, Roberts & Co. built another in 1833. The latter firm also built three 2–2–0s for the Dublin & Kingstown Railway in 1834. Their outside vertical cylinders drove the rear wheels through bell-cranks. Such locomotives tended to be unsteady at speed; this defect was alleviated to some extent in three locomotives built, with vertical cylinders and bell cranks, by J. & C. Carmichael for the Dundee & Newtyle Railway during 1833–4 – these had the wheel arrangement 0–2–4, the rear wheels being carried on a bogie.

Locomotives with a leading bogie (4–2–0) were first built in the USA in 1832 with the intention of producing a type suited to the light and roughly-laid tracks of that country. They worked well in practice and some locomotives of this type were built in Britain in 1833 for export to America. With one exception, however, which will be mentioned below, this type of locomotive was not adopted in Britain.

Some 2–2–0s built in Liverpool by George Forrester from 1834 onwards were eventually to have much greater influence here. In these, for the first time, horizontal cylinders at the front of the locomotive were positioned outside the frames. This made the connecting rods and associated machinery more accessible than it was when beneath the boiler. The space available between the wheels was put to good use for (another first) these locomotives did not have two slip eccentrics, but four fixed ones. There was a pair for each valve, one of each pair fixed in the position for forward running, the other for reverse. The rods from each pair of eccentrics diverged slightly, and terminated in gabs, or wide-mouthed V-shaped jaws, which faced one another either side of a pin on the valve rod. The gabs in each pair were linked together, so lowering the gab for forward running to engage the pin simultaneously lowered the gab for reverse running to disengage it, and vice versa. The angle of the V was such that while a gab was engaging the pin it moved the valve rod one way or other to position the valve. A single linkage worked all four gabs simultaneously from the footplate, so that the driver had to move only one lever instead of four to reverse the locomotive, and no longer had to put up with handles rocking to and fro beside him whenever the locomotive was in motion.

Locomotives of this type were supplied to the Dublin & Kingstown, Liverpool & Manchester and London & Greenwich Railways. The wide spacing of their cylinders, however, made them sway so much when in motion that they were nicknamed 'boxers', a design fault alleviated in 1836 by adding a trailing axle. Four fixed eccentrics were also introduced independently by R. & W. Hawthorn when they built the 0–4–0 *Comet* with which the Newcastle & Carlisle Railway commenced its unauthorised steam train service in 1835. They managed to combine valve gear of this type with inside cylinders and inside frames, an arrangement which, though cramped, came to be used extensively.

Six wheels

The mention above of adding a trailing axle to 2–2–0 design has been slightly out of chronological sequence, for this action was first decided upon in 1833, not to alleviate horizontal swaying, but to reduce vertical pitching. Locomotives of the Planet type, with the firebox overhanging the rear axle, were found to damage the Liverpool & Manchester's light track, and pending improvements to it Robert Stephenson & Co. introduced a 2–2–2 version with the additional axle behind the firebox. This was originally intended only to check the locomotive's pitching action and normally bore little of its weight. The first such locomotive, the *Patentee*, entered service in March 1834; the wheel arrangement proved to be an excellent one for passenger locomotives, and locomotives were to be built to it until the 1890s.

While the 2–2–0 was evolving into the 2–2–2, the 0–4–0 was simultaneously evolving into the 0–4–2: Robert Stephenson & Co. delivered their first to the Leicester & Swannington Railway in December 1833. But development did not stop there: the Leicester & Swannington needed powerful locomotives to haul its coal trains and in February 1834 Stephenson sent them *Atlas* with six wheels all coupled. The 0–6–0 with inside cylinders was to become the classic British goods locomotive, and examples remained in regular use until the last few years of steam on British Rail. Another innovation for which the Leicester & Swannington was responsible, following a level-crossing collision in 1833 between a locomotive and a market cart laden with butter and eggs, was the steam whistle.

Lion

The 0–4–2 type became popular, and when in 1837 the Liverpool & Manchester Railway placed an order for two 'luggage engines' with the newly established firm of Todd, Kitson & Laird of Leeds, they were built to this wheel arrangement and were basically of the pattern developed by Stephenson four years earlier – although a prominent firebox rising high above the level of the boiler top was reminiscent of the ideas of Bury. The two locomotives were delivered during the spring or summer of 1838 and their significance is, of course, that one of them was *Lion*, which by a remarkable course of events has survived to become the oldest workable locomotive in Britain. For *Lion* was eventually sold out of railway service to power a pump in Liverpool docks. She was discovered, rescued and restored to running order for the L&MR centenary celebrations in 1930, and overhauled again to take part in the 150th anniversary celebrations in 1980. She is remarkable as a survivor not of a particularly famous or technically advanced type, but as an example of the everyday locomotive of her period; and quite a lot of her is original, or dates from no later than the 1840s – or such is the conclusion of Adrian Jarvis and Len Morris writing in *Lion*, National Museums and Galleries on Merseyside's booklet about what must surely be their most prized possession.

Lion from time to time emerges from Liverpool Museum which is her home to take part in steam at important events, and it was at the 150th anniversary celebrations of the Grand Junction Railway, held at Crewe in July 1987, that the author, as a member of the Old Locomotive Committee, was able to assist operate her. The Old Locomotive Committee – OLCO – revives the name of the group which originally rescued the locomotive from Liverpool docks and has been established as the voluntary support group for *Lion*.

A close encounter – armed with overalls and cleaning rags – with *Lion* is indeed fascinating: for on her are to be found, in reality, period features which otherwise one knows only from drawings, engravings and written descriptions. She has gab valve gear of course, and with it a reversing lever quadrant with a single forward position and a single reverse: later locomotives have link motions the earliest of which were introduced not long after she was built and will be mentioned below. Here too are sandwich frames, a four-bearing crank axle with bearings inside and outside the wheels – no doubt a precaution against crank axle breakage – leather-padded buffers, a brass-clad haystack firebox and a working steam pressure of 50 lb per sq. in. Other features, standard on later locomotives, are on *Lion* conspicuous by their absence: there are no injectors, the boiler being fed by pumps, nor, on the locomotive, are there any brakes of the usual type. The valve gear is put into reverse some distance before a stopping place so that the cylinders act as counter-pressure brakes. Yet though simple, the locomotive is clearly not experimental: she was designed with confidence as an entity. She confirms the great strides made in locomotive design between 1829 and 1838.

In 1837 the earliest 2–4–0 locomotives, with the firebox between the coupled wheels, were built by Robert Stephenson & Co., but the first examples of this type were exported, some to France and some to the USA; the first for use in Britain were built two years later. About this period the first two tank locomotives to run regularly on a public railway were supplied by Forrester to the Dublin & Kingstown Railway. They appear to have been of his outside-frame, outside-cylinder type of four-wheeled locomotive.

Bury on the London & Birmingham

This brings us to the opening of the first trunk lines. The Grand Junction Railway, despite Locke's having superseded George Stephenson as engineer, was opened with 2–2–2s built by Robert Stephenson & Co. The London & Birmingham, on the other hand, though Robert Stephenson was its engineer, did not use Stephenson locomotives. With one exception: an improved Patentee-type 2–2–2 called *Harvey Combe* was built by Stephenson and delivered as early as 1835 for use during construction of the line. Then, partly because some of the directors were jealous of Stephenson and partly because it could quite properly be argued that the line's engineer should not also supply its locomotives, no more orders went to Robert Stephenson & Co. They went instead to Edward Bury. Bury took charge of the railway's locomotive department, and the locomotives, of his distinctive four-wheeled type, were supplied by his firm – Edward Bury & Co. until 1842, Bury, Curtis & Kennedy thereafter.

Robert Stephenson attributed all this to machinations of Cropper, Rathbone, Vignoles and Bury. But earlier the Stephensons had usurped Vignoles's position as surveyor on the Liverpool & Manchester Railway, building the line which he had surveyed: perhaps the Stephensons got their come-uppance when locomotives built by Bury, whom Vignoles supported, took over the London & Birmingham which Robert Stephenson had engineered.

By mid-1839 there were 54 Bury locomotives at work on the London & Birmingham, of which 36 were passenger engines (2–2–0s) and 18 were 'merchandise engines' (0–4–0s). A year later the total had increased to 82. Bury himself addressed the Institution of Civil Engineers on the subject of his London & Birmingham 'locomotive engines' in March 1840. He claimed that both the quantity of coke consumed, and the cost of repairs, were much less than usual, and attributed this to the construction of the engines. Boiler and firebox were designed to provide a large heating surface in a small space, and promote rapid circulation of water.

Next to a good boiler which governed economy of fuel, said Bury, the most important point in the construction of a locomotive (which influenced the cost of repair) was to connect all parts firmly together by a strong and well-arranged framing, but with outside frames it was necessary to have additional inside frames which in turn meant extra friction from the extra bearings and difficulty in keeping all the bearings true.

Bury claimed that his design enabled the driver, standing on the footplate, to inspect the whole of the machinery. His four-wheeled locomotives were balanced so that weight was nearly equally distributed on front and hind wheels: an additional axle was not merely unnecessary to support the firebox, but would be disadvantageous because of the extra friction between flanges and rails.

The workmanship put into Bury's locomotives was excellent and their use became widespread. The Midland Counties Railway, engineered by Vignoles, used Bury locomotives; the Eastern Counties used Bury-type locomotives built by John Braithwaite's firm Braithwaite, Milner & Co. A late example of a Bury locomotive, delivered to the Furness Railway in 1846, has survived to be preserved in the National Railway Museum, her name (originally a nickname) *Old Coppernob* being a reference to the prominent brass cover over her firebox. They were also exported early on to the USA where their bar frames became a standard feature of American locomotive practice, eventually evolving into the cast steel engine beds of the 1930s.

Bury himself built only small four-wheeled locomotives until the mid-1840s when he at last started to build six-wheeled versions of his type, long after locomotives with six or more wheels were commonplace elsewhere. The mainstream of British locomotive development came to be through the Stephenson school and its derivatives (and with it, plate frames became standard practice). Originally, Bury's ideas were as good as any of his contemporaries', but his London & Birmingham locomotive rapidly became outclassed, and it is a matter of regret that he seems more and more to have let himself be driven into defending what he had already done rather than to have developed his ideas further.

In 1841 the Board of Trade reported that the principal railway companies had 605 six-wheeled engines in use, and 224 four-wheeled. Of the latter, the London & Birmingham accounted for 90; this company, the Midland Counties and the Eastern Counties relied solely on four-wheeled locomotives. A curiosity, at this period, were the American-built bogie 4–2–0 locomotives which the Bristol & Gloucester Railway's management, having heard of American loco-motives' gradient-climbing ability, obtained in 1840 to work their line which included the 1 in 37½ Lickey Incline. These came complete with Bury-type fireboxes and bar frames, but had inclined outside cylinders; just why a single-driver type of locomotive was preferred to four or six coupled types to climb a such a steep gradient is not clear, although since the bogie pivot was beneath the smokebox and the driving wheels ahead of the firebox a substantial proportion of the locomotive's weight must have been on the driving wheels, and the three-point suspension probably helped to keep them firmly in contact with the track despite irregularities.

Broad Gauge

For the first locomotives for the broad gauge Great Western, Brunel imposed such strange conditions on their design as to make them, when built, almost unworkable. This is as well known as his reasons for doing so remain obscure. However as early as 1836 Robert Stephenson & Co. had received an order for two 6 ft gauge locomotives for export to Russia: they were designed, at least in part, by employee Daniel Gooch, then aged nineteen, who found the wider-than-usual gauge most attractive when arranging the engine.

In the autumn of 1837 Gooch applied to Brunel for a situation on the broad gauge, and was appointed his Chief Locomotive Assistant. Two locomotives which had been built by Robert Stephenson & Co. to the 5 ft 6 in. gauge, intended for export to the New Orleans Railway, had been left on the builder's hands: these were purchased by the GWR, and their gauge widened to 7 ft. The first of them, called *North Star*, was delivered by barge to Maidenhead in November 1837, and became the GWR's first reliable locomotive.

North Star was an enlarged version of the typical Stephenson 2–2–2 of the period; her driving wheels were 7 ft diameter. Ten more locomotives of similar design were built by Stephenson for the GWR during 1839–41. Gooch then developed the design further and 62 more express locomotives were built by seven different manufacturers. Specifications and templates were provided by Swindon to ensure interchangeability of parts – the first instance of locomotive standardisation in this way. Smaller 2–2–2s were built for local passenger trains, and eighteen 2–4–0s and four 0–6–0s for goods. The biggest order for the express locomotives – twenty of them – went to Fenton, Murray & Jackson of Leeds and it was during their construction that David Joy was apprenticed there. Later he was to recollect seeing such a locomotive steamed and tested on completion, with its driving wheels resting on pulleys.

Locomotive Components

Steam pressures throughout the 1830s were usually no more than about 50 lb per sq. in. Boilers for this pressure were made from 5/16 in. thick iron plates: plates of increased size gradually became available, so that whereas *Planet*'s boiler was made from 22 plates, by 1838 the L&MR could specify boiler barrels made from four plates only. Boilers were lagged with wood strips. Mechanical pumps fed a boiler with water, test cocks indicated its level, a spring balance safety valve indicated full pressure when it allowed the steam to blow off. Boilers were fastened rigidly to frames until 1839 when Isaac Dodds, by then locomotive superintendent of the Sheffield & Rotherham Railway, allowed for expansion by fastening a boiler at the front only and allowed it to slide at the firebox end.

One of the most important developments in locomotive technology came in the early 1840s with the introduction of link motion valve gears. It is easy to see how they evolved. Consider a gab valve gear with forward and reverse gabs one above the other, opening towards the pin on the valve rod between them. Then combine the gabs into a single parallel-sided link attached top and bottom (like the gabs) to the eccentric rods and containing within it the pin, or rather a block attached to the valve rod, able to slide when the link is moved up or down. When the block is at one end or other of the link, the effect is virtually the same as with gabs; and the valve is set so that steam enters the cylinder throughout most of the stroke of the piston. This is desirable when the locomotive is starting. Raising the link from the forward position progressively reduces the travel of the valve (until the mid-position is reached) and so cuts off steam from entering the cylinder increasingly early in the stroke of the piston: steam already there continues to expand. The link can be raised once the train is on the move; this results in a great saving in steam, and therefore in fuel costs.

This is the basic principle of link motions such as Stephenson's Link Motion which was first fitted in 1842, to a locomotive under construction in Robert Stephenson & Co.'s works. It had been originated there by William Williams, apprentice draughtsman, and William Howe, pattern maker, and taken up promptly by Robert Stephenson once he was shown a model of the proposal. Other similar link motion valve gears were developed by, for instance, Daniel Gooch, and there had been earlier attempts to design valve gears to produce expansive working such as that of John Gray who designed locomotives for the Hull & Selby Railway, which were built in 1840 with a valve gear so curious and complex that it was known from its appearance as the 'horseleg gear'. But Stephenson's link motion outlasted all of these, its only serious competitor being the valve gear invented by Belgian Egide Walschaert in 1844 but not applied in Britain until 1881.

No doubt it took some while for link motions to be adopted generally and understood. As late as 1850 David Joy, by then locomotive superintendent of the Nottingham & Grantham Railway, had a driver who was familiar only with gab gears. Joy wrote in his diary: 'What a mess the driver, old Pilkington, made of his first trip [on a locomotive with link motion]. I knew right enough about driving, with link gear and expansion, and told him after starting to pull her up on the link, but he would not believe she would pull, and let her out, to stick fast at Elton, three stations on. Then I made him link her up.' Locomotives with link motion were not intended to run continuously in full forward gear, and did not produce enough steam to do so: hence old Pilkington stuck fast for lack of steam after three stations.

Like stage coaches, locomotives were driven from a position open to the elements, although since coachmen were at least allowed to sit it is a little difficult to see why engine drivers usually had to stand – indeed seats on locomotive footplates remained rudimentary until the end of steam. As speeds increased, spectacle plates were fitted forward of the footplate to protect the enginemen. Nevertheless, beards seem to have been popular wear.

The Crewe Type

At this period, the tendency was for locomotives to be designed by builders rather than railway companies, but one notable exception, on the Great Western, has already been mentioned, and another occurred on the Grand Junction from 1840 onwards. It originated because the curves by which the Grand Junction line joined the Liverpool & Manchester were of no more than 10 chains radius (they had been laid out in the first place by the Warrington & Newton Railway), and over them a 5 mph speed limit was imposed. But, as general manager Mark Huish eventually told the Gauge Commissioners, 'it is very difficult to limit them [the engine drivers] to that, because they always like to sweep round, otherwise they run a risk of not getting through'. The consequence had been a spate of crank axle breakages.

Works manager Alexander Allan had had previous experience with G. Forrester & Co., and therefore eliminated crank axles, by reviving outside cylinders. The type of locomotive which evolved, first in rebuilds and then in new construction, was a 2–2–2 with outside frames which ran the length of the locomotive for the leading and trailing wheels, and inside frames for the driving wheels: the cylinders were secured between inside and outside frames, and slightly inclined to leave clearance for the machinery. This type of locomotive proved steady, compact, durable and successful: it was eventually used on many other railways, but was known, from the works at which many were built from their establishment in 1843 onwards, as the Crewe Type. An example survives in the form of the GJR's *Columbine* in the National Railway Museum.

Long-boiler Locomotives

Otherwise the mid-1840s became a period when not only did standard-gauge locomotive design seem to diverge from the proper path of progress to disappear up a series of blind alleys, but large numbers of locomotives of inadequate and incorrect design were built and put into service. The principal cause of this was the evident superiority of broad gauge locomotives over standard gauge, and the perceived need for standard gauge locomotives to match the performance of broad while remaining within the dimensions and other constraints imposed by the standard gauge. Of the latter the most important, it was believed, was a need to keep the centre of gravity low.

Robert Stephenson, whose designs had boilers of the maximum diameter then thought practicable on the standard gauge, attempted to increase the heating surface by lengthening the boiler from the 8 ft or so then usual to 12 ft and eventually 14 ft. He was also influenced by Bury to the extent of providing a large firebox overhanging the rear axle, and using inside frames; small turntables also appear to have restricted the wheelbase to about 12 ft. The first Stephenson 'long-boiler' locomotives were 2–2–2s built in 1841, and during the next few years many were built. Boiler efficiency improved, but at the expense of producing a locomotive which swayed from side to side and was extremely unsteady at any but the slowest speeds, a feature which was aggravated by the absence from the wheels of balance weights, which were then only slowly coming into use. To produce a steadier locomotive Stephenson built at 4–2–0 type, which enabled the outside cylinders to be moved back between the carrying wheels and so reduced lateral oscillation. The first of these was completed in 1845 for the Great North of England Railway as their engine A (it seems to have been the practice on some railways to differentiate between locomotives by giving them not numbers but letters), and as 'the great A' she became one of the locomotives used for the standard gauge side of the gauge trials. She is depicted, with her broad gauge competitor, in David Joy's drawings which appear as illustrations 14–16.

As a goods locomotive the long-boiler type was successful, for high speeds were not required, and it was perpetuated for many years, particularly for industrial lines with sharp curves where the short wheelbase was an advantage. A long boiler 0–6–0T built in 1883 for the Consett Iron Company is preserved by Tyne & Wear County Council Museums Service.

Broad Gauge

One effect of establishment of the Gauge Commission was to stimulate construction of locomotives, on both broad gauge and narrow, of much greater power than those generally in use. No new locomotives had been built for the Great Western since 1842, for the company's policy was one of repair by replacement, cylinders and boilers for instance being renewed when necessary. Apart from the unsatisfactory locomotives obtained at the very beginning, no Great Western locomotive had been withdrawn. (Question 6462 of the minutes of evidence before the commissioners, to Mr Brunel: 'Are you aware that there are persons who purchase old engines for the sake of breaking them up?' – Answer: 'I was not aware of such a thing; they must have a very small run of business in the broad-gauge way.')

In 1846 Gooch's 2–2–2 *Great Western* was built at Swindon with 8 ft diameter driving wheels, 1,733 sq. ft of heating surface and a working steam pressure of 100 lb per sq. in. That June she took a 100-ton train from London to Swindon, 77 miles, in 78 minutes – an average speed, start to stop, of just under 60 mph. Subsequently her leading axle broke, and two pairs of leading wheels were substituted. In this form she became the prototype for twenty-two more 4–2–2s built at Swindon between 1847 and 1851, and a further seven built during 1854–5. Such locomotives were to haul Great Western expresses until the end of the broad gauge.

In recent years a workable broad gauge locomotive has been one of the most conspicuous absentees from the railway scene. To fill this gap the Science Museum in 1982 arranged for a full-size working replica to be built of *Iron Duke*, the first and one of the most famous of the 8 ft 4–2–2s. To reduce costs, parts were incorporated from two 'Austerity' 0–6–0 saddle tanks withdrawn by the National Coal Board (many complete examples of this class of locomotive survive, in preservation and elsewhere); parts used included the boiler from one of them. The replica *Iron Duke* was completed in time for the 150th anniversary year of the Great Western, 1985, and operated on temporary track laid in Kensington Gardens, London. She was eventually taken to the National Railway Museum where a broad gauge track was laid for her. This replica is not a reproduction accurate to the last nut, bolt and rivet, but rather a workable locomotive of the same overall appearance as the original, which enables people once again to appreciate (after an interval of the best part of a century) just how large and imposing an express locomotive was when running on Brunel's broad gauge.

Cramptons and *Cornwall*

Two types of locomotive which were intended to combine a large heating surface with a low centre of gravity in a standard gauge machine were patented in 1842 by T. R. Crampton. Crampton (1816–1888) was at that date working under Gooch on design of GWR locomotives, but he later became a noted engineer in his own right. One of the types he patented was to be a six-wheeled locomotive with the driving axle passing above the boiler, but no locomotive of this type was built until 1847, as we shall see. The other, which was to be a four-wheeled locomotive, was to have the driving axle to the rear of the firebox, allowing a boiler of large diameter to be mounted low down in a locomotive with large driving wheels. But when the first locomotives were built to this patent, in 1846, it was found necessary to have an additional pair of carrying wheels beneath the boiler, which immediately minimised the advantages of the arrangement by reducing the adhesive weight on the driving wheels.

However, when the first two Crampton patent locomotives – 4–2–0s with 7 ft diameter driving wheels – were built in 1846 by Tulk & Ley of Whitehaven for the British-owned Namur & Liège Railway, one of them was tested before export on the Grand Junction Railway, and it performed to such good effect that in 1847 the London & North Western built one at Crewe for its own use. Simultaneously it built the sole example of Crampton's other patent type, a 4–2–2 (possibly built as a 2–2–2 and quickly modified) with 8 ft 6 in. diameter driving wheels: their axle passed through a recess in the top of the boiler. The locomotive was designed by the LNWR Northern Division's locomotive superintendent Francis Trevithick, and since he was the son of Cornish pioneer Richard Trevithick it is a fair guess that the locomotive's name *Cornwall* was given her in honour of the designer's native county.

Nevertheless *Cornwall* evidently was not, in her original form, a great success, for she was rebuilt in 1858 as a comparatively conventional 2–2–2, though she retained her enormous driving wheels and so her boiler was unusually highly pitched. In this form she was much more successful, and with another rebuild in 1897 she hauled expresses until the early years of the twentieth century, and then continued in service hauling an engineer's saloon. On eventual withdrawal she was preserved and now forms part of the NRM collection.

While *Cornwall* was not repeated, Crampton locomotives with the driving axle to the rear of the firebox were enjoying some success – to a limited extent in Britain and a greater extent on the Continent. As well as the LNWR, they were used by the Dundee & Perth, South Eastern,

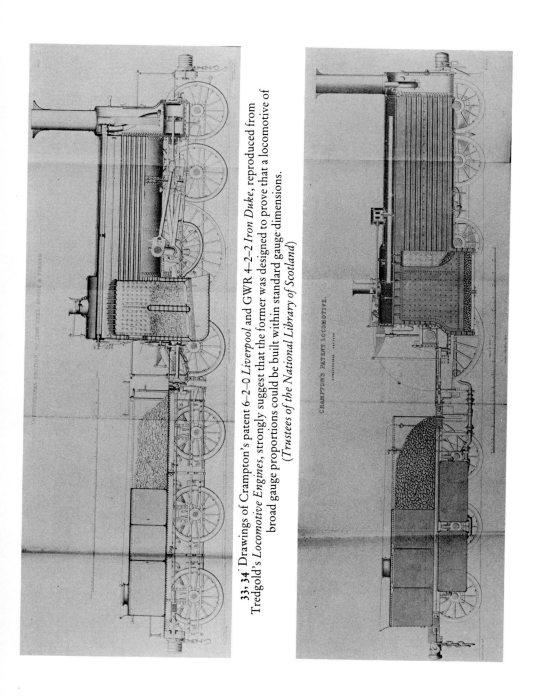

33, 34 Drawings of Crampton's patent 6–2–0 *Liverpool* and GWR 4–2–2 *Iron Duke*, reproduced from Tredgold's *Locomotive Engines*, strongly suggest that the former was designed to prove that a locomotive of broad gauge proportions could be built within standard gauge dimensions.
(Trustees of the National Library of Scotland)

35 Design of the Padarn Railway's *Fire Queen* of 1848 owed much to
Crampton's ideas. Preserved in 1890 after withdrawal, she was eventually
purchased on behalf of the Manifold Trust by John Smith M.P. and placed on loan
to the National Trust. She may now be seen at Penrhyn Castle, Gwynedd along
with other related railway exhibits.
(*D. Rendell/National Trust*)

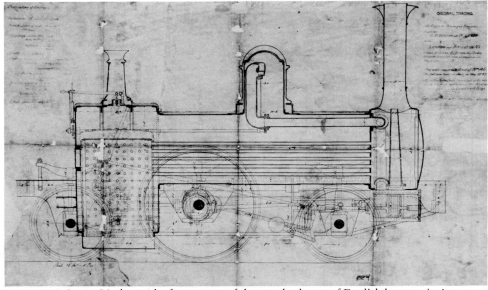

36 *Jenny Lind* was 'the forerunner of the standard type of English locomotive'
(*The Engineer*, 1896). This tracing is taken from one of David Joy's original
drawings of 1846.
(*The Institution of Mechanical Engineers*)

A First Class Train with the Mail.

A Second Class Train for Passengers.

A Train of Waggons with Goods &c.

A Train of Carriages with Cattle.

RAILWAY CONVEYANCES FROM LIVERPOOL TO MANCHESTER.

37 Ackermann's 'long prints' of Liverpool & Manchester Railway trains give a good impression of the locomotives and rolling stock of the first trunk railway, despite certain inaccuracies. These are the 1834 versions of the prints. The locomotive hauling the first class train is of the *Northumbrian* type (although no locomotive of this type appears in fact to have been named *Liverpool*); in the manner of stage coaches the first class coaches are named respectively *Times*, *Marquess of Stafford*, *Treasurer* and *Despatch*, and the mail coach is, like the mail coaches of the roads, un-named but bore their usual black and deep red livery. A privately-owned carriage is carried on a carriage truck at the rear and no doubt at the terminus its occupants will resume their usual mode of travel, hiring post-horses to draw them from stage to stage. *Fury* hauling the second class train is a *Planet* type locomotive, and *North Star* hauling the goods train is a *Rocket* type. Locomotive *Jupiter* hauling the livestock train should be shown as a 2–2–0 *Planet* type; 0–4–0 locomotives of this type had been built by the date of the print but were intended for banking heavy trains.

(Trustees of the Science Museum, London)

38, 39 D. K. Clark's *Railway Machinery* of 1855 illustrated goods rolling stock of the London & North Western Railway, including open and closed wagons, a gunpowder van and a goods train brake van.
(*Trustees of the National Library of Scotland*)

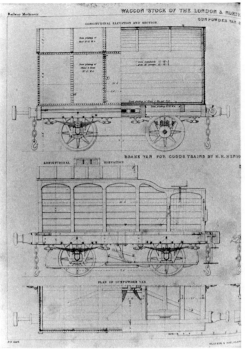

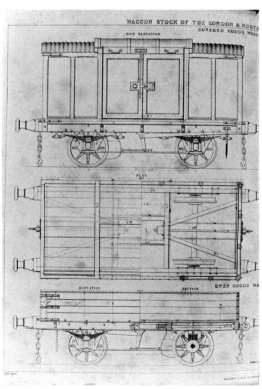

Midland and Eastern Counties Railways. Although the design appears ungainly today, it did have advantages. Cylinders mid-way along a locomotive with a long wheelbase made for lack of sideways oscillation, and since the weight was kept so far as possible on the leading wheels and the driving wheels at the rear, with the middle pair lightly loaded, there was less tendency to pitch than with an ordinary 2–2–2 which pitched about the heavily-loaded middle driving axle. And trains were light – eighty tons made a heavy train – so lack of adhesion was not so important as it would have been later.

In 1848 the Crampton design was used to produce an exceptionally large locmotive for the Southern Division of the LNWR. This locomotive, the *Liverpool* built by Bury, Curtis and Kennedy, had nothing else but the name in common with Bury's earlier productions in that city. She had the wheel arrangement 6–2–0, and one gets the impression that she was built to prove that anything that could be done on the broad gauge could be matched if not exceeded on the standard. Her driving wheels were of the same diameter – 8 ft – as an Iron Duke class locomotive, the cylinders were of the same dimensions – 18 in. by 24 in. – and the total wheelbase was the same at 18 ft 6 in. Even the suspension of the two leading pairs of wheels was similar – both axles were linked to a common spring each side. The total heating surface was greater – 2,290 sq. ft compared with 1,790, and so was the steam pressure, 120 lb per sq. in. compared with 100, although that of the GW locomotives was later increased to the former figure.

The public had the chance to make a direct visual comparison at the Great Exhibition of 1851, for *Liverpool* was exhibited there, and so was the latest Great Western 4–2–2 *Lord of the Isles*. But whereas *Lord of the Isles* represented a class highly successful in service, *Liverpool* remained something of a freak. Although she could keep time from London to Wolverton with a train of 40 carriages, the work of three ordinary locomotives, her great weight (35 tons in working order) and long wheelbase proved too punishing to track normally traversed by Bury's lightweight four-wheelers. She was soon, as D. K. Clark puts it in *Railway Machinery*, 'laid aside'. Most Cramptons in Britain were withdrawn after ten years or so of service, and all had gone by the mid-1870s. On the Continent they lasted much longer, into the twentieth century, and one is preserved by the French Railway Museum.

In view of the lack of a preserved Crampton in the UK, it is interesting to note the survival of a locomotive of this period which does, in its design, have much in common with Crampton's ideas. This is the long-wheelbase 0—4—0 *Fire Queen* built in 1848 for the 4 ft gauge privately owned Padarn Railway, North Wales, and now preserved at Penrhyn Castle Industrial Railway Museum near Bangor. *Fire Queen* was built by A. Horlock & Co. of Northfleet, Kent, and since Crampton was a native of Broadstairs it is quite possible, as R. Weaver pointed out in the *Festiniog Railway Magazine* spring 1970 issue, that he was consulted over the design. Whether this was so or not, the locomotive which Horlock produced has the rear pair of driving wheels to the rear of the firebox, and they are driven from cylinders mounted approximately mid-way along the boiler. No advantage however is taken of the arrangement to lower the centre of gravity, for the front wheels are of the same diameter as the rear ones and coupled to them by rods. These appear extremely long, for the wheelbase is 12 ft 0½ in.

The Padarn Railway carried slates from Dinorwic Quarries, Llanberis, to Port Dinorwic on the Menai Strait for shipment. *Fire Queen* was its first locomotive, and with a sister delivered soon afterwards worked all traffic until the 1880s. After withdrawal she was preserved by the quarry owners; she was eventually purchased by John Smith MP, and moved to Penrhyn Castle (National Trust) late in 1969. There is more about this railway and its rolling stock in chapter eight.

Joy and *Jenny Lind*

One person who was less than happy about the Crampton locomotive was David Joy — he found one of the earliest Tulk & Ley examples 'awfully rough to ride on, in spite of her very low centre of gravity'. But it was at this period in any event that Joy put the ship of locomotive design back on course by designing his Jenny Lind type 2—2—2. Joy had been appointed chief draughtsman at E. B. Wilson's Railway Foundry, Leeds, which was building the long-boiler engines then preferred. He was sent to Brighton late in 1846 to see about an order from John Gray, who was in charge of London & Brighton locomotives, for locomotives to his design, and get the particulars from him. Gray was a busy man and attended to this in the evenings: during the day, Joy was given an engine pass and took the opportunity to ride on as many locomotives as possible.

Back at Leeds, Joy had hardly started work on the drawings when word came that Gray had lost his job and a new engine was to be designed. In his own words:

> . . . set off scheming . . . on the lines of the last engine we had, Leeds and Dewsbury, . . . Got out 10 or 12 schemes in a week, and threw all aside – after dissension. Then – 12 noon, Saturday – Fenton [general manager] came to me and said: 'Try another, . . .' I was sick of it, and bolted for my Saturday afternoon.

But he continued:

> Arrived at home, I thought over the engine to go for – and at once it struck me what a pretty engine it would make. So abandoned the Leeds and Dewsbury type, and all the feeling in favour of the long boiler class. This was going back to the old engine, and my inoculation into Gray's ideas at once biassed me in favour of that type. I had studied very well for three weeks, and had ferretted among all the types of engines on the Brighton Railway, and had ridden on most of them, with the idea to get a definite opinion of my own which was best for big speeds.
>
> So, having a sheet of double elephant [drawing paper] mounted ready . . . I set to work and drew out with Gray tendencies a 10 ft 6 in. boiler, as big in diameter as I could get it, and as low down as I could possibly get it – for the cry was one for low centres of gravity to secure steadiness, though Gray did not seem to care for it. Cylinders, 15 in. by 20 in.; drivers single, and as far back as possible, 6 ft diameter. Inside frames, which must be made to carry the cylinders, the frames stopped at the firebox, so that the firebox was got as wide as the wheels would allow it. This, of ordinary length, gave 80 sq. ft of surface, and with 124 tubes 2 in. diameter, gave 730 sq. ft, or a total of over 800 sq. ft. Then I put on the Gray's outside frames for leading and trailing wheels, 4 ft diameter, giving the bearings below, thus making a firm wheel-base, with no overhanging weight.

Unlike Gray's locomotives, which had his own valve gear, Joy's design had Stephenson link motion. The first of these locomotives was completed in May 1847: she was finished regardless of cost – the boiler and firebox were lagged with polished mahogany and bound with bright brass hoops, the dome and safety valve covers were bright copper and there was much other bright work. She was named *Jenny Lind* after the famous opera singer. But the locomotive proved to be not just pretty to look at, but a grand performer too. Partly this was because the boiler pressure was raised (Fenton's idea) as high as 120 lb per sq. in., partly because the outside plate frame for the leading and trailing wheels had a degree of elasticity so that, in Joy's words, 'these engines, at high speeds, always rolled softly, and did not jump and kick at a curve.'

On trial on the Midland Railway the following year, a Jenny Lind locomotive hauled a train of nine coaches and two vans, weighing 64 tons, from Derby to Rotherham at an average speed of 52 mph, including an average of 47 mph up eighteen miles of 1 in 330. Locomotives of this type were soon being ordered by many other railways. In 1896 *The Engineer* magazine described the Jenny Lind type as 'in a very large measure the forerunner of the standard type of English locomotive'.

William Bridges Adams

It was the custom for the products of locomotive works to be credited to the firm rather than the individual designer, so to the general public Jenny Linds were E. B. Wilson's, just as link motion was Stephenson's. Free-lance engineer-designers of course suffered no such restrictions and their ideas and prototypes could and did get wide publicity in the press – perhaps more so sometimes than the concrete achievements of employees of the big firms. One such free-lance was William Bridges Adams, who by the mid-1840s had turned his attention to railways. He was active in design of railway coaches – as one might expect – and track – to which he was to make a contribution of lasting and world-wide importance – but he also had distinct ideas on locomotive design, about which readers of *The Illustrated London News* were kept well informed.

He was also able to put them into practice, for in 1843 he opened an engineering works, the Fairfield Works, Bow, London. Here, in 1847, was built an extremely small steam-driven inspection railcar for the Eastern Counties Railway: the idea for this probably originated with James Samuel, the ECR's resident engineer. This little vehicle, called *Express*, was 12 ft 6 in. long, had a small vertical boiler and four wheels, and could carry seven passengers as well as the crew.

The following year the concept was extended to carriage of farepaying passengers, with construction of the broad gauge 40 ft long steam railcar *Fairfield* for the Bristol & Exeter Railway, at the recommendation of its engineer, C. H. Gregory, who had tried out the *Express*. The wheels of the coach part were made of wood and ran loose on their axles, and it appears that Adams was adapting accepted (road) carriage building practice of the time to rails both in this and in mounting the body between the wheels. After trials on the mixed-gauge West London line *Fairfield* ran on the Tiverton and other branches of the B&E for several years.

In 1849 Bridges Adams built a third steam railcar, the *Enfield*, for the Eastern Counties Railway's branch to the town of that name. The power unit of this, with its horizontal boiler, resembled a small conventional locomotive, although both it and the coach body were mounted on a single eight-wheeled frame. The idea evolved further, perhaps inevitably, when later the same year Adams built for the ECR the *Cambridge*, a lightweight 2–2–0 tank locomotive to which one or two light carriages could be coupled. From this time onwards light locomotives saw limited but widespread and continuing use on many companies' branch lines.

Into the 1850s

Tank engines were gradually coming into use, the first specifically for shunting in 1847. In 1849 Gooch built a class of broad gauge 4–4–0 saddle tanks for the GWR with leading bogies. The late 1840s and early 1850s saw construction of several designs of locomotive in which driving wheels to the rear of the firebox were driven from inside cylinders by means of an intermediate driving shaft mounted ahead of it. None of them had any lasting influence. Much more important was the appearance in 1848 for the first time of 0–6–0 locomotives in which inside frames were combined with rear wheels mounted to the rear of the firebox – a type to be familiar for many, many years to come.

The most remarkable locomotives constructed during the early 1850s were some broad gauge 4–2–4 tank locomotives with two bogies and 9 ft diameter flangeless driving wheels, built for the Bristol & Exeter Railway in 1853–4. These apart, however, the 1850s were a period when locomotive design was settling down, and when less experimental work was done than during the previous decade.

Locomotives for express trains, during the early part of the 1850s, were mostly built as 2–2–2s. Notable among them was a class designed by J. E. McConnell for the southern division of the LNWR and built from 1851 onwards. In McConnell at last appeared a designer prepared to pitch his boilers high – with a centre line 7 ft 1 in. above the rails. With this were combined 7 ft diameter driving wheels, inside cylinders and inside frames: to the enginemen it seemed these locomotives showed a lot of their wheels and, since Mrs Amelia Bloomer's attempts to persuade ladies to replace long dresses by a costume combining a short skirt with trousers were then getting much publicity, these locomotives gained the nickname 'Bloomers'. Their boilers at first contained steam at 150 lb per sq. in. pressure, though this was later reduced, and their springs were of india rubber. The Bloomers performed well on Euston-to-Birmingham expresses for many years, notwithstanding McConnell's construction (perhaps because of outside pressure) during 1852–4 of a class of 2–2–2s with low-pitched boilers and outside frames.

As to further developments in this decade, in 1853 Robert Stephenson & Co. built some 2–4–0s for the Chester & Birkenhead Railway in which inside frames were combined with rear driving wheels to the rear of the firebox. They were the first of what was to become a common type. In 1855 the first standard gauge locomotives for the Great Western were built, 2–2–2s designed by Gooch and built by the newly established firm of Beyer Peacock & Co. The same year Robert Stephenson & Co. built some 4–4–0 tank locomotives with leading bogies for the North London Railway, the forerunners of many. The first passenger tank locomotives to have six coupled wheels were some 0–6–0 saddle tanks built in 1856 by the Lancashire & Yorkshire Railway for use on steeply graded branches. The first instance of construction of a large quantity of locomotives of a standard class came with the DX class 0–6–0s of the London & North Western Railway. The design was due to John Ramsbottom and the first example built in 1858 at the LNWR's north-eastern division works at Longsight, Manchester; but construction moved to Crewe with Ramsbottom's promotion there the same year. By the time it ceased in 1874, no less than 943 of these locomotives had been built, including 86 for the Lancashire & Yorkshire Railway. For express passenger trains Ramsbottom built sixty Lady of the Lake class 2–2–2s, from 1859 onwards, departing from earlier Crewe practice by giving them inside frames.

Boilers and Boiler Mountings

Ramsbottom is perhaps best remembered, however, for the safety valve of his design. During the 1840s and 1850s most locomotive boilers were fitted with spring balance safety valves which had the disadvantage that they could be screwed down to increase steam pressure. This device was on occasion resorted to by drivers faced with steep gradients and inevitably it became a cause of boiler explosions. Ramsbottom's safety valve had two equal-sized valves held closed by a single spring, and was immune from tampering, for the adjusting nut was inaccessible to the enginemen, although a lever enabled them to relieve the pressure on the valves to check that they had not stuck.

By the mid-1850s, though, tampering with safety valves was becoming not so much a common cause of explosions as an excuse for them, for boiler explosions which had been remarkably rare during the 1830s and 1840s were regrettably becoming comparatively common. The real cause was not, either, that there were many more locomotives in service, but that the boilers of some of the early ones had been in service for long enough to be approaching the end of their safe lives. Originally, of course, no one had any idea of how long a boiler might last, what the effects of corrosion might be, or how often it should be inspected internally. When, for instance, in 1855 the boiler of GWR Firefly class 2–2–2 *Actaeon* (built 1841) blew up, it was found that corrosion had reduced the thickness of the boiler's bottom plates from $5/16$ in. to, in places, no more than $1/10$ in. – and it was five years since the boiler had last been inspected internally. Information on safe boiler design and maintenance was dearly bought: C. H. Hewison's *Locomotive Boiler Explosions* makes interesting reading.

Steel started to replace iron as a material for boilers about 1856; the injector for boiler feed was invented in France by Henri Giffard in 1859 and applied to locomotives in the UK soon afterwards. Some of Ramsbottom's 2–2–2s were among the first locomotives to be fitted with injectors. A preoccupation of several locomotive engineers during the 1850s was to find a means of burning bituminous coal effectively without production of excessive smoke, since this fuel was cheaper than coke. Many complicated types of firebox were designed – McConnell for instance used a firebox divided longitudinally with a combustion chamber forward of it within the boiler barrel – but the best solution proved to be the simplest in the now-familiar form of the brick arch, an arch of firebricks within the front part of the firebox, abutting on to the tubeplate but below the tubes themselves, which principally has the effect of lengthening the path taken by burning gases from the front of the fire to the tubes and so improves combustion within the firebox. This, together with a deflector plate within the box above the firehole door to allow, when the door is slightly open, some 'secondary air' down into the fire, was developed on the Midland Railway by Charles Markham under Matthew Kirtley between 1856 and 1860, and coal then gradually superseded coke as fuel. By 1860, there were some 5,800 locomotives owned by railways in the British Isles, and most of the features which were to be typical of locomotives for the rest of the century had already appeared. Of those which were still to come, the most important were the introduction of compound expansion from France during the 1880s, and a gradual increase in size of locomotives, to match increasing weights of trains. Locomotives of the 4–4–0 type with inside cylinders and frames and a front bogie were first built for the North British Railway in 1871: this type became the typical passenger locomotive of the late Victorian period. At the other extreme, the first locomotives of very narrow gauge were 0-4-0 tank locomotives built for the Festiniog Railway in 1863 by George England & Co., who had made a name for themselves building light locomotives derived from the ideas of W. B. Adams. When the Festiniog needed more powerful motive power, a double-ended, double-boiler 0-4-4-0, mounted on bogies to Robert Fairlie's patent, was built in 1869. The impressive performance of this locomotive, the *Little Wonder*, when demonstrated to visiting engineers, did much to influence the spread of narrow gauge railways mentioned on page 110.

8 : Wagons and Carriages

The Chaldron Waggon

Since goods, or at least mineral, vehicles came a long time before those
to carry passengers, it seems best to take them first. The traditional
vehicle of the wooden waggonways of North East England, and the iron
railways which succeeded them, was the chaldron waggon mentioned in
chapter one. Where locomotives were in use, as at Wylam, Middleton
and Hetton, such waggons were coupled together, by chains, into long
trains. Their timber frames which lay inside or between the wheels,
were extended to form dumb or unsprung buffers.

One would have expected the Stockton & Darlington Railway to have
been equipped similarly, but according to Tomlinson this was not
initially so. In an effort to keep S&DR coal out of the London market,
coal owners from competing areas had successfully persuaded Parliament to allow the railway only a low and supposedly unremunerative
toll on coal for 'export'. Expecting only local rather than 'export' trade,
the company had had built small waggons, many of which seem to have
been end-opening rather than bottom-opening. Presumably they were
similar to other contemporary waggons such as those of the Belvoir
Castle and Stratford & Moreton Railways. These had timber frames and
bodies with low vertical sides, end-opening, and set between the
wheels. Examples were illustrated in *The Archaeology of the Transport
Revolution*. The tender of *Locomotion* in Darlington Railway Museum
repays examination in this context, too, for it appears to have accompanied her since first preserved in the 1850s and to be based on a low
vertical-sided waggon of this type.

Shortly before the S&DR opened it became clear that coal for
shipment was going to be carried, and the coal waggons, which had
come in for some criticism anyway, had to be altered so as to open at the

bottom. Some had their sides heightened to increase capacity. Chaldron waggons remained the usual vehicle for coal-carrying in North East England: the North Eastern Railway, when formed by amalgamation in 1854, inherited over ten thousand of them, and they did not finally go out of use on colliery lines until the 1960s.

Improved Waggons

Goods waggons were unremarkable things, and detailed records of them are few. F. W. Simms, however, in *Public Works of Great Britain* does illustrate a timber waggon designed for the Stockton & Darlington Railway by John Dixon, one of its resident engineers under Stephenson. As was usual, it lacked springs. The S&D management evidently felt that some improvement in waggon design was needed, and carried out experiments to that end. In 1828 it ordered a waggon mounted on springs from Robert Stephenson & Co., which was dispatched on 27 November of that year. Not only did it have springs, the frames and axleboxes were outside the wheels. This type of construction proved satisfactory enough to be adopted by the Liverpool & Manchester Railway also, and thus unobtrusively the standard British railway wagon made its appearance.

Fortunately a clear and probably fairly accurate record of the wagons used by the L&MR in its earliest years does survive, in the form of the long prints of goods trains published by Ackermann (see illustration 37). The tender provided by the railway company for the locomotives in the Rainhill trials used the same form of construction, so that examination of the tender attached to the NRM's replica *Rocket* gives us an idea of the appearance, and probably the dimensions, of the railway's goods wagons. The most distinctive feature is that the outside frames, to which the springs are attached, are below the level of the tops of the wheels, so that the floor is inevitably mounted several inches above it, with a gap between through which the top part of the wheels can be seen.

The L&MR used flat wagons of this type for general merchandise, covering it with tarpaulins when necessary; the long prints also show an open wagon, and another with slatted sides. Open wagons with slats more widely spaced were used for pigs and cattle, and a roofed-in double deck version for sheep. Bringing up the rear of Ackerman's livestock train is an open-sided covered van containing a horse, but Donaghy's

Liverpool & Manchester Railway Operations states that only two horse wagons were built, in 1831, and after that no more, horses being carried in open wagons. Timber was carried on wagons similar to those designed by Dixon for the S&DR, but fitted with springs.

Coal was conveyed by two means on the L&MR: in high-sided open wagons, which probably resembled chaldron wagons, and in small containers or 'loose boxes' carried two to a flat wagon. Such containers were in constant use on canals in the Manchester area for many decades both before and after the railway was built. Similar containers were also used on the Long Eaton Gangway, a tramroad, for transfer between tramroad waggon and canal boat and, possibly, road waggon; they were used for a time in the North East for transfer between waggonway waggon and barge, and they were proposed, but not adopted, for the Stockton & Darlington Railway. On the L&MR they were used for many years to carry coal into Liverpool where they were transferred to road carts. J. U. Rastrick however was later to tell the Gauge Commissioners, to whom loose boxes had obvious potential for transfer between the gauges, that he had tried them out on the London & Brighton Railway, so that coal merchants at Brighton could transfer them to road and make their deliveries; in fact, the Brighton coal merchants preferred to unload the coal and stockpile it for future deliveries.

Some of the lithographs and other engravings of railways published during the late 1830s and 1840s include rolling stock in the scenes depicted, and it is clear that by then sprung buffers had come into general use, and that the frames to which the springs were attached had moved above wheel-level to become solebars of the type since conventional. Low-sided goods wagons were common and small covered vans were in use. J. C. Bourne's lithographs of the Great Western depict low-sided wagons with low-level solebars outside the wheels and the body proper between them – the wheels in some instances can be seen to protude above the solebar. The Great Western also favoured wagons with tarpaulin covers carried on semi-circular hoops, similar to the road waggons of the period. According to E. T. Lane, who was a pupil at Swindon Works during 1848–9 and whose notebooks survive at the Science Museum, the wheelbase of these 7 ft gauge wagons was in at least some instances no more than 9 ft 9 in. Pickford's William Bass, in evidence before the Gauge Commissioners in 1845, stated that standard gauge wagons held up to 4 tons 10 cwt of goods, broad gauge 6 tons.

Transhipment between the Gauges

Written records, although limited and imprecise ones, do come down to us about one aspect of goods rolling stock which nevertheless concerns things never put into regular practice. These were the various expedients proposed to remedy the evil of break of gauge, so far as they concerned specialised rolling stock. There were four upon which the Gauge Commissioners reported: sliding or telescopic axles, upon which wheels would be slid further apart or closer together at the break-of-gauge station; broad gauge wagons fitted with rails upon which to carry standard gauge wagons; removable bodies to vehicles, which could be transferred from frames and wheels of one gauge to those of another; and use of loose boxes for merchandise and minerals. All were discounted by the Gauge Commissioners, and all, or something like them, have subsequently been used at various break-of-guage points as railways of various gauges have spread throughout the world. The commissioners were probably justified in thinking that telescopic axles, at first sight the simplest solution, could not be used safely, given the technology and skills of the period. Their reasons for rejecting the others were far more abstruse.

The real reason why none of them was adopted is to be found in Brunel's answer to question 4048 of the Gauge Commissioners. The question, which related to transfer of goods at Rugby following construction of the proposed broad gauge Oxford & Rugby Railway, was: 'Having dealt with the passengers, and having had now some considerable time to think of the question of goods . . . have you made up your mind at all as to the mode in which you would arrange respecting them?'

Brunel replied: 'No, because it must depend upon what the other companies choose to do on the other side; if they do not afford assistance, I will not say if they throw impediments in the way, but if they do not afford assistance to exchange, the mode must be different from that which it would be if they did.'

In other words, if the standard gauge companies had wanted to make it easy to exchange traffic between the gauges, then they could have.

Further question and answer are worth following, however. Brunel continued: 'As regards coal, there is no doubt that there would be every facility, because the mode of carrying . . . will, no doubt, be influenced by the wishes and desires of the coal-owners, and the coal-owners will, of course, be desirous of doing whatever will encourage their trade with Oxford.'

Question 4049: 'You would have no difficulty with them?' – 'I think we shall have no difficulty whatever with them. As regards general goods, it must depend upon what the other companies may choose to do; the worst that could happen, of course, would be the entire unloading and reloading of the goods . . .'

Question 4050: 'It would involve, I suppose, a detention of four or five hours, at least by the goods trains?' – (Brunel:) 'Oh dear, no; I think nothing of that kind; even two or three hours' detention would not necessarily . . . be an increase of two or three hours upon the time occupied between a northern town and a southern town, because from Rugby the goods will consist of goods coming from more than one place, and by more than one railway; they will not arrive at Rugby exactly at the same time . . . and therefore the reloading on to Great Western trains of goods . . . by any of what may be called the Rugby lines, may be going on, and the moment of the departure of the Great Western train would not be delayed. . . .'

Question 4051: 'Supposing that the system of unloading should not be adopted, to which of the other systems should you give the preference?' – 'It would depend entirely upon the extent of the trade, and upon the nature of that trade. If there were large quantities of goods in bulk, I think the transhipping of the body of the waggon would be a very convenient way of doing it; if there were frequently waggons with various goods, and no assistance whatever afforded to us by the other companies, and assuming then that we did not unpack, I think taking waggon and all would be one way that we should adopt.'

Question 4052: 'Upon another truck?' – 'Upon another truck.'

Question 4053: 'To which you see no practical difficulty?' – 'No; it is merely the useless weight carried that would be the drawback.'

Question 4054: 'Are you inclined to think that the introduction of another pair of rails, or another rail to diminish the gauge, would be a less objectionable mode on the whole?' – 'No; I should say that on that line it would be more objectionable. . . .'

Transporters at Dinorwic

Other answers make it clear that a broad gauge wagon was in fact equipped with rails to carry standard gauge stock and demonstrated at

Paddington. Since such vehicles never went into regular use on the Great Western, it is notable that a railway using precisely this arrangement, of carrying small narrow-gauge wagons on a larger transporter wagon of wider gauge, was completed at this period and continued in regular use for well over a century. This was the Padarn Railway, North Wales, to the early locomotives of which reference was made in the last chapter.

The origins of the Padarn Railway lay in a horse tramroad of nominal 2 ft gauge built in 1824–5 by quarry owner Thomas Assheton-Smith to carry slates to Port Dinorwic from his quarry near Llanberis. This line was some seven miles long with three rope-worked inclined planes, and in this form it was no doubt modelled on the earlier tramroad from the quarries at nearby Bethesda to Port Penrhyn. In 1828 Assheton-Smith was succeeded by his son, also called Thomas, and by the 1840s the main focus of quarrying at Llanberis had moved to a point from which loads were having to be taken uphill to the tramroad's inland terminus. A new line was therefore built on a low-level alignment.

The form taken by the new line was a 4 ft gauge railway over which the locomotives of 1848, described in the last chapter, hauled trains of transporter wagons each of which could carry four 2 ft gauge slate wagons. The 2 ft gauge remained in use in the quarry and at the port, and also on a new inclined plane adjacent to the port: the 4 ft gauge ran a comparatively level course from the quarry to the head of this inclined plane.

Of the reasoning behind the reconstruction of the line in this form, at first sight extraordinary, no record appears to survive. However Assheton-Smith II was both knowledgeable about steam power and keen to use it. He was a pioneering owner of several successive steam yachts, built for him from 1830 onwards by the noted shipbuilder Robert Napier, and resigned in consequence from the Royal Yacht Squadron which at that date would allow members only to have sailing craft. One of his steam yachts, under new ownership, was subsequently used for the Liverpool-Ardrossan service mentioned in chapter three. In 1848 he installed a stationary steam engine to power the quarry slate mills, and the locomotives that he obtained, however curious and archaic they may appear to us now, were as we have seen in line with the most up-to-date thinking on locomotives at the time they were built.

In the light of contemporary railway developments generally, it is reasonable to suppose that Assheton-Smith wished to introduce steam locomotives on his railway but faced the difficulty of the tramroad's extremely narrow gauge. Twenty years or so were to pass before the Festiniog Railway would demonstrate that steam was practicable on the 2 ft gauge: in the 1840s many engineers held the opinion that the 4 ft 8½ in. gauge itself was uncomfortably cramped for locomotives and a broader gauge was desirable. To Assheton-Smith, however, anything wider than 2 ft within the quarry workings would have been extremely inconvenient.

The most attractive hypothesis is that unable to introduce steam locomotives on the 2 ft gauge he used the narrowest gauge upon which they did appear practicable, that is to say 4 ft, and adapted contemporary thinking on broad/standard gauge transporters to produce 4 ft gauge transporter wagons upon which his 2 ft gauge wagons were carried. Unfortunately this hypothesis stumbles, if it does not break down, over the date at which the Padarn Railway was built on the revised alignment. One of the few things about the railway's origin which is clear is that it was built during 1841–3, and came into use, with horses, in March 1843. Although there are records of modifications to it prior to the introduction of locomotives, there is little doubt that it was built to the 4 ft gauge, and used transporter wagons from the first. However it was not until 1844, when the Bristol & Gloucester Railway was opened, that break-of-gauge became an issue of national interest and importance.

Assheton-Smith, however, was well placed to have been aware of coming problems earlier than this. Construction of steam railways through North Wales to either Porthdinllaen or Holyhead had been in the air since 1837, and Brunel's broad gauge line to Porthdinllaen was proposed to the commissioners investigating communications between London and Dublin in the spring of 1840. Assheton-Smith is known to have been a strong supporter of the broad gauge Worcester and Porthdinllaen scheme of 1845 and his interest is unlikely to have originated only at that date.

On the Padarn Railway there would have been no point in building transporter wagons for a line to be worked indefinitely by horses, for they would have done no more than add unnecessarily to the limited load which horses could haul. It seems likely to me that quarrying necessity led to the construction of the new line in the early 1840s, but that the economic depression of the period led to postponement of the introduction of locomotives for a few years until times were better. Whether the concept of its transporter wagons originated from broad gauge/standard gauge proposals, or whether it was a development of the then common practice of carrying road coaches on railway vehicles (described in chapter ten), or whether it arose in some other way, remains a matter of conjecture.

There are other unanswered questions about the origins of the Padarn Railway which it would be fascinating to pursue, but this digression, in a general history, into the origins of a line of local importance and limited influence is already long enough. It is justified, however, because of the survival of items of its equipment – the locomotive mentioned in the last chapter and a transporter wagon carrying its load of smaller vehicles at the Narrow Gauge Railway Museum, Tywyn. The precise date of construction of the latter is not known but there is no reason to suppose that the design of these wagons varied down the years. Together these form two most important relics of a vital period in railway history from which physical relics are very rare.

What is also interesting, in view of contemporary reservations about the transporter wagon system in the 1840s, is that when the original Padarn locomotives and track wore out in the 1880s the quarry management did not re-lay the 4 ft gauge section to 2 ft gauge and introduce 2 ft gauge locomotives on it, as it very well might have done by then, but evidently found the system satisfactory enough to perpetuate its two breaks of gauge. It obtained replacement 4 ft gauge locomotives and re-laid the line with heavier materials. In this form it continued in use until 1961.

How the railway coach evolved

For the goods wagons of early steam railways, there was some sort of established prototype readily available in the form of the chaldron waggon, and other horse-drawn tramroad waggons. For their passenger coaches, the only possible prototypes were the stage and mail coaches of the roads, and to a lesser extent private carriages. How these had evolved has been described in chapter one. Nevertheless it must be remembered that use of coaches private or public was restricted to the wealthiest among the community. Others, if they rode in a vehicle, used the carriers' waggons which principally carried parcels and goods; many, if they travelled at all, simply walked.

From the limited descriptions of it that survive, it seems that the

Oystermouth Tramroad's pioneer passenger coach of 1807 was constructed mainly of iron. The horse-drawn coaches which operated over the Stockton & Darlington Railway in the late 1820s and early 1830s were closely based on contemporary road coaching practice. Or at least their bodies were, although they were made double-ended so that they need not be turned: the usual forward facing guard's seat was replaced by a second driver's seat facing the other way. This body was mounted on a wooden underframe closely derived from that of the chaldron waggon, with small flanged wheels. Being so derived, it also had brakes, which could be operated by the driver. This was a distinct advance on the road coaches of the period; but it was also much more necessary, for so easily did these coaches run, compared with road coaches, that a single horse took the place of the road coach's four. Nevertheless on occasion a greater passenger complement carried. These coaches had, however, no springs, though they were considered to ride smoothly by their passengers. Tomlinson says that the first spring-mounted railway vehicle was a rail-mounted landau specially built in 1827 for the Duke of Wellington to travel on the Londonderry waggonway in Co. Durham.

As the Liverpool & Manchester Railway approached completion, various types of coach were considered. On 14 June 1830, according to Booth's *Account* of the railway, the locomotive *Arrow* hauled two carriages – one 'a closed glass coach, the other an open carriage' – to take the directors on a journey of inspection. Unfortunately he does not describe the coaches in detail. To convey the Duke of Wellington at the opening, various types of triumphal car were designed, and one eventually built, on eight wheels – they were like nothing ever built to run on rails before or since. The aquatint *Coaches &c employed on the Railway* by T. T. Bury, published by Ackermann in 1831, includes a curious vehicle carrying the inscription *Chinese Liverpool*. Windows run the full length of the upper part of the sides; along their lower part, to left and right of a central door, are projections which serve no obvious purpose, unless they are to accommodate the feet of passengers sitting lengthways, back-to-back, within. The end view of this coach is reminiscent of the side of a stage coach body, with boots attached. In any event, the layout did not catch on. What did catch on is the layout of the other two passenger coaches shown in the same print. In this, three ordinary road coach bodies are mounted next to one another on an underframe similar to that used by the railway's goods wagons. This type of coach was designed by Thomas Clarke Worsdell and his son Nathaniel who were in business as coachbuilders Worsdell & Son in Liverpool. George Stephenson had been introduced to them: to whom else but a coachbuilder would he turn to have coaches built? From 1828 they were building coaches for the L&MR.

There is no question of this type of railway coach just *looking* as though three stage coach bodies had been put on to a railway underframe: that is exactly how such coaches were built. This is made clear by the specification for the first London & Birmingham Railway coaches, quoted by F. W. Simms in *Public Works of Great Britain*. These were modelled on the L&MR coaches and were to have three 'bodies or compartments', the 'bodies to be fixed firmly upon the under carriage with strong bolts secured with nuts'. The specification is in two parts, one for the bodies and the other for the undercarriage. To make this distinction cannot have seemed novel to those who studied it: as we have seen, contemporary road coach design called for a body mounted upon a separate undercarriage, and Bridges Adams in his book makes a clear distinction between body-makers, their skills and tasks, and carriage makers and theirs.

To revert to the Liverpool & Manchester coaches, Ackermann's print shows two types of underframe, one with outside frames, the other inside. The lower part of the side of each body is rounded in the conventional manner, and on the inside-framed vehicle the recesses thus formed between adjacent bodies accommodate the tops of the wheels: on this type the body is mounted lower than on the other, though it was the outside-framed type that became usual, and is shown in the Ackermann Long Print illustration number 37. The wheelbase, in the first L&MR coaches, was only 7 ft; this proved too short, for the coaches had a see-sawing motion. Within the coaches, passengers sat three-a-side upon upholstered seats, and were separated by armrests. Luggage, as usual, was carried on the roof; the guard too was outside, up aloft as usual, though his seat was upon the end of the roof. Like stage coaches, the Liverpool & Manchester coaches bore names, and they were painted yellow and black, colours familiar to stage coach travellers. Initially, they were loose coupled by chains, and buffers were minimal. Little thought seems to have been given to what was needed: perhaps those responsible, having put as many as three coach bodies on to a single undercarriage, did not appreciate how many such coaches would be formed into trains. Sprung buffers seem to have been fitted to the coaches in 1833; Henry Booth invented the screw coupling soon after.

For passengers who preferred on stage coaches to travel 'outside', the L&MR provided open-air coaches with wooden seats, upon which passengers travelled four-a-side. Some resembled open wagons with doors, some even lacked doors having a series of crosswise bench seats. Roofs or awnings were subsequently fitted, as much to protect passengers from sparks as from the weather. These coaches came to be considered second class, those with stage coach bodies first class. For those who would otherwise have walked, or gone by carrier's waggon, there were railway carriages which were no more than open wagons, with doors but without seats. To the 'mechanics and labouring people' who, according to T. T. Bury (*Coloured Views on the Liverpool & Manchester Railway*), travelled in them in great numbers they were no doubt a vast improvement on their other options. Such 'stand-up' coaches received the punning nickname 'Stanhope': the allusion no doubt was to a well-known variety of light two-wheeled carriage, invented by and named after a gentleman of that name.

By 1831 the mails between Liverpool and Manchester were being carried on the railway, and the mail coaches which the railway built provided improved comfort for passengers. They had three compartments, but seats were only two-a-side; in one compartment the cushions could be rearranged to form a bed with an opening to a boot for the occupant's legs, as in the Dormeuse road coach. On the railway the arrangement seems to have been intended for invalids. The Post Office mail guard took his place on a seat bracketed out from one end of the coach, but facing towards it so that he could watch the boxes containing the mails which were carried on the roof. These coaches were finished in the famous maroon-below, black-above, livery of the mail coaches on the roads, and like them they bore the royal coat of arms. For the wealthiest people who were accustomed to travel post in their own coaches, flat-decked carriage trucks were provided upon which private coaches and their occupants were carried for the railway stage of their journeys.

1830s Railway Coaches

The Garnkirk & Glasgow Railway equipped itself with two coaches similar to the L&MR first class ready for its official opening in

September 1831. But patrons of the Garnkirk & Glasgow were evidently less wealthy than the merchants of Liverpool and Manchester: such splendid coaches were subsequently left in the carriage shed in favour of humbler vehicles which the G&G, which mingled horse-drawn coaches with steam passenger trains, found that its customers preferred. The best of these coaches were enclosed, with small glass windows; others were open.

Demand for passenger accommodation on the Leicester & Swannington Railway, which was principally a coal-carrier, was also modest. When opened in 1832 it possessed but one passenger coach, an open vehicle built in its own workshops. A closed first class coach was built there to join it later the same year, and in 1833 a composite first and second class coach was built with a central first class compartment flanked by two roofed but open-sided second class compartments. No more seem to have been added over the next decade.

The opening of the Leeds & Selby Railway in 1834 produced a second railway with a substantial demand for medium-distance passenger traffic. The railway had coaches of the Liverpool & Manchester type from the start: the first train comprised three named first class coaches painted yellow with glass windows and six open second class coaches. In the same year the Stockton & Darlington Railway introduced coaches of the same type on to its line, although this was not the end of the single-compartment type used there previously. These continued in use for some years, sometimes drawn by horses, sometimes by locomotives, and when the first part of the Whitby & Pickering Railway was opened in 1835 it used such coaches, horse-drawn.

One of the very few railways to attempt putting seats for outside passengers on top of its coaches was the Newcastle & Carlisle; these, with passengers, appear in several of J. W. Carmichael's engravings of the line which were published in 1837. They were placed lengthways and intended for passengers wishing to admire the scenery: but speed, smoke and smuts meant that there was little pleasure in this, and they were used by passengers seeking cheap accommodation. Coaches on the London & Greenwich Railway, opened in 1836–8, had the solebars, and with them the headstocks, below the axles, so that should they derail – which might have had serious consequences on a line carried on continuous viaduct – the coaches would drop only a few inches on to the rails.

Probably the oldest coaches to survive are three from the Bodmin &

Wadebridge Railway which are now in the collection of the National Railway Museum. This railway was opened, on the standard gauge, in 1834; in 1845 during the mania it was bought by the London & South Western company which did not, however, succeed in building a standard gauge line so far west to link with it until the 1880s. In the meantime it was isolated beyond the broad gauge lines, and early rolling stock remained in use, to be preserved by the LSWR when eventually withdrawn after the standard gauge link was complete. Unfortunately, of the three coaches held by the NRM, neither the precise building dates nor the extent to which they are original rather than later rebuild is now known, but it is probable that the frames at least date from the mid-1830s even though the bodies may be later.

To W. Bridges Adams, considering the state of the art of railway carriage building about 1837, it seemed that there was considerable room for improvement. Wheels were too small and bodies, placed above the wheels, too high; and since the most up-to-date private road coaches were dispensing with a separate undercarriage and attaching wheels and axles directly to strengthened bodies, it seemed practicable to him that railway coaches, intended for a much smoother road surface, should be designed similarly. Furthermore, the action of four flanged wheels on curves, where even coned wheels had partially to slide, seemed defective. What he proposed was a train of two-wheeled carriages, each seating twelve passengers in two compartments, articulated together after the manner of his equirotal road coaches; each was to have a single pair of large-diameter wheels with the body between them, the wheels set mid-way along the body. His ideas were among the most sensible of many peculiar ideas for railway vehicles produced at this period; but so far as I am aware they did not at this stage take concrete form.

Coaches for the Trunk Lines

In fact, when the Grand Junction and London & Birmingham Railways were opened during 1837–8 their coaches were closely modelled on those of the L&MR. The specification for L&BR coaches, which has already been mentioned, required the workmanship of the bodies to be equal to that of the most recent coaches built by the L&MR at their yard at Crown Street, Liverpool, and the framing of the undercarriage was to be substantial and modelled on a recently-built carriage of the L&MR.

Prospective builders could inspect a model in London or a full-size 'pattern coach' in Liverpool.

The specification rewards further examination. The 'extreme length' of the three bodies or compartments was to be 15 ft 6 in., their inside breadth 6 ft, their inside 'height from floor to roof' 4 ft 6 in. Clearly a coach (like a modern car) was something one got into and sat down in: the concept of a railway coach as a vehicle within which one could move around had yet to emerge. Hamilton Ellis (*Railway Carriages in the British Isles*) gives the inside height as 6 ft, so the builders' ideas about headroom may have been more generous than the railway company's. The body framework was to be of well seasoned ash, the flooring of American pine. Seats at each end of the roof were to hold two persons on each, the roof proper was to be fenced in with iron luggage rails. The exterior was to be panelled with well-seasoned board, covered with canvas glued on. As for painting, the body was to receive three coats of white lead or colour, and four coats of 'filling up'; after being well pumiced, it was to have three more coats of the same colour, and be finished with two coats of a colour 'to be approved by the directors' (green-and-black seems to have been the scheme approved, at least in some instances) followed by four coats of the best varnish. The panels were to be lettered in gold and ornamented with a coat of arms or other device. Within were to be Brussels carpet and horsehair-stuffed cushions. In all of this the strong influence of contemporary road coach building practice can be discerned.

The 'under carriage frame' was to have an extreme length of 15 ft 8 in., and to be made of well-seasoned ash with axle guards and other components of wrought iron. Buffers were to extend 1 ft 9 in. beyond the end of the frame, with ends of ash, and covered with stout leather and stuffed with horsehair. Three chains were to be fitted each end, the central one for drawing the coach, the others for safety. Even the under-carriage was to receive five coats of paint and two of varnish.

Whishaw, writing about 1840, gives very similar dimensions for Grand Junction Railway first class coaches. The body length is the same at 15 ft 6 in., and the width (i.e., outside) 6 ft 7 in. From the scale drawing which accompanies his description, it appears that the inside height is less than 5 ft. The length of the undercarriage is 20 ft, which includes buffers with lengthy shafts sprung by mounting them in contact with horizontal semi-elliptic springs beneath the floor. Such coaches could carry eighteen passengers inside, and two outside. He also describes second class coaches, with three compartments, which were roofed in and closed at the sides and ends, and held twenty-four passengers within a body measuring 13 ft long by 6 ft 5 in. wide. Third class carriages, as Whishaw puts it, 'are also in three compartments, and hold the same number as those of second class, but have neither roofs nor sides; but the seats are as comfortable as in the second class carriages'.

The carriage stock of the Grand Junction, Whishaw tells us, included twelve 'mails', which were similar to those on the Liverpool & Manchester, fifty-four first class carriages, thirty-seven second class carriages and fourteen third class carriages. These figures give an indication of the popularity of each class of travel, and of the extent to which the company catered for it. So do the figures for carriage trucks and horse-boxes (each able to hold three horses) — fifty of each. The carriage trucks would have been used not only for private carriages but also for stage coaches and mail coaches which by now were often carried for parts of their routes by rail. The GJR's stock also included two travelling Post Office carriages and the Post Office bag tender.

The mails, seating two passengers abreast, were well-liked. In 1845 the Gauge Commissioners asked Capt. Mark Huish, General Manager of the GJR, apropos of the number of passengers who could sit beside one another on broad and standard gauge coaches, 'Do you find that any objection is made to your having only three seats in a carriage instead of four abreast?' He replied: 'So far from it, that the public always select the carriages in which there are only two seats abreast, if they have the option, which is the construction of the old mail.' We are fortunate that an excellent example of this pattern of coach survives in the coach built by the London & Birmingham Railway about 1842 for Queen Adelaide, which is now preserved in the National Railway Museum. The body, built by coachbuilder Hooper, has furnishings and finish luxuriously appropriate to royalty, but the layout of the coach is that of contemporary mails, complete with two-seater coupé at one end and bed compartment with boot at the other. It was last used in 1849.

Broad Gauge

Today we are so accustomed to railway vehicles which are much wider than the rail gauge that it seems remarkable that no attempt was made to build broad gauge vehicles out to the maximum widths which would have been practicable. But of course this is totally to misunderstand the thinking of engineers of the period, Brunel, Bridges Adams et al. To them, the great advantage of the broad gauge was that it enabled vehicles of useful width to be built *without* much overhang, and even to be built with their bodies in the conventional place for carriage bodies, between or inside the wheels.

In practice, broad gauge passenger vehicles with bodies inside the wheels seem to have been limited to two principal types. These were four-wheeled carriage trucks, to carry road coaches both public and private, which remained in use for many years, and 'posting carriages' which were intended to provide a service similar to that of post-chaises. Sides splayed outwards from a floor 6 ft wide enabled inwards-facing sofas within the body to be placed directly above the wheels. But the windows were above the sofas along the sides, and the sofas themselves continued around the ends of the coach. Mid-way along each side was a door, above which the roof was raised to provide headroom, and a longitudinal clerestory gave sufficient headroom within the body for passengers to reach their seats.

Although the clerestory roof was eventually to become a common feature of Victorian railway carriage design, the posting carriages themselves do not seem to have had a long life, for passengers seem to have preferred the ordinary first class. These had the usual cluster of compartments resembling stage coach bodies mounted on a wheels-below railway underframe, but the broad gauge enabled the bodies to be 9 ft wide, which meant that passengers sat four-a-side in comfort; furthermore a central partition could be closed to divide an eight-seat compartment into two four-seat ones. There were four compartments to a carriage, for except for a very few early examples all GWR coaches had six wheels. The Gauge Commissioners, after experiencing travel on all lines radiating from London, grudgingly admitted their opinion that 'at the higher velocities the motion is usually smoother on the broad gauge'.

Passengers occupying coaches of lesser classes were treated appropriately less well. Second class coaches were open above the waist at the sides, but did have doors; third class passenger coaches, some with six wheels, some with four, and with plank seats, were in at least some instances enclosed to a height of only two feet above the floor. By the mid-1840s, however, some were being built with iron frames and iron bodies also.

Standard Gauge in the 1840s

On the standard gauge lines, the four-wheeled coach with three compartments was well established by the 1840s, and continued to be so for the next couple of decades. In some instances – such as the Stockton & Darlington examples preserved in the National Railway Museum and Darlington Railway museum – a central first class compartment was flanked by two wooden-seated second class ones. On the Manchester & Leeds Railway such composite coaches had the first class compartment flanked by open-air second class. The finish of coaches was still closely based on that of stage coaches. Many still bore names; some had coats of arms painted (not transferred) on their sides. Liveries of bold colours were favoured – yellow & black, green & white, claret, crimson, maroon. Most first class carriages had sprung buffers, and brakes. Superior coaches for royal use were built by various companies, notably the London & Birmingham and the London & South Western. The London & Birmingham's was laid out as an open saloon.

At the opposite extreme, the lot of the third class passenger was ameliorated by Gladstone's Act of 1844 which obliged railways to provide third class carriages with seats and protection from the weather. The following year the Board of Trade was paying tribute to the 'prompt and generous way' in which railways had interpreted the relevant provisions of the Act. In practice this meant, for instance, that they had third class carriages with windows, and third class continued to be spartan by later standards for many years. Some companies, such as the Edinburgh & Glasgow, provided fourth class also.

By the late 1840s, luggage was coming down off the carriage roofs and being carried in vans – the Grand Junction and the London & Birmingham both introduced baggage vans in 1845.

An unusually spacious type of coach was developed in 1847 by W. Bridges Adams – the first was built for the Eastern Counties Railway in that year. Great length of 40 feet was achieved by making the body in two parts, each carried on four wheels with limited sideplay, and articulated together in a manner reminiscent of his equirotal road carriages. His thoughts on the width of railway carriages had evidently advanced, however, for the bodies, positioned above the wheels, were 9 feet wide, which was wider than some broad gauge carriages. Each part of the body was divided into two compartments only, to give one first class and three second class compartments in all: the first class contained two U-shaped upholstered couches with a central table, the second class two U-shaped wooden seats with three additional central and backless wooden benches. Such coaches were first used on the North Woolwich branch. The first eight-wheel coaches to go into regular express train service in Britain were six 38-ft long coaches put into use by the Great Western in 1852 and nicknamed 'Long Charleys'. These coaches had iron frames and a wooden body containing three first class compartments flanked by two second class at each end. Two pairs of wheels, with some sideplay, were positioned at each end of the coach.

One of the advantages claimed for coaches with eight wheels was greater safety in event of wheel breakage compared with coaches with four or six. This was justified, for tyre breakage, followed by disintegration of the wheel and derailment of the vehicle, was a fruitful cause of disaster at this period. Tyres were commonly fastened by countersunk rivets through the rims; an improved form of construction, which was to bear his name, was introduced in 1848 by Richard Mansell of the South Eastern Railway. The wheel was formed from segments of teak around a wrought iron boss, with iron – later, steel – tyres shrunk on.

The 1850s, and After

By the 1850s, many coaches had oil lamps, and some upholstery was being fitted in second class coaches. Footwarmers, tinplate containers of boiling water already in use in France, were introduced to Great Britain by the then-new Great Northern Railway in 1852 and came into general use. Headroom was increasing. In the guard's compartment of passenger coaches, the guard often continued to occupy an elevated position, but within a glazed lookout above the general roofline. Communication cords between guards and driver were recommended by a House of Commons select committee in 1858 and then introduced widely; unlike the later 'communication cord' they did not initially operate the brakes, for continuous brakes operating throughout a train had yet to come into general use. Already in limited use, though, were continuous brakes operated by a chain beneath the carriages, and so was Fay's brake operated by a jointed revolving rod beneath the carriage floors.

As early as 1850 the LNWR had some sort of saloon carriage available for hire for the use of invalids – the seats could be turned into beds, there was a wc and accommodation for servants and luggage. A comparable vehicle was provided a decade later by the South Eastern Railway, and during the 1860s such coaches came into use as family saloons which could be hired and, for long journeys, attached to the trains of successive companies so that their occupants need not change. In their function they were clearly descended from the post-chaise, though in their layout they were the first widespread departure from the road coach precedent. But the typical coach of the 1860s was still four- or six-wheeled, with its body divided into several compartments, without continuous brakes. Bridges Adams was already forecasting a need for corridor trains with kitchens and lavatories, but these and other improvements would come only slowly during the seventies and eighties. The first proper sleeping car was introduced in 1873, the first dining car in 1879, the first side-corridor compartment coach in 1882. Bogie coaches were first used in Britain in 1872. Continuous automatic brakes, which would be applied automatically on all coaches if a train became divided, did not become compulsory until 1889.

9 : Buildings and Civil Engineering

The Railway Heritage

This chapter, by contrast with earlier ones, is about features which date from the earliest main line railways, yet remain in many cases in everyday use. Their civil engineering works – cuttings, embankments, tunnels, viaducts and so on – and buildings notably station buildings, are still familiar to present-day travellers. Even the prototype of much track still in use had already appeared 150 years ago.

There has been a welcome re-awakening of interest in surviving original mid-nineteenth century railway buildings and structures. The most notable single example was the dawning realisation that the most important buildings of the original Manchester (Liverpool Road) terminus of the Liverpool & Manchester Railway were still in existence, followed by formation in 1977 of the Liverpool Road Station Society to press for their preservation with, eventually, a large degree of success, and establishment of Greater Manchester Museum of Science and Industry at this location.

British Rail too has a new awareness of the worth of its buildings. One effect was publication in 1983, with the backing of British Rail, of *The Railway Heritage of Britain*. Here and readily available for the first time is a comprehensive, indeed encyclopaedic, detailed guide to historic railway buildings and other structures. Publication was followed in 1984 by a conference, held at the Royal Society of Arts, on 'The Future of the Railway Heritage'. At this it was announced that British Rail was setting up the Railway Heritage Trust, which would become an independent body. Its main functions are twofold: to augment the efforts of British Rail with its listed buildings on the operating railway, and to assist in the transfer of buildings and property no longer used by the railway to other bodies which would help to preserve them. For the first of these functions, £1 million was made available by BR during 1985–6.

Meanwhile railway preservation groups have increasingly come to realise that it is desirable to preserve, maintain or re-create not just locomotives and coaches but the entire steam railway scene, buildings and all. One consequence of this was establishment of the Best Preserved Station Competition in 1979. Now re-named Ian Allan Railway Heritage Awards, it gets a great many entries not only from preservation groups and other owners of former railway stations, but also from British Rail itself: and it is hotly contested.

Level Roads and Inclined Planes

Civil engineering works are the foundation of all railways, so it seems logical to consider first the civil engineering works and structures of the early main lines, followed by the permanent way laid upon the roadbed they provided, and followed in turn by the station and other buildings associated with it. So far as the first and third of these are concerned, the task is made easy by *The Railway Heritage of Britain*: for to attempt to give a geographical survey of the structures and buildings which survive from that era in the space available here would simply be to provide an inadequate summary of what is readily available in great detail there. Rather I shall attempt an outline in historical perspective.

The most distinctive feature of the main lines built by the Stephensons, and in the Stephenson tradition, is the great pains that were taken to provide a level road, or one as nearly so as possible. This was a consequence of experiments made by George Stephenson in his Killingworth days when, according to Samuel Smiles (*The Lives of George and Robert Stephenson*), he found that a locomotive would use up three-quarters of its power in ascending a gradient of 1 in 100, and half its power on a relatively easy gradient of 1 in 260. So the Liverpool & Manchester Railway was built with, for the most part, a ruling gradient of 1 in 880, and the London & Birmingham with one of 1 in 330.

Where steep gradients could not be avoided, engineers continued to use cable haulage and fixed engines. Certain early main lines were famous for approaches to termini laid out as cable-hauled inclines – notably, Liverpool, Euston and Glasgow Queen Street. The extent of cable haulage in 1841 on railways which later formed part of the North Eastern Railway is indicated by Tomlinson: seventeen inclined planes worked either by gravity or partly by gravity and partly by steam, with a total length of 13 miles, and powered inclines with a further total mileage of 42½. He does not unfortunately state how many individual inclines made up this total, but there were 30 engines to work them.

On many inclined planes it proved possible eventually to introduce locomotive traction: the steepest example was the Cromford & High Peak Railway's 1 in 14 Hopton incline, worked by steam locomotives from 1877 until the line closed in 1967. Elsewhere, deviation lines were built to avoid cable-worked inclines considered too steep for locomotives, and in some places cable haulage continued to be used, as it still is in specialised situations such as cliff railways. Traditional techniques of cable haulage are demonstrated in preservation uniquely by the Bowes Railway, Tyne & Wear. Here, operating skills, which would otherwise have been lost, can still be seen – such as detaching the cable from a rake of wagons on the move, as they reach the summit of one incline and roll forward on a slight down gradient to await descent of the next. The Bowes Railway is a section of a longer mineral line, laid out as the Springwell Waggonway in the mid-1820s by George Stephenson. Cable haulage was thought of well enough here for stationary steam engines eventually to be replaced by electric haulers by the National Coal Board; the railway remained in use until 1974.

On a few early main lines engineers persisted in the curious technique of inserting short steeply graded sections into routes that were otherwise easily graded, and operated by locomotives. The Rainhill level on the Liverpool & Manchester was flanked by the 'inclined planes' of Whiston and Sutton, both of 1 in 96, although throughout the rest of the locomotive-powered line there was no gradient steeper than 1 in 880. For these inclines of course there was originally the possibility of cable haulage, but this was never so with the best-known example, the Birmingham & Gloucester Railway's Lickey Incline, over two miles long and with a gradient of 1 in 37. The line appears to have been located for economy in the cost of land, and the incline was intended for locomotive haulage from the start. But the phase did not last long, for by the mid-1840s engineers, notably those led by Joseph Locke, were becoming much more confident of the abilities of locomotives (as, indeed, demonstrated on the Lickey) and gradients as steep as 1 in 50 became generally permissible.

Tunnels

At the approaches to Crown Street and Lime Street, Liverpool, and Queen Street Glasgow, there was a second reason for cable haulage. All three termini were approached through tunnels, from which cable haulage eliminated smoke and steam, and helped to reduce the fears of passengers.

The first tunnels though which passengers were conveyed in locomotive-hauled trains appear to have been those at Glenfield near Leicester on the Leicester & Swannington Railway, opened in 1832, and at Marsh Lane, Leeds, on the Leeds & Selby opened in 1834. Glenfield Tunnel, for which Robert Stephenson was the engineer, was single track, level and 1 mile 36 yd long. The chimney of the locomotive hauling the opening-day ceremonial train struck the roof, at a place where platelayers had packed the track too high. One would have supposed this tunnel more claustrophobic than the Leeds tunnel, which was only 700 yards long and double track. Nevertheless the latter seems to have attracted more criticism, possibly because the Leeds line carried far more passengers than the Leicester one. At one stage the interior of Marsh Lane tunnel was whitewashed. Later it was opened out. The line through Glenfield Tunnel was closed in 1966 and the tunnel subsequently sold to Leicester Corporation.

Kilsby Tunnel, 1 mile 638 yd long, in Northamptonshire on the London & Birmingham was the first of the great railway tunnels. The story of its construction, a heroic struggle against the quicksands which flooded the workings, has often been told elsewhere, in Rolt's and Smiles's biographies of the Stephensons for instance. Drawing perhaps on experience at Glenfield Tunnel, which had been found unpleasantly smoky despite provision of ten ventilating shafts (seven of 4 ft diameter and three of 7 ft) Robert Stephenson planned that at Kilsby, in addition to sixteen working shafts, there would be two great shafts of 60 ft diameter to ventilate the tunnel and allay passengers' fears of suffocation. To this day they continue to provide a momentary flash of daylight for passengers in the electrically hauled and air-conditioned trains which speed through the tunnel.

The western portal of Kilsby Tunnel can clearly be seen from the Watling Street, now the A5, where it crosses over the railway. This road, though important in coaching days, did not present Stephenson with a public relations problem comparable to that presented to Brunel

213

by the Bath Road, which lay in similar proximity to the western portal of Box Tunnel. For at Box Hill between Chippenham and Bath on the Great Western not only was Brunel boring a tunnel which at 1 mile 1,452 yd was to be the longest in Britain when complete, he was working in full view of alarmists among his potential passengers – for the Bath Road (now the A4) was the principal coach road between London, Bath and Bristol. Perhaps it was for this reason that not only was the portal ornamented architecturally, but the bore was made considerably taller at the entrance than through the rest of the tunnel concealed within. Timid passengers continued to avoid Box Tunnel for some years, travelling by road over that section.

The Great Western had six more tunnels between Box Tunnel and Bristol; the London & Birmingham six others apart from Kilsby. Two of these, at Primrose Hill and Watford, 1,120 and 1,830 yd long respectively, would have been famous engineering works in their own right were they not overshadowed by the longer and more difficult bore at Kilsby. The London & Brighton Railway, with a ruling gradient of 1 in 264, had three long tunnels, at Merstham, Balcombe and Clayton. Clayton Tunnel was lit by gas.

Yet within a few years as understanding of the locomotive's powers increased, the need for such tunnels diminished. The Lancaster & Carlisle Railway, built through much more rugged country than the early lines, climbed up and over Shap without a tunnel, and the Caledonian which continued the line over Beattock to Glasgow was equally tunnel-free. Where long tunnels were being built during the mid-1840s, it was because it was still difficult or impossible to avoid them. A forerunner of such tunnels was the Manchester & Leeds Railway's Summit Tunnel, 1 mile 1,100 yd long, opened in 1841 through the Pennine ridge between Littleborough and Todmorden. The Sheffield, Ashton-under-Lyne & Manchester Railway's tunnel beneath the Pennines was to be longer, and took longer to complete: it was 1845 before the 3 mile, 22 yd Woodhead Tunnel was opened. This in turn was exceeded in length by the Huddersfield & Manchester Railway's Standedge Tunnel, 3 miles 66 yd long and completed in 1849. No longer was the public scared of long tunnels. The 4¼-mile Severn Tunnel, longest of all British railway tunnels apart from those on urban underground lines, was eventually completed in 1886.

40 Carriage of standard gauge wagons on broad gauge transporters was proposed by the Great Western during the Battle of the Gauges, but not put into practice because of lack of co-operation by the standard gauge companies. From the same period, however, dated the Padarn Railway which carried 2 ft gauge wagons on 4 ft gauge transporters and continued in use until 1961.
(*L. King*)

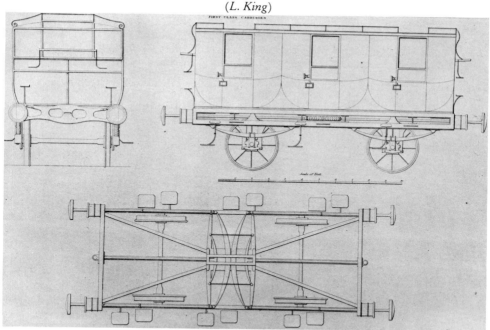

41 Drawings of the London & Birmingham Railway's first class carriages appeared in Simms's *Public Works of Great Britain*, published in 1838. Doors were no more than 4 ft 6 in. high, suggesting that, as with a road coach (or a modern car) one got in and sat down – railway coaches to walk around in had still to develop.
(*Trustees of the National Library of Scotland*)

42 Examination of this photograph of the east end of Waverley Station, Edinburgh, during the 1860s suggests a mixture of coaches built over the previous twenty years.
(D. Rendell)

43 Long-disused viaduct by which the London & Blackwall Railway crossed over the Regent's Canal was being renovated early in 1986 for incorporation into the Docklands Light Railway.
(Author)

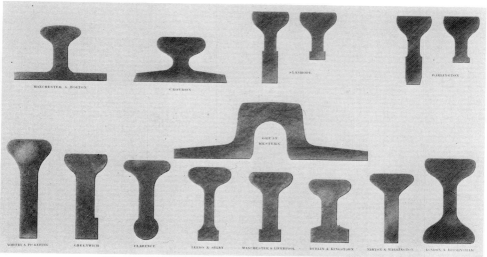

44 The many different types of rail in use in the late 1830s are exemplified in this plate of comparative cross-sections, which originally appeared in Simms's *Public Works of Great Britain*. (*Trustees of the National Library of Scotland*)

45 This print in the National Railway Museum's collection is said to depict Abingdon Road Halt on the GWR, although the gauge appears to be standard and the Bury locomotive suggests London & Birmingham. Wherever it may be, it is evocative of the interwoven nature of rail and road travel at the end of the 1830s, with horses being prepared to take the coaches when they regain the road at the loading dock on the right. (*Courtesy of the National Railway Museum, York*)

STEAMED OUT.
or the Starving Stage-Coachman and Boys.

46 The collapse of coaching, as seen at the time.
(*Mary Evans Picture Library*)

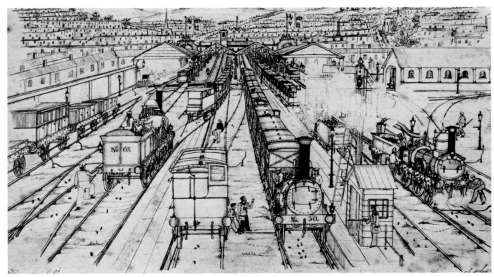

47 In 1850 the author's great grandfather Joseph Lucas, aged fifteen, drew 'A Busy Scene at a Railway Terminus' as a birthday present for his brother.
(*Author's collection*)

Viaducts and Bridges

While the London & Birmingham Railway had to contend with ridges of great hills which lay across its route, the route of the Grand Junction had to cope with sudden deep valleys. So whereas the London & Birmingham was a line of long and numerous tunnels, the Grand Junction had some imposing viaducts. Certainly it had two short tunnels also, but the viaducts were its notable feature, and the most notable of these was Dutton Viaduct over the valley of the River Weaver in Cheshire. Dutton Viaduct, twenty sandstone arches with a total length of about a quarter of a mile, carries the line some sixty feet above the river: it was completed in 1836 and was the first of the great main line viaducts, just as Kilsby was the first of the great main line tunnels – and, like Kilsby, it is still traversed by West Coast main line expresses. A few miles to the south the Grand Junction crossed the Weaver a second time, by Vale Royal Viaduct, and further south still, at Penkridge, Staffordshire, it crossed the valley of the River Penk by the seven-arch viaduct which gave to Thomas Brassey, later perhaps the most famous of all Victorian railway contractors, his first experience of railway building.

The London & Greenwich Railway was originally carried for its entire length of three and three-quarters miles upon a continuous viaduct of 878 brick arches. The origin of this feature, later to be a familiar one on many South London railways, is obscure, but it may be that the line was elevated so as to avoid crossing on the level the many streets that already existed at its London end. Certainly its engineer, Col. George Landmann RE, when giving evidence before the Gauge Commissioners, said that it was originally intended to carry the line on arches as far as the Grand Surrey Canal (about two and a half miles from the London Bridge terminus) and then to descend to ground level and pass beneath Deptford High Street: but that opposition in Parliament compelled construction of the line on arches the whole way.

The London end of the viaduct was in due course widened so that two extra tracks could be provided for use by trains of the London & Croydon, London & Brighton and South Eastern Railways. But further out, Brighton trains had a much grander structure to cross in the form of the thirty-seven-arch viaduct, 92 feet high, by which veteran engineer J. U. Rastrick carried the line across the Ouse valley. Other examples of great viaducts, built for the early main lines, which remain in use

215

include the Manchester & Birmingham Railway's twenty-seven-arch viaduct above Stockport, completed in 1842; Crimple Viaduct of 1848, thirty-one arches which take the Harrogate branch of the York & North Midland 110 feet above the Crimple Beck; Ballochmyle Viaduct, completed in 1848 for the line which soon after became known as the Glasgow & South Western Railway's route to Carlisle – its central span of 181 ft is said to be the longest masonry arch; and, perhaps the best-known if only because its curved approach gives passengers an unusually excellent view, Robert Stephenson's magnificent Royal Border Bridge, the viaduct of 28 arches which was completed in 1850 to carry the York, Newcastle & Berwick Railway – now part of the East Coast main line – 126 feet above the River Tweed.

As the last-named suggests, the distinction between viaduct and bridge is not clear-cut, but of brick or masonry bridges provided to carry a railway over a watercourse or similar feature, rather than to elevate it over low-lying ground, Brunel (as usual) provides the outstanding example. This is of course the bridge which takes the Great Western across the Thames at Maidenhead: two elliptical brick arches of 128 ft span but a mere 24 ft high allowed headroom for sailing craft without excessive approach gradients on the railway.

Towards the western end of his railway, between Bath and Bristol, Brunel provided bridges with Gothic features. In general, though, bridges on early main lines are distinguished less by decorative features than by the quantity that had to be provided – to cross roads, rivers and canals and restore access between parts of properties severed by the railway – and by the quantity which remain in use. Their builders followed the earlier and contemporary practice of canal builders whose techniques they adopted. Even the skew bridges of which early railway engineers were so proud had originated on the canals; and where, to suit the whim of a landowner an ornamented railway bridge or tunnel portal was provided, this practice too had its canal precedents. The same applies to earthworks: deep cuttings and high embankments are a particular feature of those early main lines built as level as possible, such as the London & Birmingham and Great Western, but they had their immediate predecessors in the cuttings and embankments of the Birmingham Canal Navigation improvements and the Birmingham & Liverpool Junction Canal.

Timber and Iron

Limited use was made of timber as a material for viaduct spans. On the Newcastle & North Shields Railway, opened in 1839, the arches of two viaducts, and of two road bridges, were formed of several thicknesses of deal planks, curved and laminated together by trenails; the spandrels and decks were made of timber also. With these arches the railway's architect brought to Britain for the first time a method of bridge-building which had originated on the Continent. It was successful enough to be used by some twenty other railway companies down to 1850. Among them were the Great Western — Brunel put in a laminated timber bridge across the Avon at Bath — the Sheffield, Asthon-under-Lyne & Manchester, and the Great Northern.

Despite his use of laminated timber at Bath, Brunel subsequently used a simpler construction in which substantial struts of Baltic pine radiated from the tops of masonry piers to support the timber decks. A great many timber viaducts of this type were built in Devon, Cornwall and South Wales. The advantage of timber as a bridge-building material was low first cost, particularly in an era when high quality timber was available cheaply. The disadvantage, in course of time, was high maintenance cost, as the most suitable timber for replacements ceased to be available. In consequence timber viaducts and bridge spans were replaced with masonry arches or spans of iron or steel: so far as I am aware no timber viaducts or bridges from this period survive. Barmouth Bridge across the estuary of the River Mawddach in North Wales, which is the largest timber railway viaduct surviving in use, was built by the Aberystwyth & Welsh Coast Railway in the 1860s.

But if timber proved ephemeral as a bridge-building material on the early main lines, iron certainly did not. Small bridges of cast iron had been built for horse railways and tramroads, and George Stephenson carried the horse-worked western section of the Stockton & Darlington Railway across the River Gaunless by a bridge in which short spans principally of wrought iron rested on cast iron piers. Much of it has survived to be re-erected at the National Railway Museum. On the London & Birmingham Railway Robert Stephenson built bow-and-string bridges in which an arch of cast iron — the bow — was tied by a wrought iron 'string', and used the principle again for his greatest example of the type, the High Level Bridge at Newcastle upon Tyne, completed in 1849. Here six spans carried the railway, as they still do,

217

120 feet above the river and the design was adapted to provide a second deck beneath the railway for road traffic – one of very few examples in Britain of physical co-ordination of the two means of transport.

Robert Stephenson's experience with a second type of bridge in which cast iron girders were reinforced by wrought iron truss rods was much less happy. In this design each girder had a truss rod either side and each of these comprised three linked portions: the centre portion was horizontal and supported the middle of the girder, the outer portions inclined upwards so that their extremities could be fastened to large bosses cast on top of the girder-ends. A bridge of this design was built across the Dee at Chester for the Chester & Holyhead Railway, and completed in 1846; seven months after its opening it collapsed under a train, with a noise like thunder and several fatalities. The cause was that the top flange of one of the girders had given way due to stresses imposed by the method of fastening the truss rod to the boss.

This accident not only made cast iron highly suspect as a material for railway bridges, it encouraged the development of the bridges with box-section tubular spans of wrought iron by which the Chester & Holyhead was to cross the Conwy estuary and the Menai Strait. The track passed through the tubes. The method was already, at the time of the accident, under test by shipbuilder William Fairbairn for Robert Stephenson, and the single-span bridge (two tubes side by side) at Conwy provided a trial of the method before construction of the Britannia Bridge over the Menai. The latter took shape as a bridge of four spans, the central ones being the longest at 460 feet, carried by three piers sufficiently high above the water to give (at the insistence of the Admiralty) clearance for sailing ships beneath. It was completed in 1850: the detailed story of its design and construction has been told so often and so well that, despite the risk of appearing dismissive, it seems superfluous to repeat it here. By contrast it is almost forgotten that Robert Stephenson engineered a third tubular bridge at this period: according to Tomlinson (*The North Eastern Railway*) it was completed in 1851 to take the Knottingley branch of the York & North Midland Railway across the River Aire at Brotherton, and so to link the Great Northern into Hudson's YNM. Of the three bridges, only Conwy remains in use in its original form.

The story of Brunel's two greatest bridges is as familiar as that of the Conwy and Britannia Bridges. Brunel too was able to use a lesser version of his chosen form of construction, the South Wales Railway's Wye bridge at Chepstow completed in 1852, as the prototype for the greater, his Royal Albert Bridge over the Tamar at Saltash completed in 1859 shortly before his death. The principal component of each span was a wrought iron tube, but in these bridges a separate deck was rigidly suspended from it; and in this case although the smaller bridge has been rebuilt, the greater survives to carry the main line into Cornwall.

Rails and Sleepers

The term 'permanent way' was first used, as every schoolboy knows, to distinguish the permanent way of a new railway from the temporary way of the contractor. It was in use during construction of the London & Birmingham Railway in 1837, and possibly earlier. 'Track', in railway context, seems originally to have been an Americanism adopted early here.

In any case, the permanent way, or track, call it what you will, of the Liverpool & Manchester Railway when it was opened comprised fish-bellied wrought iron rails, fifteen feet long, weighing 35 lb per yard. These were carried in cast iron chairs mounted upon stone blocks or, in places where it was thought the line might settle, wooden sleepers; blocks and sleepers were embedded in a layer of ballast, comprising broken stone or small coal (the latter is mentioned by Whishaw, writing c.1840). Joints were held in common chairs.

Design of the track had of course been settled before Rainhill, before it was known what sort of locomotives might run over it, or at what speeds. In fact, it soon proved inadequate for Rocket-type locomotives, swaying from side to side at 30 mph, and more so for Planets which weighed nine tons to *Rocket*'s five, and, with the firebox overhanging the rear axle, pitched badly. Bent rails and broken rails soon became commonplace. It was partly to alleviate the problem that the more steadily-running 2–2–2 type was developed: but the long-term solution lay in heavier rails and improved track. The track was progressively re-laid with rails of increased weight, and parallel rails were introduced to replace fishbelly. By the time Whishaw was writing, most of the line was laid with parallel rails weighing between 60 and 75 lb per yard, though there was still some 50 lb fishbelly. Stone blocks had been found to split and many had been replaced by wooden sleepers.

Second-hand fishbelly rails from the Liverpool & Manchester were used to lay the Storeton Tramway in Wirral in 1837–8, and from there

219

some eventually found their way to National Museums & Galleries on Merseyside. An example is also displayed at the National Railway Museum.

The space between the tracks on the Liverpool & Manchester Railway was no more than 5 ft 2 in. No doubt when the track was laid people had still to appreciate the amount of overhang with which railway vehicles would eventually be built, but even early on this narrow space was certainly a contributory factor in the Huskisson accident. It seems nevertheless to have persisted on the L&M line for several decades, though the next generation of main lines were built with wider spaces between the lines – 6 ft on the Grand Junction and 6 ft 5 in. on the London & Birmingham, according to Whishaw.

F. W. Simms records that the London & Birmingham Railway in 1834 offered a prize of 100 guineas for 'the most improved construction of railway bars, chairs and pedestals, and for the best manner of affixing and connecting the rail chair and block to each other, so as to avoid the defects which are felt more or less on all railways hitherto constructed'. The Rainhill approach: even two of the judges were identical – J. U. Rastrick and Nicholas Wood. The third was Professor Peter Barlow, who has been mentioned in chapters three and four. This appears to have been his introduction to railway work: facilities at Woolwich were used for tests. The outcome of this competition, however, was nothing like so decisive or spectacular as the locomotive trials, for although many plans, models and descriptions of track were received, there was insufficient data to determine which proposed rails would be strongest and stiffest in use. Simms notes that recommendations for the prize were made, but omits to mention to whom!

There appear, however, to have been three types of rail on the London & Birmingham as built: fishbelly rail weighing 50 lb to the yard, and 'parallel', i.e. double-headed, rail weighing 65 lb and 75 lb. All were held in chairs mounted on stone block sleepers most, possibly all, of which were positioned diagonally to the line of track. Rail joints were held in common chairs. During the early 1840s L&B track was being maintained by contract – T. Jackson, one of the contractors, told the Gauge Commissioners that he had been responsible for maintenance of 83 miles of line from Euston Square to Rugby, including providing replacement materials. His contract had been terminated in March 1845 when the company decided to make alterations to its line.

Perhaps the use of some double-headed rail on the London &

Birmingham was an outcome of the prize competition; certainly during May 1835 Joseph Locke, by then building the Grand Junction, carried out tests at Edge Hill on seven different types of rail, finding that the strongest of them was double-headed rail weighing 62 lb per yard. The rail he actually laid on the GJR was of this type, but even heavier at 84 lb. It was carried in chairs and both stone blocks and wooden cross-sleepers were used: the latter were intended as a temporary expedient to be replaced in due course by the former, but in fact gave a better ride and in due course became a permanent feature. Locke used wooden sleepers again on the London & Southampton.

Longitudinal Timbers

On the broad gauge Great Western, Brunel used 'bridge' rails (of inverted U cross-section) supported on longitudinal timber baulks. At intervals of fifteen feet or so the longitudinals rested on cross-sleepers or 'transoms' which extended beneath both tracks, so that they not only maintained the gauge of each pair of rails but also kept each track the correct distance apart. Since vehicles were expected to have little overhang, the distance between the tracks was less than the gauge of each – the inner rails of up and down lines were only 6 ft 2 in. apart. To hold them down, the transoms were bolted to piles driven deep into the roadbed.

Brunel's aim was to minimise the amount of timber and at the same time, by using longitudinal supports to the rails, to minimise the weight of rail needed: his bridge rails weighed 43 lb per yard. Railway track in the USA at this period commonly comprised timber longitudinals with iron straps along them to provide the running surface: the Brunel family had connections with the USA but whether Isambard Brunel himself was aware of the American method of building railway track I do not know; at any rate his form of track was considerably more highly developed. In America, track was simply in the process of evolving quickly from the wooden railway to the steam railway without the intervening plateway stage.

As is well known, Brunel's track was at first unsatisfactory. The effect of the piles was not to hold the track down, but when the roadbed settled to hold it up. The cross-sleepers had a similar effect: after a few days' work in wet weather, the track tended to be supported by the cross-sleepers rather than the longitudinals. The effect of this on the riding of trains can be imagined. The cure was to abolish both piles and cross-sleepers. The former went without replacement; as for the latter, Brunel explained to the Gauge Commissioners how the track was kept to gauge: 'the two longitudinals are kept apart by a strut of wood; they are kept together by two iron bolts and strap, the strap being bolted to transoms. That appears at first rather a clumsy arrangement, inasmuch as a simple bolt sent through would . . . tie the whole together. But the reason for using it is this, that if any accident occurs by which the transom is broken, the gauge is not disturbed, whereas we find that, with single bolts running through, the longitudinals are drawn in and collapse, and we adopt therefore a simple truss, with a bolt and strap at each end.' The frequency of derailments which this explanation implied went without comment!

Even so small but vital a detail as the means of fastening the rails to the timbers underwent step-by-step improvement. At first the rails were simply screwed to the timber, but deflection and creep of the rails loosened the screws and after they had been tightened a few times it was found that they would no longer hold firm. They were first replaced by bolts with nuts beneath the timbers; then the bolts were reversed so that the nuts might be accessible for examination. The corners of the bolt heads were turned up to bite into the timber and prevent the bolt from turning.

In its modified form, with the longitudinals resting directly on the ballast, this type of track became satisfactory and lasted as long as the broad gauge, and indeed longer, for the gauge could be narrowed simply by shortening the trusses and moving one of the rails closer to the other. In recent years, broad and mixed gauge tracks have been laid at Didcot Railway Centre by the Great Western Society, using original materials which had been re-used, after the end of the broad gauge, to lay standard gauge sidings at Burlescombe, Devonshire; the complications of track and pointwork which arose from addition of an extra rail for standard gauge trains have been faithfully re-created. Broad gauge track has also been laid at the National Railway Museum for the benefit of the replica *Iron Duke*. In this case some of the rail used was new material, for even in the 1980s bridge rail of the correct pattern is still available, having applications in industry to provide tracks for cranes and so on.

Bridge rail on longitudinal sleepers was also used on standard gauge lines. The London & Greenwich Railway used this form of track between Deptford and Greenwich, with the longitudinals resting on cross-sleepers at 4 ft intervals. Although most of the London & Brighton was laid with parallel rails on either stone blocks or cross-sleepers, that notable member of the engineering old guard, J. U. Rastrick, adopted bridge rail on longitudinal timbers on a viaduct, probably over the Ouse. He used 80 lb per yard rail and found it so satisfactory that he recommended the same form of construction where additional tracks were to be laid (on viaduct) on the London & Greenwich Railway, for use by Croydon, Brighton and South Eastern trains, and the recommendation was adopted. On the widened section of the Greenwich line, the cross-sleepers were omitted and thicker longitudinals used with cross-ties.

Flat-bottom Rail

Like the Deptford–Greenwich section of the Greenwich railway, the London & Croydon Railway's track used timber longitudinals on cross-sleepers at short intervals. But the rails laid upon the longitudinals were of the flat-bottom type, though with a very broad base and squat compared with modern rails. Screws passed through the base of the rails to secure them to the longitudinals. Design of London & Croydon track is credited by F. W. Simms to the railway's engineer Joseph Gibbs in conjunction with Charles Vignoles.

Flat-bottom rail had been invented by the American R. L. Stevens about 1830 and rolled in Britain for use in the USA. Vignoles may have known Stevens through his earlier American contacts, or he may simply have come to know of the rail being manufactured this side of the Atlantic. He was certainly coming to the conclusion that the combination of iron rails and chairs and stone sleeper blocks produced track so rigid that it caused damaging wear both to the trains and itself, and in 1836 as consulting engineer to the Croydon company he successfully recommended the more flexible form of track they eventually used. Flat-bottom rail then became so closely associated with him that it became known as Vignoles rail. Other railways which used it included the Hull & Selby, the Newcastle & North Shields and the Manchester & Bolton. All used longitudinal wooden sleepers, although the Manchester & Bolton also used continuous longitudinal stone sleepers and the Hull & Selby for about one third of its length used cross-sleepers, upon which the rails were mounted on chairs. Rail of the London & Croydon type was considered by Rastrick for use on the London & Greenwich viaducts but rejected on the ground that it was weaker than bridge rail. The present author therefore was particularly intrigued to observe, a few weeks before writing this, that most of the Forth Bridge is even now laid with squat, wide based flat-bottom rails of that type screwed to longitudinals, and that on a short length where it is not used, bridge rail is used instead.

Back in the 1830s and 1840s there were rails of many other cross-sections in use. Some of them appear in illustration 44. Perhaps the most exotic of all was the Barlow rail, named after its inventor W. H. Barlow (son of Peter Barlow) and patented in 1849. In cross-section similar to a bridge rail of enormous size – 13 in. across its feet – it was intended to be embedded in ballast without any sleepers at all, and was used by the Great Western. Weights of rails generally steadily increased, in proportion to increasing weights of locomotives and speeds of trains, so that by the date of the Gauge Commission rails of 85 lb per yard were in use. Bullhead rail started to replace parallel rail from the early 1860s, and the LNWR was using steel rails by 1862. Flat-bottom rail became standard for main lines in Britain, after decades of regular use elsewhere, only in 1949.

Stone block sleepers tended to become loose in their beds, and chairs worked loose on the blocks. Trains got a rough ride and passengers found the noise a nuisance. Improved processes for preserving timber – first by steeping it in mercuric chloride, called Kyanising after its patentee, then by creosoting – gave the balance of advantage to wooden sleepers and these gradually replaced stone blocks. The latter were still in use on the Bodmin & Wadebridge line in the 1880s.

Fishplates

Brunel used joint plates beneath the joints between his bridge rails, and J. U. Rastrick, on extensions to the London & Brighton, used joint plates for bridge rails which had their edges turned up to grasp the feet of the rails and hold the rail-ends in position relative to one another. But throughout the 1830s and 1840s the normal means of securing joints between double-headed rails continued to be to hold them together in a larger-than-usual chair. This was the weak point in this form of permanent way: chairs tilted, rail-ends were hammered by wheels and damaged. For the solution, the still-familiar fishplate, we are indebted to that prolific inventor W. Bridges Adams. Adams had realised early on that improvements in railway track were as necessary as improvements in railway vehicles. Here is how the fishplate was developed, in the words which Adams himself used to address the Institution of Civil Engineers in 1852. Referring to damaged rail-ends, he said:

'Supporting the joint by extra sleepers appears a simple remedy, but the sleepers are not practically supports, as they only bear on loose ballast and not on any continuous surface. It becomes necessary, then, to join the rails firmly together. The operation of "fishing" by the addition of pieces of metal to each side then presents itself; but to secure these "fishes" becomes the next question. The simplest mode is to take the rail joint wholly out of the chair, and to place a sleeper, with a chair on it, on each side of the joint, thus suspending the joint between the two chairs. The "fishes" being then driven in on each side of the rails, the rails and chairs are connected together. This was practiced by the author in 1847.

'The damaged rails were thus supported by the chairs in the undamaged part, and they were made practically continuous, while permitting expansion and contraction, by the sliding of the fishes. But putting the fishes into the chairs involved the necessity for fresh castings, and it was found a simpler operation to punch holes in the rails and connect the fishes together by four bolts passing through them all. . . .'

The first 'fishes' were of cast iron but wrought iron was soon substituted. So perfect was the arrangement, Adams claimed, that old rails, which were so battered that one end projected nearly a quarter of an inch above the next, when firmly connected by 'fishes' gradually rolled under the working of the trains into a perfectly level surface. Nevertheless fished joints came into use slowly at first. The Eastern Counties Railway tried them in 1849, and by the time Adams addressed the Civil Engineers in 1852 had twenty miles of fishplated rails, which it was expected would reduce maintenance costs by half. Subsequently fishplates became the most widespread and long-lasting of all Adams's inventions, and his name deserves to be remembered in connection with them.

Accidents, or Lack of Them

With track so bad that it was apparently not uncommon for one rail end to project a quarter of an inch above the next, and with the rails loose too, it seems amazing to us now that railway history of this period did not consist of a series of appalling derailments. But in fact accidents from this cause were few – probably a result of speeds which, by later standards, were low and which no doubt were themselves in turn a consequence of imperfect track. Between September 1840 and the end of October 1844 the Railway Department of the Board of Trade recorded only six accidents in which 'the Engine or Carriages or some part of the Train have run off the line, without any known obstruction', and three of those had not resulted in fatalities.

David Joy, as a boy, witnessed a derailment in 1841:

> Walking home on our side the canal one evening about five, I saw the train which ran on the other side, about a mile off. The engine ran off the line, and moving off to our side crossed the other rails, and ran down the embankment, pulling part of the train with it. I was too tired to go round by the lock gates and across the fields. But I went in the morning to see the removing. There was no one hurt; my old uncle was in the train, but was only bumped off the seat on to the floor.

This accident does not appear to be recorded in the Board of Trade returns. Perhaps it was considered too trivial to be worth reporting.

Turntables and Points

Another cause for accidents during the 1840s was wagons strayed from sidings. They would be left on the main line during shunting operations, or merely blown there by the wind, and a train in due course would collide with them. The consequence was the development of trap points. Earlier this seems to have been less of a problem, possibly in part because of the means used to transfer vehicles from one line to another. Wooden waggonways used turnplates or turntables for this purpose, and their use persisted through the tramroad era and into that of steam railways, particularly in the vicinity of stations. Locomotives, cumbersome things, were at first used mainly to haul trains from one place to another: at termini, individual vehicles were marshalled by man-power, or by horse, and it remained convenient to install turntables as the principal means of access to sidings.

But where it was necessary to divert a train of waggons from one line to another, plateways used pivoted pointed switch rails, and iron edge railways adopted them also. So did public railways such as the Stockton & Darlington and Leeds & Selby. At first the switch rails were mounted on vertical pivots at their heel ends, and shifted individually by hand. Subsequently the switch rails were linked together and worked by trackside levers, and points or turnouts of the type which remains usual evolved. Tomlinson, in *The North Eastern Railway*, notes that these began to come into use between 1839 and 1841, the first pair for the Stockton & Darlington Railway being made in 1839 from 60 lb rail. The type did not come into use without competition, however, for some railways preferred the alternative arrangement in which a pair of rails pivoted at their ends were moved by lever to align with the butt ends of the rails forming one track or another at a divergence. Lines which used such stub points included the Newcastle & Carlisle and the Brandling Junction. No doubt their obvious defect, that a train could not trail through them without derailment, caused them to be superseded by points with switch blades.

Station Layouts

The passenger termini of the Liverpool & Manchester Railway, Crown Street Liverpool and Liverpool Road Manchester, had respectively three and four parallel tracks passing in front of the passenger building. During the year after Crown Street opened, a wooden roof was added over its tracks, supported on one side by the passenger building and on the other by a wall opposite. It protected both passengers and stationary coaches from the weather and was the prototype of the train shed which became a familiar feature of early Victorian stations. Platforms were vestigial – despite the opening day disaster, to judge from contemporary illustrations of L&M stations no attempt seems to have been made to prevent passengers from wandering about on the tracks. Indeed at Liverpool Road which was approached by double track, passengers arriving by train would then have had to cross at least one track on the level, unless the track nearest the station building was used for both arriving and departing trains. A separate platform for arriving trains was not added on the opposite side of the railway until 1837.

From the Liverpool & Manchester Railway onwards, railways were generally built with double track, each track being reserved for trains in one direction. It must have made sense, at termini, to widen the space between the tracks and place carriage sidings between them, through which coaches from arriving trains could pass eventually to the departure line. Certainly this arrangement became the usual layout for early main line termini, with single arrival and departure platforms adjacent to the appropriate lines and the whole covered by a train shed. Access to sidings was often through turntables rather than points.

Some important early termini were laid out like those of the L&MR with the main station building alongside the departure platform. Euston was laid out like this, and King's Cross and Paddington still show traces of it. But the arrangement which was to become general, of putting the main building across the end of the tracks, originated early – Brighton was arranged that way, and so was Nine Elms. One cannot help but think it originally a somewhat hazardous arrangement, given the limited braking power of contemporary trains.

The principal intermediate stations on the GWR were laid out by Brunel so that trains stopping at them would be diverted off the main line. This meant stations with a single long platform to one side of the railway, at Reading, Slough and elsewhere. The principal advantage seems to have been in passenger safety – passengers had neither need nor temptation to wander across the lines. The layout was adopted at other stations – Derby for instance. Cambridge retains it to this day. Acworth, writing in the 1880s (*The Railways of England*) described it even then as old-fashioned. Increased traffic had made such stations excessively difficult to work and most had been rebuilt. The Great Eastern Railway had likewise obtained powers to rebuild Cambridge station at considerable expense, but to do so needed a small piece of common land. Even though the company was prepared to purchase land elsewhere to add to the common, opposition was too strong: the scheme went into limbo from which it seems never to have been recovered.

Island platforms seem to have originated from the need for interchange of passengers between trains at important early junctions such as Swindon and Normanton.

Station Buildings

At first, both passengers and railway managements saw rail travel in the same light as the coach travel with which they were familiar. At Liverpool Road, Manchester, what we would think of as the station building was described during its construction as the 'coach office'.

However R. S. Fitzgerald in his *Liverpool Road Station, Manchester* quotes a pamphlet* said to have been on sale on the opening day: '. . . a spacious building with a Grecian front to the Liverpool Road. This will be the Station for the reception of passengers . . .' But the term *station* evidently did not come fully into use immediately. *The Railway Companion* of 1833 simply refers to '. . . the railway office in Liverpool-road. This is a fine stuccoed building, with ample convenience for transacting a business equal to the largest coach-office establishment in London.' And at Liverpool it refers to '. . . the office for passengers, in Crown-street . . .'. Elsewhere, however, the same publication does mention, 'The company keep a police establishment who have station-houses at intervals of about a mile along the road. These stations (sic) form also depots for passengers and goods from or to any of the intervening places.' So it appears that the term *station* in its railway sense came gradually into use at this period.

Although neither of the original passenger termini of the L&MR survives as such, Edge Hill station, which dates from 1836 and the opening of the line down to Liverpool Lime Street, still has part of its original buildings in use. Indeed they were handsomely restored, and later accretions removed, for the 150th anniversary celebrations in 1980. It must be one of the oldest station buildings still in use for its original purpose. However, Hexham station on the Newcastle & Carlisle line is probably even older. It was opened in 1835, and examination suggests that the original building forms part of the larger building still in use.

The Newcastle & Carlisle Railway was the first to build a series of station buildings in uniform architectural style. It provided many of its stations with neat little stone buildings in more-or-less Tudor style. Happily many of them survive, although all except Hexham are now at unstaffed halts. The coach-office influence may be inferred from their locations, bearing in mind that this line was promoted as a horse railway. The convention of placing station buildings along a platform had, at the time of their construction, yet to arise. So, physically, had raised platforms, for the N&C stations seem not to have had them originally. In some instances the buildings are by later standards awkwardly close to the track, as at Wylam, and in others set back some distance from it (Riding Mill in particular, if memory serves correctly).

---

*J. Scott Walker, *An Accurate Description of the Liverpool and Manchester Railway* 1830.

Certainly Whishaw seized on this point as a criticism of the line as early as 1842. They also show a tendency to be unusually low to the ground compared with later station buildings. At Wylam for instance passengers pass at ground level between the station house and the railway before ascending a ramp to the present day platform.

The Great Stations

Since the early main lines were the greatest engineering works then known to man, the companies which built them often provided a suitably grandiose building as an introduction to them. A forerunner of this tendency was the Liverpool & Manchester Railway's Moorish Arch at Edge Hill, beneath which all trains – and passengers – setting out from Liverpool had to pass. In fact of course it was an architectural disguise for the engine houses of the inclined planes by which the L&MR reached its actual termini. The Doric Arch which the London & Birmingham Railway built at the road approach to Euston, however, served no utilitarian purpose beyond that of providing intending passengers with a fitting introduction to the great new means of transport. Even Whishaw, who hated extravagance in railway buildings, managed to approve: 'We are inclined to think that the grand Doric entrance to the Euston station, from the design of Mr. Hardwick, which is, as it were, the key to all the railways north of London, is perfectly allowable.' At its other terminus, Birmingham Curzon Street, the L&BR provided another suitably impressive entrance building with a fine Ionic portico; and though the Euston Arch has gone, the Curzon Street building happily survives, now in local authority ownership.

At Bristol Temple Meads, Brunel placed his neo-Gothic building containing the railway offices across the end of the tracks – it was flanked by two arches, departing passengers passing beneath one and arriving passengers beneath the other. The building, less the latter archway, survives – part of the Brunel Engineering Centre Trust. The station's greater glory, however, is its great hall of a train shed, with mock hammerbeam roof. Drawings, dating from the mid-1840s, of the station are reproduced in my *Archaeology of the Transport Revolution*. Because the main station at Bristol was moved to the curve connecting the GWR and Bristol & Exeter lines, the original terminus became of secondary importance – which enabled it to survive with little modification. In 1981, railway use having ceased, it was leased to the trust.

The train shed at Temple Meads, apparently of wooden construction, is in fact an iron-framed building. Lesser train sheds were built of wood by Brunel, and became typical features of medium-sized stations throughout the Great Western and associated railways. Elsewhere they were rare – iron was the preferred material for the framework. Development of iron train sheds originated from the plain iron-framed pitched roofs supported by cast iron columns which were built over the tracks at Euston, and designed according to Gordon Biddle (*Victorian Stations*) by Robert Stephenson and Charles Fox – the latter presumably, being he with whom Wheatstone held inconclusive discussions about an electric telegraph. Such train sheds were built throughout the LNWR system; other companies developed their own decorative styles as variants on the theme. At Haymarket, the original (1842) Edinburgh terminus of the Edinburgh & Glasgow Railway, part of the original train shed remained in existence, though latterly no longer spanning tracks, until 1982. Then, in connection with reconstruction of the station, it was dismantled – and re-erected by the Scottish Railway Preservation Society at its new station at Bo'ness. The classical station building at Haymarket was not directly affected by the reconstruction and happily remains on site and in use.

At Newcastle-upon-Tyne Central architect John Dobson for the first time used malleable iron ribs to form train sheds with arched roofs. The station was completed in 1850 and remains in intensive use; the effect is the more striking because of the curve upon which it is situated. Train sheds with arched roofs could cover wide spaces and were much used subsequently. The most notable early example is Paddington, completed in 1854 to replace the earlier Great Western terminus. Brunel designed it with the assistance of architect Digby Wyatt – it was strongly influenced by the Crystal Palace built to house the Great Exhibition, with the construction of which both men had been concerned. Its three great bays provided an overall roof covering a large enough area to last the Great Western for over sixty years before extension was needed, and remain the heart of the station to this day.

At King's Cross, however, which was completed a couple of years before Paddington, Lewis Cubitt supported the two adjoining overall roofs by arches of laminated timber. These were eventually found to place too great a sideways pressure on the walls: one roof was replaced by iron girders in 1869–70, the other in 1886–7. Meanwhile the Midland Railway, arriving in London in 1868, had built next door the very much more ostentatious station of St Pancras, with its train shed 689 ft long and 240 ft wide, and ornate Gothic hotel frontage, completed in 1873.

King's Cross, with its frontage consisting mainly of two vast brick arches, was considered plain to excess by Victorians. Of station buildings which received the full architectural treatment, one of the finest dating from before 1860 – certainly one of the finest to survive – is no London terminus, but the station completed in 1847 in the provincial town of Huddersfield. It is classical: a large central building is fronted by an imposing Corinthian portico, and matching colonnades on either side terminate in pavilions which were once the booking offices for the companies which used the station – the Huddersfield & Manchester Railway & Canal Co. which was absorbed by the LNWR, and the Lancashire & Yorkshire Railway. Behind all this, originally, was a single long platform.

These were great stations. But at intervals along all the main lines of the 1840s and 1850s were provided innumerable lesser stations: their buildings in timber or stone or brick, in style Tudor or Italianate or Classical, according to architect's whim or local custom, or both. Cottage orné style was popular for country stations. The buildings of many wayside stations of this period survive. Even though many of the stations themselves have been closed, buildings sometimes survive in non-railway use. Once again one refers to *The Railway Heritage of Britain* for comprehensive details not only of passenger station buildings but also of other surviving railway buildings, those erected for goods traffic, for maintenance and so on.

Museum Pieces

There is however a select band of stations and other buildings from this period which merit individual mention for, like Liverpool Road, their buildings have survived by achieving museum status or similar. Notable among them is Monkwearmouth, completed in 1848, not large but with a magnificent classical frontage. Originally Monkwearmouth, north of the River Wear, was the station for Sunderland on its south bank – but its first station, although terminus of the Brandling Junction Railway, was so small and inconveniently sited that one diarist passenger is quoted by Tomlinson as having supposed it located 'for the purpose of escaping public observation'. Its replacement was quite the opposite. The line was extended three-quarters of a mile to terminate close to the road bridge across the river, and its station of some splendiferousness built to celebrate George Hudson's position as member of parliament for Sunderland.

In 1879, however, a railway bridge was built across the Wear and the line extended into Sunderland itself. Monkwearmouth became a suburban station of little importance. It was eventually closed in 1967 – but the building was saved from demolition when purchased by Sunderland Corporation. Subsequently restored as Monkwearmouth Station Museum, it has become an excellent transport museum.

Darlington North Road was opened by the Stockton & Darlington Railway in 1842, by which date the company evidently considered it needed a proper station in one of the principal towns it served. Important for many years, it was eventually eclipsed by Darlington Bank Top station on the East Coast Main Line. Only one platform remains in use by British Rail as an unstaffed halt – but the rest of the station has, since 1975, been a museum. Originally called North Road Station Museum, it is now known as Darlington Railway Museum, and has as its most notable exhibit S&DR *Locomotion No. 1*.

A recent addition to museums of this type is at North Woolwich, in East London on the north bank of the Thames. Here is the terminus of what was originally the Eastern Counties & Thames Junction Railway; opened in 1847, it in due course became part of the Great Eastern. On it operated the first of W. Bridges Adams's articulated coaches mentioned on page 207. The original wooden station building at North Woolwich was replaced about 1854 by the surviving handsome Italianate building, larger than might be expected, for the station was not the terminus of a dim branch line but the interchange point for the ferry to Woolwich itself and for steamer services on the river. By the 1970s it was – the familiar story – too large for British Rail needs. BR retained one platform, with a small modern building. The old building came to feature filthy brickwork, boarded-up windows, sprayed-on graffiti. From this it was rescued by the Passmore Edwards Museum Trust, the Passmore Edwards Museum being an important local municipal museum concerned with the heritage of Essex and east London. With the financial aid of the London Docklands Development Corporation the station building was restored to pristine state, and North Woolwich Old Station Museum was opened to the public in 1984 as a museum of the Great Eastern Railway.

Cheddleton station on the North Staffordshire Railway line from

Leek to Uttoxeter has an attractive Victorian-Tudor station building, built in 1849. The railway through the station remains open, but for freight traffic only. Demolition of the building was planned in 1974 but prevented when Councillor N. Hancock parked his car in the path of the bulldozer which was about to commence the task. The station building was subsequently listed. Its long-term maintenance however was assured not by municipal effort but by establishment of a voluntary preservation group, the North Staffordshire Railway (1978) Ltd, which has set up a steam centre based on the station.

Dating from before the main-line period, a goods shed erected by the canal-feeder Mansfield & Pinxton Railway has been carefully demolished and transferred to the Midland Railway Trust, Butterley, for re-erection, and covered coal-drops from the Stanhope & Tyne Rail Road have been reconstructed at Beamish. The Liverpool & Manchester Railway's goods warehouse at Liverpool Road has strong canal warehouse affinities, notably rail entrances at right angles to the running lines, which were approached via turntables. Its brick walls concealed a many-floored interior constructed largely of timber – sadly present-day concern for fire risk has meant removal of much of the timberwork so that the building could be incorporated into the museum. Didcot Railway Centre has the goods transfer shed, now on a new site, but originally constructed at Didcot in 1863 with parallel standard and broad gauge tracks on either side of a platform – it was used for transfer of goods between wagons of each gauge. The main line west to Bristol was still solely broad gauge at that date. On its new site within the railway centre tracks of both gauges have once again been laid into it, and so it has become a tangible reminder of 'the evil of break-of-gauge'.

10 : Traffic by Rail, Road and Canal

Passengers and Freight

'You find the passengers almost universally prefer the railway to the high road?' – 'Universally'.

The questioner, on 18 December 1837, was the chairman of the House of Commons Select Committee on Railroad Communications; the respondent, Mr W. Chaplin. And Chaplin (despite having words put into his mouth by the chairman) was of all people the best placed to speak with authority – an extensive coach proprietor and mail coach contractor, he had recently had to abandon the Manchester and Liverpool mails which ran parallel to the Grand Junction Railway, and was preparing to do the same with mails to Birmingham so soon as the London & Birmingham Railway should be open.

The early trunk lines saw their great and immediate success with passenger and parcels traffic – their freight traffic grew much more gradually. Grote Lewin notes that in the first half of 1841, passenger receipts represented 87 per cent of the total on the Great Western Railway, 84 per cent on the London & South Western, 82 per cent on the London & Birmingham and 77 per cent on the Grand Junction. In 1843 the national figure for railways then open was passenger traffic, 68.5 per cent of receipts; freight traffic grew steadily but it was not until 1852 that it accounted for more than half the total receipts. Throughout the period when the railway system was expanding at its fastest, the emphasis was on passenger traffic.

Coaching Practices

The rapid growth of the railway system and its eclipse of road coaching were without precedent. Some coaching practices, terminology and personnel transferred naturally to the newer form of transport. 'Six carriages commenced running regularly upon the road', says *The Railway Companion* of 1833, referring to the introduction of regular train services – three trains each way daily – upon the Liverpool & Manchester Railway in 1830. Coaching terms which made the transition survive in railway use to this day, among the much wider specialised terminology which subsequently developed. Apart from 'coach' itself, 'guard' for the man in charge of the train is a notable example. So are 'up' and 'down' for trains to and from London (and, by extension, the lines used by them): coaches went up to London and down to the country, coaching's 'upper grounds' being the roads nearest to the capital, the high place of the kingdom. Indeed 'road' itself is sometimes used by railwaymen to refer to a railway – a driver new to a route 'learns the road', a derailed locomotive is 'off the road'. It seems more likely that use of 'road' in these senses has been continuous since the early days of railways than that it originated later.

With passengers, the habit of treating trains in the same way as coaches died hard. As late as 1850, David Joy recalled of the newly opened Nottingham & Grantham Railway, 'One of the funs of the place was its being a new line, everybody and everything was strange to the engines. People used to come and get on the line at the road crossing gates and wave their umbrellas at us to stop as if we were an old stage coach . . . We didn't.'

The Stockton & Darlington Railway based its horse-drawn passenger coaches on lineside coaching inns, at least one of which gave its name to a subsequent station, Fighting Cocks. The Leicester & Swannington hired a room in an inn close to the line, and later incorporated it into a station. The Garnkirk & Glasgow, conscious of the lack of facilities at its eastern extremity, actually built an inn, at Gartsherrie.

Early railways continued to name stations after inns. Such were Four Ashes and Spread Eagle stations on the Grand Junction, Dartmouth Arms and Jolly Sailor on the London & Croydon. The early main lines also inherited the custom of locating refreshment rooms, analogous to coaching inns, every fifty miles or so – at Swindon, for instance, and Wolverton. Here passengers descended to refresh themselves, and these early refreshment rooms seem quickly to have acquired coaching inns' reputation for sharp practices, such as producing soup so hot that the purchaser could not drink it before leaving to board his coach, or train, and the soup could be poured back into the pot to be sold again.

To direct and manage the new railways came men from the coaching and carrying industries. Chaplin, having sold out his coaching interests, became chairman of the London & South Western Railway. Joseph Baxendale, manager of Pickford & Co. for twenty years, became superintendent of the London & Birmingham Railway and deputy chairman of the South Eastern. Others came from the Army and the Navy: middle-ranking officers with experience of accountancy and control of large staffs but (it seems likely) limited chances of promotion. Captain Huish was one of many. As for the staffs they commanded, Tomlinson remarks of railways in the North East by 1841 that the only really trained men were the enginemen, many of whom had gained experience at Killingworth (or, one may add, on the Stockton & Darlington), a few of the guards who had served on stage coaches, and platelayers who had previously been employed on waggonways. Other parts of Britain had even more limited reservoirs upon which to draw, and it is remarkable that railways were able to expand so quickly in apparent safety when the staff were so inexperienced.

Traffic Increases

That expansion was not only in the number of routes, but also in the traffic over them. D. K. Clark in *Railway Machinery* (1855) quotes some figures derived from one of Huish's reports. On the Liverpool & Manchester Railway between 1831 and 1848 the number of trains daily to and from Manchester had increased from 26 to 90, the average weight of passenger trains from 18 tons to 70, of goods trains from 52 tons to 126. On the Grand Junction the number of trains serving Stafford daily increased between 1837 and 1848 from 14 to 38, the weight of passenger trains from 60 tons to 70, the weight of goods trains from 133 to 176.

By the time the Gauge Commissioners reported, there were three types of trains in general operation. The first were 'Fast, or Express Trains'. The gauge war had encouraged their operation; those on the Grand Junction comprised four coaches and a luggage van. Larger numbers of passengers were carried by the 'Ordinary, or Mixed, Trains'. ('Mixed' meant mixed as to classes of passenger accommodation, rather than the later sense of a mixed passenger and goods train.) These also conveyed private carriages on carriage trucks and horses in horse boxes; this traffic is so typical a feature of the period that it is mentioned at greater length below. The third were goods trains.

Some goods trains carried third class passengers. So, of course, did carriers' waggons on the roads: and of the Manchester & Leeds Railway in 1841 Bradshaw had noted: 'The Manchester 7 a.m. train is the only one by which passengers can go to London in waggons.' At the same date the London & South Western had two goods trains daily in each direction between London and Southampton which took third class passengers.

Seymour Clark was traffic superintendent of the GWR for the area London–Oxford–Swindon–Gloucester. In 1845 he was questioned on GWR traffic by the Gauge Commissioners, and here in their own words are the commissioners' questions and the replies of the man responsible for traffic on the principal broad gauge railway:

What is the total number of passenger trains which leave Paddington daily? – Seventeen.

How many of such trains carry third-class passengers? – Only one of those.

Which train is that? – That is at half-past six o'clock in the morning.

What is the speed of that train? – Twelve miles an hour. It is obliged to be by Act of Parliament 12 miles an hour, but, in fact, it is quicker than that. . . . It is about 15 miles an hour.

Then that is exclusively a third-class train? – Yes, we carry first and second-class passengers with that for the convenience of parties who might wish to go to intermediate stations . . . because that train, by the regulation of Government, stops everywhere. It is not because it pays us at all that we carry those passengers, but we do it for their convenience; but, in fact, it is almost nominal; very few avail themselves of it.

No other passenger train carries third class? – No, only this; but there is a goods train at half-past nine at night which carries passengers.

How many luggage-trains leave Paddington daily? – Two.

At what hours? – One at half-past four in the morning, and the other at half-past nine at night.

Do they both carry third-class passengers? – No; the half-past four does not.

What class of passengers are carried by the express-trains? – First and second.

At what hours do they leave Paddington? – The express-train leaves Paddington at a quarter to ten.

What is the total number of passenger and luggage or goods trains, which leave daily the termini of the lines worked by the Great Western Company and which of those trains carry third-class passengers? – Of the goods trains, the one at half-past nine runs to Exeter and Gloucester, and, in fact, all over the line. The half-past four train runs only to Oxford and Bristol. All the long passenger trains run to Exeter, Oxford, and Gloucester; but some of those that I have given of the 17 are only short trains. Out of those 17 daily trains, there are seven which we call short trains; one of them running to Oxford, one of them running to Reading, three of them running to Maidenhead, and two to Slough.

Tickets

Railways at first naturally adopted the stage coach practice of issuing passengers with paper tickets. 'The check ticket given to the passenger on the payment of his fare will be required from him on leaving the coach or at the station next before his arrival at London or Birmingham; and if not then presented he will be liable to have the Fare again demanded', explained Bradshaw of the London & Birmingham Railway in 1840, and added, 'A Passenger may claim the seat corresponding to the number on his ticket, and when not numbered he may take any seat not previously occupied.'

Such tickets were generally supplied to stations in books, pre-printed, but details had to be completed in ink by the booking clerk, and each ticket torn from the book in which usually there remained the counterfoil. This was a laborious process, particularly in view of the much greater number of passengers on a train compared with a coach. Booking of tickets was made much easier – and so was keeping records of them – by Thomas Edmondson's invention in 1837 of card tickets, pre-printed, pre-numbered, stored in racks from which they were issued in order, and dated by pushing them into a small dating press. Such tickets have still not entirely disappeared even in this computerised age. At the time of his invention Edmondson was a booking clerk on the

Newcastle & Carlisle Railway, from which he was soon lured away to the Manchester & Leeds and, one hopes, well-deserved promotion.

Coaches on Carriage Trucks

Originally, when the Liverpool & Manchester Railway was the sole example of a trunk railway among a network of turnpike roads, it seems likely that the practice of letting passengers travel in their own carriages, carried on carriage trucks, was intended to enable the new type of road to take its place in the existing road network. Between Liverpool and Manchester, those wealthy enough to have their own carriages would take advantage of the railway's speed by having them put on carriage trucks: elsewhere, before and after the railway stage of their journeys, they would continue as before to hire relays of post horses to take them from stage to stage. The Liverpool & Manchester first class train in Ackermann's long print has at the rear a carriage truck conveying an open carriage in which three fashionably-dressed ladies are travelling, accompanied by their servants.

As with private carriages, so with public. As early as 1832 Liverpool–London stage coaches were commencing their journeys by being carried by rail, complete with passengers, to Warrington. In 1835, when the Newcastle & Carlisle Railway was opened as far as Hexham, the Newcastle–Carlisle coach was carried by train to the latter place. During the late 1830s and early 1840s it was not unusual for stage coaches to perform part of their journeys mounted upon carriage trucks, and this practice in relation to mail coaches has already been mentioned in chapter five. Just when it eventually ceased I have been unable to establish, but it seems unlikely to have outlived the great expansion of the rail network which took place in the late 1840s.

The delightful and apparently accurate engravings of London & Birmingham and Grand Junction Railway trains, which appeared at the heads of the maps of those lines included in Osborne's guides (and which are here reproduced as illustrations 9 and 10, both show carriage trucks bearing travelling chariots included in the trains. John Moss of the Grand Junction referred twice to the practice of carrying private carriages in his evidence before the 1838 Select Committee on Railroads, referring on one occasion to 'three or four gentlemen's carriages going to Ireland . . . by a particular train' and on the other to the company's trains 'containing perhaps 60 passengers, and four or five gentlemen's carriages'. In 1840 Bradshaw was informing readers that gentlemen riding in their own carriages were charged second class fares by the GJR.

The tables for both the London & Birmingham and the Birmingham & Derby Junction at the same date indicated that carriages and horses were to be at their departure station a quarter of an hour before train departure time. This does not seem long, and suggests that practised ease enabled railway staff to load carriages and horses quickly. As the railway network rapidly expanded and the road components of journeys became correspondingly shorter, it became more and more preferable for carriage-owners to take their horses with them by train as well as their carriages. Nicholas Wood introduced the subject as one of his objections to breaks-of-gauge, when giving evidence before the Gauge Commissioners. There were two grounds to his objection. The first was that it would be impossible to have a wagon body carrying a private carriage transferred from an underframe on one gauge to one on another, so the carriages themselves would have to be transferred from wagon to wagon with consequent delays. The other was that gentlemen required their horses to be conveyed on the same train as themselves, and it was extremely difficult when horses were taken out of a horsebox to get them to enter another: they had to be kept quiet for some time to cool them.

By this date it is unclear to what extent owners of carriages were actually travelling in them on board trains, and to what extent they travelled in accompanying railway passenger coaches. Those who attempted to travel in their own open carriages must soon have found the speed, smoke and smuts unpleasant (even though most locomotives burned coke at this period which minimised the smuts) and have retreated into railway coaches. No doubt the change was a gradual one. Hamilton Ellis, in *British Railway History* remarks that the Duke of Wellington continued to travel in his own carriage on a carriage truck as late as 1852.

In view of the popularity of travel in this manner it is surprising that few contemporary descriptions of it survive. Acworth does quote a contemporary newspaper account of the alarming experience which befell a gentleman travelling in his own carriage on a truck attached to the rear of a train on the London & Brighton Railway. In Balcombe tunnel the truck became uncoupled from the train which disappeared into the distance, leaving the gentleman afraid to alight yet scared out of his wits awaiting collision by the next train. 'He had not been long in this suspense, when an engine entered the tunnel, puffing away and the whistle screaming. He now considered his doom sealed; but the engine proved to be a pilot one sent to look after him, the truck and carriage having fortunately been missed on the train arriving at the next station.' The carriage and occupant were then taken on their way to Brighton.

Jorrocks arrives at Handley Cross

Another account appears in R. S. Surtees's *Handley Cross*, first published in 1843. It is fiction – indeed, it is satire, not to say farce – but none the less contains an excellent word picture of how railway travel appeared to contemporary observers, which is well worth quoting. The hero is Mr Jorrocks, a Cockney of enormous girth and 'a great city grocer of the old school', yet a 'natural born sportsman' whose lot had been cast behind a counter instead of in the country. Jorrocks has accepted an invitation from Captain Doleful, master of ceremonies at Handley Cross spa (and something of a charlatan) to become Master of Fox Hounds there: in that era fox hunting was a highly fashionable sport. Here his arrival is awaited by Captain Doleful and a large crowd at the station:

> Eyes were strained up the railway in the direction he was to come, and ears were open to catch the first sound of the engine. All was anxiety and expectation. Hope and fear vacillated on every countenance. 'Should he not come, what a bore!' 'Oh, but he's certain to arrive, and Mrs. Jorrocks too, arn't they, Captain?' The Captain looked thoughtful and mysterious, as all great men should, but deigned no reply.
>
> Precisely at three-quarters of a minute before three, a wild shrill whistle, that seemed to issue from the bowels of the earth and to run right up into mid-air, was heard at the back of Shavington Hill, and, in an instant, the engine and long train rounded the base, the engine smoking and snorting like an exasperated crocodile. Nearer and nearer it comes, with a thundering sort of hum that sounds throughout the country. The wondering plough-man stops his team. The cows and sheep stand staring with astonishment, while the horses take a look, and then gallop about the fields, kicking up their heels and snorting with delight. The guard's red coat on the engine is visible – next his gold hat-band appears – now we read the Hercules on the engine, and anon it

pulls up with a whiff, a puff, and a whistle, under the slate-covered shed, to give the Hercules his water, and set down and take up passengers and goods. Seven first-class passenger carriages follow the engine, all smart, clean, and yellow, with appropriate names on each door panel – The Prince Albert, Queen Victoria, and the Prince of Wales, The Venus, The Mercury, The Comet and The Star; next came ten second-class ones, green, with covered tops, and half-covered sides, but in neither set is there anything at all like the Jorrocks' party. Cattle-pens follow, holding sheep, swine, donkeys and poultry; then came an open platform with a broken britzka, followed by a curious-looking nondescript one-horse vehicle, containing a fat man in a low-crowned hat, and a versatio or reversible coat, with the preferable side outwards. Along with him were two ladies muffled up in cloaks, and at the back was a good-looking servant-maid. From the bottom of the carriage swung a couple of hams, and a large warming-pan.

'Pray is Mr. Jorrocks here?' enquired the elegant M.C. [i.e., master of ceremonies], who had persuaded the station-master to let him in upon the line, riding his white charger near the door of the first-class carriage, and raising his hat as he spoke; but getting no answer, he continued his interrogatory down the whole set until he came to the end, when casting a despairing glance at the cattle pens, he was about to wheel round, when the gentleman in the versatio coat, in a very stentorian voice, roared out 'I say, SIR! Bain't this the 'Andley Cross station?'

'It is, Sir,' replied Captain Doleful, in his most dignified manner, 'the Datton station for Handley Cross at least.'

'Then I want to land,' responded the same sweet voice.

'Here's a gentleman wants to be down,' observed Captain Doleful to the scarlet-coated guard, who came bustling past with a pen of Cochin-Chinas to put upon the train. [Surtees seems to have mistaken both the function of the mail guard and, earlier, the location in which he travelled.]

'Yes, a gentleman and two ladies,' roared our friend; 'MISTER AND MISSIS JORROCKS in fact, and MISS JORROCKS!'

'Bless my heart,' exclaimed Captain Doleful in ecstasies, 'how delighted I am to see you! . . . But hadn't you better alight and get your carriage and things off the train? . . . they'll be off with you if you don't mind', and thereupon the Captain beckoned the guard, . . . the porters cut off the last joints of the train, when away it went, hissing and snorting through the quiet country. . . .

Now Jorrocks had made his first appearance in the 1830s in the pages of the *New Sporting Magazine.* Surtees had started this in conjunction with Rudolph Ackermann junior, whose father, also Rudolph, was the noted fine art publisher who had produced the Liverpool & Manchester Long Prints. So there can be no doubt that Surtees was familiar with these, and in his description of Jorrocks's arrival in his carriage upon a carriage truck, hams, warming pan and all, one is tempted to see a satire on the ladies of fashion who bring up the rear of the L&M train in the print. A more remarkable coincidence is that Surtees, who came from County Durham, was closely related to the Blacketts of Wylam, Christopher Blackett being his uncle. In view of this it is a pity – from the railway historian's point-of-view – that he did not spend more time writing about the contemporary railway scene, which he was so well placed to describe authoritatively, than he apparently did.

Special Trains and Excursions

Excursion traffic is as old as the steam railway. During the summer of 1830 the Liverpool & Manchester Railway was running free shaking-down excursions for the proprietors and their friends to view the almost completed railway, and soon after the opening day it thriftily re-used the Duke of Wellington's triumphal car in excursions which took the fare-paying public sightseeing to Sankey Viaduct. Other early railways to operate excursions were the Garnkirk & Glasgow and Dublin & Kingstown. When the London & South Western Railway announced eight trains to Kingston upon Thames on Derby Day 1838 – within a week of opening – its Nine Elms terminus in London was swamped by 5,000 would-be passengers. In 1840 the Newcastle & Carlisle offered cheap return fares by certain trains to Newcastle, and followed this by cheap Sunday excursions, one of which (in 1841) was denounced in placards by a noted Sabbatarian:

A Reward for Sabbath Breaking
People taken safely and swiftly to Hell!
Next Lord's Day, by the Carlisle Railway, for 7s 6d.
It is a Pleasure Trip!

Nevertheless the excursion seems to have been successful, so perhaps even then all publicity was good publicity.

Thomas Cook

The name best-known in connection with early excursions is of course that of Thomas Cook. In his own words, as recollected twenty years later:

> My first project was in connection with the Temperance Movement, to which I had been warmly attached for five or six years previous to 1841. It was in the spring of that year that I was walking from Market Harborough to Leicester, to attend a temperance meeting . . . when the thought suddenly flashed across my mind as to the practicability of employing the great powers of railways and locomotion for the furtherance of this social reform . . . on the temperance platform that evening, I proposed to the friends assembled to get up a Special Train to Loughborough, a distance of twelve miles, at the time of an approaching District Meeting of Delegates. The proposal was . . . submitted . . . to J. Fox Bell Esq., in whom centred the Secretaryship and the Leicester management of the Midland Counties Railway [opened in 1840]. A special train was arranged, and on the day appointed about 500 passengers were conveyed in 24 open carriages, the amazing distance of a dozen miles! I believe this was either the second or third train of the kind ever run on the Midland Railway . . .

Over the next three years Cook as a philanthropic amateur arranged similar special trains to temperance gatherings in the Midlands. But this laid the foundation for more ambitious excursions. In 1845 he organised a special train from Leicester, Nottingham and Derby to Liverpool. It travelled via Normanton and Manchester, and at Liverpool a special steamer was arranged to carry the excursionists along the North Wales coast to Caernarfon and back. The excursion was so heavily over-subscribed that it had to be repeated, and the success of both encouraged him to run an excursion to Scotland the following year. This took the route via Fleetwood and steamer to Ardrossan. Tourists by the trainload were an unprecedented phenomenon: they were met at the

'Ayrshire Railway Station, Glasgow' by a band, guns fired a salute as the train drew up at the platform, and a welcoming meeting was held in a public hall. As the railway system was extended, both to and through Scotland, Cook started to organise four trips a year to Scotland, alternating between East and West Coast routes. It is the lot of the satirist to be overtaken by reality: within a few years Cockney tourists were indeed providing useful traffic for railways in places almost as remote as Glenmutchkin.

Meanwhile Cook expanded his operations into tours to many other places, and was particularly active in arranging excursions from the Midlands and Yorkshire to the Great Exhibition of 1851. The Great Exhibition provided a notable traffic boost for many companies: Grote Lewin notes that Great Western passenger traffic for July 1851 was 56 per cent up on the same month the previous year, and comparable figures for the LSWR and the LNWR were 40.9 per cent and 28.9 per cent respectively.

Goods Traffic, by type

Fast coaching on the roads had first enabled perishable foodstuffs to be despatched from remote country districts to the cities: a brace of pheasants or a hare were common sights among the parcels carried by stage coaches. Railways, however, enabled cities to be supplied with perishables such as milk, butter, eggs, vegetables and fruit from a distance on a large scale. Fish, too: turbot and sole, for instance, previously unknown in Newcastle, were being conveyed thither from the Irish Sea by the Newcastle & Carlisle Railway from 1837, and once the rail link through East Anglia was eventually completed in 1845, fish from Yarmouth became an important traffic to London.

Livestock – pigs (from Ireland), sheep and cattle – were first conveyed on the Liverpool & Manchester Railway in 1831. When the London & Birmingham Railway was being promoted, its potential for carrying livestock to supply Londoners with meat was an important point in its favour. Cattle and sheep then arrived in London on the hoof having been driven, sometimes, over very long distances. The prediction proved true in practice, and livestock became an important traffic on the L&BR. T. C. Mills, manager of the railway's goods department at Camden Town, London, told the Gauge Commissioners that on a single Saturday in August 1845 it had delivered 229 wagons to London containing 550 Oxen, 5,571 sheep, 349 pigs and 3 calves. The Eastern Counties Railway also carried many cattle to London, and they were an important traffic elsewhere on the Grand Junction and Newcastle & Carlisle Railways.

Along with perishables and livestock grew traffic in merchandise — mostly general merchandise such as groceries though there was specialised traffic too: the Liverpool & Manchester had cotton, the Leeds & Selby wool and woollen goods. Bulk goods and mineral traffic grew more slowly, although the Liverpool & Manchester was carrying coal in increasing amounts from 1831, and timber was being carried in the 1830s on the Stockton & Darlington and Newcastle & Carlisle Railways. But the railways of North East England were exceptions to the general rule: in this area, where there were no canals, coal for shipment was the staple traffic of steam railways of the 1830s and early 1840s. By 1845 the Grand Junction had a substantial traffic in iron ore, the precursor of increasing bulk traffics over the London & North Western, encouraged by Huish with low rates. Coal traffic, which accounted for 4.7 per cent of LNWR goods receipts in the first half of 1846, had climbed to 10 per cent in 1851.

Carriers by Rail

Much of the freight traffic conveyed over the early steam railways was provided by firms of carriers which were already in existence and in some instances old-established. They carried by canal, river and turnpike road and added railways, the new form of public highway, to the list. The Stockton & Darlington Railway in its early years did indeed resemble a public highway, even to the extent that it was used by people on foot and on at least two occasions, according to Tomlinson, by funeral processions which paid for the privilege.

The Liverpool & Manchester Railway, having elected to operate its own carrying department from the opening in 1830, in 1831 opened its line for public use on payment of tolls. It saw only limited use of this type, although in the mid-1840s one coal dealer at least was still running his own locomotive on it against payment of tolls. The adjoining Bolton & Leigh Railway, however, was leased to carriers John Hargreaves & Son who provided locomotives and rolling stock and operated it until the company amalgamated with the L&MR and the Grand Junction in 1845.

By 1839 it was clear that the original Parliamentary concept that railway companies should provide a road for all comers had broken down, and this was accepted by a House of Commons committee enquiring into railway matters. Although scales of tolls had been inserted into railway Acts, there was nothing to prevent railways making prohibitive charges for use of stations, sheds and locomotive water supplies. In effect railway companies had monopolies of the use of their lines.

There were still, however, good reasons why a new railway should continue to co-operate with carriers. Some or all of the capital cost of setting up a carrying department could be avoided. Established carriers had experience of collection, loading, sorting, invoicing and delivery which the new railway companies lacked; their commercial connections were valuable to railways, and the public were accustomed to dealing with them. Carriers were established in cities and towns throughout the land, and at this period, long before railways themselves could provide a national network, it was still most convenient to the public to be able to hand over a parcel in, say, London, to a carrier who would arrange for its through conveyance to a distant town, using rail, canal or road transport according to availability and economy and irrespective of operator. Where railways were used, the carrier contracted with the railway companies to convey the goods for them. There was at this date no parcel post.

The London & Birmingham Railway certainly saw things in this light. T. C. Mills told the Gauge Commissioners that it did not carry: the general carriers on its line were 'Pickford & Co., Chaplin & Horne, Crowley and Co., Sutton, Deacon, Alexander, Hunt, and several other minor carriers'. Pickford was the most extensive of these, followed by Chaplin & Horne. Chaplin & Horne, formerly the greatest of mail coach contractors and stage coach proprietors, had sold out their coaching interests with the coming of railways and, using their old coaching connections and parcels offices, set up as carriers. The railway company supplied wagons for use by the carriers, who rented sheds from the company in which their own staffs loaded and unloaded the wagons, transferring the goods to and from carts for delivery and collection. Goods of different carriers were not mixed within wagons. Carriers were charged by the weight of their goods; wagons were subject to inspection by the railway company, were weighed before departure, and again, largely as a precaution against pilferage, before delivery to the carrier at rail destination. Wagons loaded at Camden Town were dispatched not only to Birmingham but also ran through on to the railways leading to Derby and into Yorkshire. Pickford's operations on the Gloucester railways have already been mentioned in chapter four.

But other railways followed the example of the L&MR in setting up their own carrying departments. Evidently they saw no reason why carriers should benefit from business which would be theirs if they dealt direct with the public — and they could justify their action as elimination of the middle man's profit. In retrospect it seems surprising that there was little if any opposition to railways by carriers; and also that there seem to have been few if any attempts by railway companies to take carying firms over.

The Newcastle & Carlisle and Leeds & Selby carried their own goods traffic; so, with far more important consequences, did the Grand Junction. This operation did not originate with Huish, indeed shortly before Huish left the Glasgow, Paisley & Greenock Railway for the GJR in 1841 the former railway arranged for a local carrier to introduce goods traffic to its line. Perhaps it is relevant that John Moss, GJR chairman, had earlier been instrumental in establishing the Liverpool & Manchester's carrying department. It seems that when goods traffic started on the GJR early in 1838 carriers were at first admitted, but within a year the company was collecting and delivering goods, and then, by adjusting rates squeezed carriers' profits to the point at which they became unremunerative, and became in effect the sole carrier on its line between Birmingham and Lancashire. (For goods: several carriers of coal ran their own locomotives and wagons on the line.) The railway company then endeavoured to extend its control to goods between Lancashire and London, appointing Chaplin & Horne as its London agents for collection and delivery and allowing them rebates which were not allowed to other carriers.

This brought the railway company up against Pickford, and the result was a celebrated legal test case. In November 1840 Pickford packed several small parcels, which had been entrusted to it for conveyance, into a large hamper and tendered it to the Grand Junction for carriage from Birmingham to Manchester. Each of the parcels individually weighed less than 112 lb; the total weight of the hamper was over 8 cwt. Pickford offered to pay the legal rate for goods of that weight, which amounted to £1.6s.6d. The railway company demanded the rate for each parcel as a 'small', i.e., weighing less than 112 lb, which would have totalled £4.1s.8d. The hamper did not travel, at least not by the Grand Junction Railway, and Pickford took the railway company to court. The hamper was not so fatuous as it may appear to us: what was at stake was whether the operator of the new and advanced form of transport should be allowed to monopolise carriage by it, to the detriment of established carriers. Besides, the carrier was performing a real service in consolidating small parcels into a larger unit for the railway to convey. The court decided in Pickford's favour.

There was, however, another aspect to the case. The Grand Junction rate for goods from Manchester to London was 65s a ton; this included delivery by Chaplin & Horne to whom the railway company paid 10s a ton for their work. But the rate to Pickford was also 65s a ton, although goods were handed over to Pickford on arrival in London for the carrier to deliver. In other words, Chaplin & Horne were in effect being charged 10s a ton less than Pickford. Once again, the court found in Pickford's favour, that the railway should not discriminate between the two carriers.

Unfortunately for Pickford, however, the findings proved ineffective. Ramifications of freight rates and legal obligations were so complex that the railway company, while appearing willing to comply, was in fact able to evade them. In this it must be admitted that Huish was most active in promoting his company's interest. In 1845 only Chaplin & Horne's wagons were working through between London and Liverpool/ Manchester. Other carriers' goods were unloaded and re-loaded at Birmingham (a process which afforded much interest to the Gauge Commissioners). Pickford was sending much of its goods north of Birmingham by canal boat. The opposite – one almost wrote opposing – attitudes to carriers held by the London & Birmingham and Grand Junction Railways can have done nothing to ease the friction between them at this period. Then, after the two companies amalgamated to form the London & North Western, the new company started to carry over the whole of its line in 1847. Carriers were excluded, but Pickford & Co. were enabled to join Chaplin & Horne as agents for the LNWR, collecting and delivering goods to and from stations.

The controversy, in effect, was over, although court cases between carriers and railways rumbled on into the 1860s. Railway companies set up their own collection and delivery services. Probably it was inevitable, as T. R. Gourvish remarks*, that once the railway companies had

* In *Mark Huish and the London & North Western Railway*

learned about the carrier business they would seek to assume control of it. By the late 1840s, in any case, the Railway Clearing House was doing much to facilitate through goods traffic between the companies, and railways were becoming so extensive as to approach being a national system. Once that happened the public no doubt found it preferable to deal direct with railways rather than through carriers as intermediaries. The 'private owner' wagon, operated by coal merchants and such, remained until nationalization in 1948 as a reminder that railways had once been thought of as public highways.

Competition with Canals

It was of course a considerable irritant to railway companies that carriers could, and did, carry alternatively on canals, so it is worth now seeing what effect the development of the steam railway network was having on the canal system.

Originally, this was small. Rainhill in 1829 did not immediately bring canal development to a halt. The Macclesfield Canal, direct from the Potteries to Manchester, was opened in 1831, and during the mid-1830s there were further proposals for an improved canal from Birmingham to London. It was never built, but so that it might become part of this the Oxford Canal shortened the northern part of its line, building in effect a new canal which used cuttings and embankments to cut across the winding contour loops of the old one. The new works, engineered by Vignoles, were completed in 1834; as late as 1840 heavy traffic obliged the canal company to build duplicate locks alongside the originals at Hillmorton, Warwickshire. Other canals too were having to duplicate locks at this period.

The last great canal of the canal era, the Birmingham & Liverpool Junction, was opened in 1835, nearly five years after the Liverpool & Manchester Railway, and only two years before the Grand Junction Railway, which also linked Birmingham with Liverpool. The Aire & Calder Navigation completed an improved line from the Yorkshire Ouse estuary up to Leeds in 1835, a year *after* the parallel Leeds & Selby Railway had been opened. Steam paddle tugs had been introduced successfully on the Aire & Calder Navigation in 1831, but successful introduction of steam power on canals generally, where vessel width was restricted, was delayed until the 1840s after the invention of the screw propeller. The Forth & Clyde experimented in 1839 with haulage of boats by a locomotive running on a railway specially laid along the bank. Probably a Monkland & Kirkintilloch locomotive was used. Swift passenger boats, originally introduced to counter competition from fast coaches on the roads, were taken up by several canals to meet the threat of competition from rail.

In all this, proprietors of canals and river navigations must have been encouraged, at least in the early 1830s, by the course of events in Lancashire. There, as mentioned in chapter three, the Bridgewater Canal's traffic held up, despite competition from the Liverpool & Manchester Railway, and even the lowered tolls which enabled it to do so were introduced as much to counter competition from the Macclesfield Canal and a general depression of trade as competition from the railway. But a rate war, of varying intensity, between the L&MR and the waterways became a continuing feature of the 1830s. Hargreaves on the Bolton & Leigh Railway found the Leeds & Liverpool Canal a continuing threat to profitable operation of the line, and the coal-carrying St Helens & Runcorn Gap Railway was at first quite unable to compete satisfactorily with the St Helens Canal; when the two concerns eventually merged in 1845, the canal was still the more profitable.

The pattern was repeated on a wider scale when the first long-distance railways were opened in the late 1830s and early 1840s. Although some merchandise now went by rail, particularly where speed of conveyance was important, much remained on canal, as did coal and bulk goods. Canal tolls, however, were reduced to meet the competition. Canals would have done even better if the companies had been able to agree a general policy on this, but in many instances their local short-term interests continued to take precedence over national long-term ones. This was unfortunate, for important through routes were often owned by a succession of different companies.

In 1846 Sir F. B. Head, chairman of the Grand Junction Canal, told the House of Commons Select Committee on Railways and Canals Amalgamation that between London and Birmingham, 144 miles, the Grand Junction and four other canal companies were involved. One of these, the Oxford Canal, was maintaining particularly high tolls. The Grand Junction's revenue on trade interchanged with the Oxford Canal at Braunston in 1837, the last year before the London & Birmingham Railway was opened, was £63,045 on 292,988 tons of goods; in 1845, revenue was down to £41,873, although traffic was stable at 299,608 tons. On the route from London to Leicester, on the other hand, the

Grand Junction had been able to agree toll reductions throughout with the other two canals concerned. In 1839, before the opening of the Midland Counties Railway, the figures for Buckby, where the Grand Junction Canal joined the Leicester line, were £11,762 for 86,535 tons. In 1845 both revenue and traffic were substantially up, to £17,902 for 181,228 tons.

Canals in the Railway Mania

It is clear therefore that at this date the well-established canal system was capable of competing effectively for goods traffic with the new railways. Canal passenger traffic, of course, did not (with a few exceptions) long outlast the opening of competing railways, although there were instances, on the Lancaster Canal for example, where swift passenger boats provided feeder services to railways for a few years until the rail network was extended.

For goods traffic there were two main ways in which railway companies met canal competition. One was for a railway to exploit its ability to quote artificially low freight rates, subsidising them from passenger business with the intention of ruining the competing canal. The Birmingham & Gloucester Railway was said to have treated the Worcester & Birmingham Canal thus, though without total success.

The other was to take over canal companies complete. In some instances their canals were drained and converted into railways. Straws in the wind had been suggesting this possibility for some years – as early as 1830 the Manchester, Bolton & Bury Canal obtained powers to convert its canal into a railway, then thought better of it and built a separate railway on a distinct course. In 1836, however, the Croydon Canal was sold to a railway company, closed, and much of its course used for the London & Croydon Railway.

For the most part, though, railway takeovers of canals were a side effect of the Railway Mania. During the three years 1845, 1846 and 1847 alone, 948 miles of waterways came under railway control. It was not so much the existing railways which purchased canals, although this did happen, as the promoters of new lines who did so to buy off opposition to their schemes. Prices of canal shares had declined sharply: to canal shareholders it was no doubt uncomfortably obvious that the big money was being made in booming railway shares rather than in staying with canals.

253

That, for instance, is how the pioneer and important Trent & Mersey Canal came into railway hands. One of the consequences of the Grand Junction Railway's defeat of proposals for a direct railway from Manchester to the South, described on page 106 had been that the Potteries, through which such a line would have passed, were left without rail connection. Parts of the proposals were therefore resurrected and combined with other schemes to serve the area, to become the North Staffordshire Railway, with several lines centred on Stoke-on-Trent authorised in 1846. Now serving the Potteries was the principal function of the Trent & Mersey Canal, with which the railway would have been in strong competition, had not the canal proprietors in 1845 realised that opposition was likely merely to delay construction of the railway rather than defeat it. They sought amalgamation instead. Agreement was reached that year and the takeover finalised in 1849 after the railway was opened. According to E. F. Clark,* G. P. Bidder, who was the railway's engineer, estimated in 1846 that possession of the canal would mean a saving of £272,000 to the railway company. The results can be seen to this day at Stoke-on-Trent in, for instance, support of railway bridge girders upon the brickwork of the tail of the lock beneath.

Some canal companies pre-empted railway proposals by seeking themselves to convert their canals into railways. In 1845 the Birmingham & Liverpool Junction merged with other canals with a view to converting much of their lines into railways and building more: the Shropshire Union Railways & Canal Co. was formed by Act of Parliament in 1846. The proposal had been supported by the London & Birmingham Railway which saw in conversion of the Birmingham & Liverpool Junction Canal the possibility, among others, of reaching the Chester & Holyhead Railway without troubling the Grand Junction. But in 1846 also the L & B merged with the GJR to form the London & North Western: now another railway running northwards from Wolverhampton parallel to the LNW represented only competition, and later in the year, with slump replacing boom, the LNWR arranged to take the Shropshire Union on lease. Most of its canals were to remain canals.

By 1865 it was calculated that 1,271 miles of inland waterways, one third of the total, had passed into railway ownership or control. Such

* *George Parker Bidder, The Calculating Boy.*

takeovers required the consent of Parliament and, particularly at the time of the select committee on amalgamations mentioned above, canal companies were justifiably concerned that where one canal forming a link in a continuous route came under railway control it would be injurious to the others. Partly because of this, canals came into railway ownership complete with a public right of navigation, in other words the new owners had an obligation to keep them in navigable order. There were a few instances in which powers were obtained to drain canals and build railways among their beds. Such was the fate of much of the Shropshire Canal which had seen the early use of steam-powered inclined planes. In most cases, however, railway companies had to maintain their canals, although the total extent of the canals which had come higgledy-piggledy into railway ownership was sufficiently great to split apart those which remained independent.

Railway companies in due course got a bad name for neglecting their canals, and for discouraging traffic on them. This had been foreseen at the time of the 1846 select committee; it was both justified, and understandable. Canal companies in the early 1840s generally did not have powers to act as carriers, and few if any canal carriers came into railway ownership: where it owned a canal, a railway company was in the position only of toll-taker, of providing a track for carriers to use. Now the extent to which carriers should be admitted to railways themselves was, as we have seen, at the time a controversial matter: by the late 1840s, railways were tending more and more do their own carrying by rail, and a railway company might well be in direct competition with canal carriers for traffic between places served both by its canal and its railway. It is not surprising that it would discourage canal traffic, and encourage traffic by rail, where it could profit not only from providing the track but also from carrying the goods. Only where a railway owned a canal which went to places served by other railways, but not by its own, was there any great inducement to a railway to develop canal traffic: in this way the Trent & Mersey Canal, which extended beyond the area served by the owning North Staffordshire Railway, continued to be busy for many years.

It was not until 1845 that an Act of Parliament gave canal companies general powers to operate as carriers so that they might counter rail competition. Many canals which remained independent eventually set up carrying departments. Notable among them was the Grand Junction Canal, which set up a carrying department in 1848 just about the time that Pickford, leant on no doubt by the LNWR, withdrew. The Act covered also railway companies which owned canals, but few railway companies set up canal carrying departments: the only real inducement for a railway company so to diversify lay once again in the possibility of carrying traffic by its canal to and from districts served by rival railways. The Manchester, Sheffield & Lincolnshire Railway, for instance, set up a canal carrying department in 1848 on its connected Ashton, Peak Forest and Macclesfield Canals. This lasted until 1894 when it was discontinued because the traffic had become largely one-way with insufficient return loading.

By that date, however, industry had largely tended to relocate itself away from canals to places where it could be served by the far more extensive railway system, and canals had become, as Acworth put it in *The Railways of Scotland* (1890) 'a very small item in the vast mass of miscellaneous property . . . which has come into the possession of modern railway companies'. The Regulation of Railways Act 1873 had reinforced railway obligations towards specific canals by placing on railway companies a general obligation to maintain the canals they owned; but the railways still had no obligation or inducement to improve or enlarge canals, and they had several good reasons for not doing so. Of waterways which remained independent, some died away from loss of traffic during this era – these being mainly in rural districts – while others, serving industrial areas, enlarged their navigation works to take bigger vessels and continued to be active. The railway/canal controversy has continued into our own time, and its effects are with us yet.

Horse Railways

Of other predecessors of steam railways, wooden railways for the most part were re-laid with iron, or simply abandoned, though some remained in use until the 1840s. Tramroads, too, were generally either upgraded into steam railways (either as public lines or for private industrial use) or abandoned. In a few isolated instances they remained in use until as recently as the middle years of the present century. Horses continued to be used extensively as a secondary form of motive power on steam railways. Horse-drawn passenger coaches did survive, particularly on short branch lines, for some decades, but the principal use of horses was for shunting. In 1889 Acworth noted in *The Railways of*

England 'six engines and from fifty to a hundred horses . . . constantly at work' shunting goods trains in the Midland Railway marshalling yard at Chaddesden, Derby, and about fifty more horses at work sorting mineral wagons at nearby Toton. Railway shunting horses lasted for many years: as recently as 1948 when railway companies were nationalized, the British Transport Commission inherited from them 238 shunting horses, and a further 8,555 horses for hauling road vehicles.

Ports and Shipping

The emerging relationship between steam railways on the one hand and ports and coastal shipping on the other was a complex one, but can be summarised. Where passenger steam boats operated along the coast, or up and down estuaries, they found it difficult and in many cases impossible to compete successfully with railways: but where they provided a ferry service, across estuaries, to islands and to Ireland and the Continent, steamers and railways co-operated and prospered. In some instances – the prime example was the Clyde – railways largely superseded steamers on the upper reaches of an estuary, but ran in connection with steamers serving places further down which were not served by rail. For freight, particularly coal from North East England to London, coastal shipping proved much more resilient. Ports, and the railways serving them, prospered or not according to their function. Usually, during the rest of the nineteenth century, they prospered.

Collapse of Coaching

The calamitous effect of the opening of the Liverpool & Manchester Railway upon the stage coaches between its termini has already been mentioned, in chapter three, and the equally catastrophic consequences for the mail coach system of the opening of the Grand Junction Railway and subsequent main lines have been described in chapter five. The consequences for stage coaches were as catastrophic as for mails. Furthermore, although both stage coaches and railway passenger traffic were taxed by the government, the taxes bore more lightly on railways than on coaches. Wherever railways were built and quicker, cheaper trains started to run, then stage coaches were withdrawn. Occasionally a coach proprietor would fight back: three months after the opening of the Grand Junction Railway, the famous proprietor Edward Sherman attempted to reintroduce the *Red Rover* coach from London to Manchester which had been discontinued when the railway was opened. It was unsuccessful, and Sherman eventually was ruined. Elsewhere occasionally a railway would raise its fares enough to tempt, for a while, some coaches back on to the roads. But in general, throughout the 1840s, coaches were withdrawn as the railway system spread. Travel by 'posting', by post-chaise, or in one's own carriage, disappeared equally.

The stage coach driver's skills, the successive ostlers' quick changes of horses, had made operating a fast, long-distance coach into a spectacular performance carried out very much in the public eye. The sudden disappearance of such coaches did not go unregretted by the public. Comic song writers denigrated the 'steam pot', newspaper leader writers produced mock obituaries of coaches. Coaches had their adherents, their enthusiasts. Unfortunately, like enthusiasts for branch line railways in a more recent period, they tended to travel by a newer, more convenient form of transport when they actually had to go somewhere. The branch line closures of the 1960s and 70s are probably as closely akin to the discontinuance of stage coaches as any experience known to us today: but whereas branch lines had looked old-fashioned for decades previously, and one knew in one's heart of hearts that their closure must surely come, long-distance coaching had scarcely reached its prime and its collapse was sudden and unexpected.

With coaches, it was the branch routes that, for a time, survived: stage coaches ran in connection with railways over routes where railways had still to be built. In 1845, for instance, coaches from stations on the North Midland Railway were providing connections to Matlock, Mansfield, Lincoln, Retford and Doncaster, and in the late 1850s coaches connected with trains at Shrewsbury to take travellers to Aberystwyth, Tywyn and Aberdovey. In a few areas where railways were never built – such as parts of the Lake District and the Scottish Highlands – horse-drawn coaches survived until replaced by motor vehicles in the twentieth century. (In the same way, passenger steamers on the Caledonian Canal, which was never paralleled throughout by a railway, survived until 1939.) In cities, horse-drawn omnibuses flourished, often running to and from railway stations – the Liverpool & Manchester Railway was a pioneer in this – and in the country carriers' waggons continued to provide local transport to villages off the railway system.

Diversion of long-distance road traffic to railways left turnpike trusts with insufficient funds to carry out their tasks of road maintenance, and indeed their work was now found scarcely necessary. Eventually after the mid-1870s turnpike trusts were gradually extinguished – the last was dissolved in 1895 – and responsibility for road maintenance devolved upon newly-formed local authorities. Just in time, one might add, for the internal-combustion powered revival of traffic on the roads: but that is outside our story.

Railways Established

Let us rather leave railways in the 1870s as they enter their prime. We have seen how in 1830 the first steam trunk railway had made its appearance in a Britain already well and comprehensively served by coaches, canals and coastal shipping. Indeed it was only the excellence of existing transport services that provided communications good enough to enable the railway system to be built up quickly. Building the railway system had been a task on an unprecedented scale, but technical, administrative and financial developments had alternated with one another, and contributed to one another, so that it was achieved in a remarkably short space of years.

The watershed had been about 1848. By the 1870s earlier means of transport, where they survived at all, were relegated to comparative insignificance and obscurity. The railway had become the normal means of travel for passengers and of transport for freight. Fundamentals of design of locomotives and rolling stock, track and structures, were all established. So were operating practices, and indeed the routes represented by the railway map itself. Ahead lay detail developments – and immense prosperity, consonant with an immense contribution to public well-being during the most prosperous period in British history. The Victorian railway had, largely, evolved: a means of transport was established which would be unrivalled for five decades, and which even today provides the most pleasant way to travel.

Bibliography

Nineteenth Century Works
(Contemporary with their contents or nearly so)

'A Tourist', *The Railway Companion Describing an Excursion along the Liverpool Line*, Liverpool Road Station Society, Manchester, 1980 (first published 1833)

Acworth, W. M., *The Railways of England*, John Murray, London, 1889

Acworth, W. M., *The Railways of Scotland*, John Murray, London, 1890

Adams, W. B., *English Pleasure Carriages*, Adams & Dart, Bath, 1971 (first published 1837)

Butterworth, A. K., *A Treatise on the Law relating to Rates and Traffic on Railways and Canals*, Butterworth, London, 1889

Clark, D. K., *Railway Machinery*, London, 1855

Cockburn, Henry, Lord, *Circuit Journeys*, Byway Books, Hawick, 1983 (first published 1888)

Cook, T., *Cook's Scottish Tourist Official Directory*, London, 1861

Cooke, W. F., *Telegraphic Railways*, London, 1842

Cooke, W. F., *The Electric Telegraph: Was it invented by Professor Wheatstone?* Parts I and II, W. H. Smith, London, 1856/7 (contains both Cooke's case and Wheatstone's case to be considered inventors, as laid before arbitrators)

Freeling, A., *The London & Southampton Railway Companion*, London, 1838

Osborne, E. C., and Osborne, W., *Osborne's Guide to the Grand Junction Railway*, London, 1838

Osborne, E. C., and Osborne, W., *Osborne's London & Birmingham Railway Guide*, Birmingham, 1840

Reports of the Commissioners appointed to enquire into the manner in which railway communication can be most advantageously promoted in Ireland, 1837 and 1838

Report of the Gauge Commissioners, 1846

Reports of Select Committees of the House of Commons:
Railroad Communications, 1838

Railway Communications, 1840

Guards of Mails, 1841

Railways and Canals Amalgamation, 1846

Simms, F. W., *Public Works of Great Britain*, London 1838

Walker, C. V., *Electric Telegraph Manipulation*, London, 1850

Webb, F. H. (editor), *Extracts from the Private Letters of the late Sir William Fothergill Cooke 1836–39 relating to the Invention and Development of the Electric Telegraph*, with a memoir by L. Clark, E. & F. N. Spon, London, 1895

Whishaw, F., *The Railways of Great Britain & Ireland*, David & Charles (Publishers) Ltd, Newton Abbot, 1969 (first published 1840)

Wilmot, Sir J. E. E., *Reminiscences of the late Thomas Assheton Smith Esq*, John Murray, London, 1860

Recent Works

Ahrons, E. L., *The British Steam Railway Locomotive, 1825–1925*, Locomotive Publishing Co. Ltd, London, 1927

Baxter, B., *Stone Blocks and Iron Rails*, David & Charles, Newton Abbot, 1966

Biddle, G., *Victorian Stations*, David & Charles, Newton Abbot, 1973

Biddle, G., Nock, O. S., and others, *The Railway Heritage of Britain*, Michael Joseph Ltd, London, 1983

Bird, A., *Roads and Vehicles*, Arrow Books, London, 1973

Birse, R. M., *Engineering at Edinburgh University*, School of Engineering, University of Edinburgh, Edinburgh, 1983

Body, G., *The Blackwall & Millwall Extension Railways*, Avon-Anglia, Weston-super-Mare, n.d.

Bowers, B., *Sir Charles Wheatstone FRS 1802–1875*, HMSO, London, 1975

Boyd, J. I. C., *Narrow Gauge Railways in North Caernarvonshire*, vol. 3, *The Dinorwic Quarry & Railways, Great Orme Tramway and other Rail Systems*, Oakwood Press, Oxford, 1986

Boyd, J. I. C., *The Narrow Gauge Railway Museum*, Oakwood Press, Lingfield, 1972

Bushell, J., *The World's Oldest Railway*, Turntable Publications, Sheffield, 1975

Bushell, J., *Yorkshire's First Main Line* (Leeds & Selby Railway) West Yorkshire Metropolitan County Council, Wakefield, 1984

Carlson, R. E., *The Liverpool & Manchester Railway Project 1821–1831*, David & Charles, Newton Abbot, 1969

Clark, E. F., and Linfoot, J., *George Parker Bidder, The Calculating Boy*, KSL Publications, Bedford, 1983

Clinker, C. R., *The Leicester & Swannington Railway*, Avon-Anglia, Bristol, 1977

Coleman, T., *The Railway Navvies*, Penguin Books, 1968

Darby, M., *Early Railway Prints*, HMSO, London, 1974

Day, L., *Broad Gauge*, HMSO, London, 1985

Dendy Marshall, C. F., *A History of British Railways down to the Year 1830*, Oxford University Press, Oxford, 1938

Dendy Marshall, C. F., *A History of Railway Locomotives down to the End of the Year 1831*, Locomotive Publishing Co.Ltd, London, 1953

Dendy Marshall, C. F., *Centenary History of the Liverpool & Manchester Railway*, London, 1930

Dickinson, H. W., and Titley, A., *Richard Trevithick*, Cambridge University Press, Cambridge, 1934

Dictionary of National Biography

Donaghy, T. J., *Liverpool & Manchester Railway Operations 1831–1845*, David & Charles, Newton Abbot, 1972

Elis-Williams, M., *Packet to Ireland – Porthdinllaen's Challenge to Holyhead*, Gwynedd Archives Service, Caernarfon, 1984

Ellis, H., *British Railway History*, George Allen & Unwin Ltd, London, vol. I, 1954, vol. II, 1959

Ellis, H., *Railway Carriages in the British Isles*, George Allen & Unwin Ltd, London, 1965

Ellis, H., *The Midland Railway*, Ian Allan Ltd, London, 1955

Ellis, H., *Twenty Locomotive Men*, Ian Allan, London, 1958

Gourvish, T. R., *Mark Huish and the London & North Western Railway*, Leicester University Press, Leicester, 1972

Hadfield, C., and Skempton, A. W., *William Jessop, Engineer*, David & Charles, Newton Abbot, 1979

Hendy, J. G., *History of the Mail Bag Exchanging Apparatus*, unpublished typescript dated 1905 in Post Office Archives

Hendy, J. G., *History of the Travelling Post Office compiled from official records*, unpublished typescript in Post Office Archives

Hewison, C. H., *Locomotive Boiler Explosions*, David & Charles, Newton Abbot, 1983

Hubbard, G., *Cooke and Wheatstone and the Invention of the Electric Telegraph*, Routledge & Kegan Paul Ltd, London, 1965

Jackman, W. T., *The Development of Transportation in Modern England*, Frank Cass & Co. Ltd, London, 1966

Jaggers, K. A. (compiler), *Penrhyn Castle Industrial Railway Museum*, The National Trust, Beckenham, 1982

James, L., *A Chronology of the Construction of Britain's Railways 1778–1855*, Ian Allan Ltd, London, 1983

Jarvis, A., and Morris, L., *Lion*, Merseyside County Museums, Liverpool, 1980

John Saxby and his part in the Development of Interlocking and of the Signalling Industry, Westinghouse Brake & Signal Co. Ltd, London, n.d.

Johnson, P., *The British Travelling Post Office*, Ian Allan Ltd, London, 1985

Kieve, J., *The Electric Telegraph, A Social and Economic History*, David & Charles, Newton Abbot, 1973

Klingender, F. D., *Art and the Industrial Revolution*, Paladin, St Albans, 1972

Kyle, I., *Steam from Lowca*, author, Workington 1974

LMS Centenary of Opening of First Main-Line Railway, supplement to *The Railway Gazette*, London, 16 September 1938

Lascelles, T. S., *Green for Allright – An Outline of the Development of Signalling in the United Kingdom*, typescript dated 1957 in National Railway Museum library

Lead, P., *The Caldon Canal and Tramroads*, Oakwood Press, Blandford, 1979

Lee, C. E., *Narrow Gauge Railways in North Wales*, Railway Publishing Co. Ltd, London, 1945

Lee, C. E., *The First Passenger Railway*, The Railway Publishing Co. Ltd, London, 1942

Lewin, H. G., *Early British Railways*, Locomotive Publishing Co., London, 1925

Lewin, H. G., *The Railway Mania and its Aftermath*, David & Charles, Newton Abbot, 1968 (first published 1936)

Lewis, M. J. T., *Early Wooden Railways*, Routledge & Kegan Paul, London, 1970

MacDermot, E. T., revised by C. R. Clinker, *History of the Great Western Railway*, Vol. I, *1833–1863*, Ian Allan Ltd, London, 1964

Makepeace, C. E. (editor), *Oldest in the World – The Story of Liverpool Road Station, Manchester 1830–1980*, Liverpool Road Station Society and Manchester Region Industrial Archaeology Society, Manchester, 1980

Marshall, J., *A Biographical Dictionary of Railway Engineers*, David & Charles, Newton Abbot, 1978

Martin, D., *The Garnkirk & Glasgow Railway*, Strathkelvin District Libraries & Museums, Glasgow, 1981

Martin, D., *The Monkland & Kirkintilloch Railway*, Strathkelvin District Libraries & Museums, Glasgow, 1976

Mather, F. C., *After the Canal Duke*, Oxford University Press, London, 1970

Owen-Jones, S., *The Penydarren Locomotive*, National Museum of Wales, Cardiff, 1981

Patterson, E. M., *The Great Northern Railway of Ireland*, Oakwood Press, Oxford, 1986

Peacock, A. J., and Joy, D., *George Hudson of York*, Dalesman Books, Clapham, Yorks, 1971

Ratcliffe, R. L., *The Canterbury & Whitstable Railway*, Locomotive Club of Great Britain, London, 1980

Rees, G., *Early Railway Prints*, Phaidon Press Ltd, Oxford, 1980

Ripley, D., *The Little Eaton Gangway*, Oakwood Press, Lingfield, 1973

Rogers, H. C. B., *Turnpike to Iron Road*, Seeley, Service & Co., Ltd, London, 1961

Rolt, L. T. C., *George and Robert Stephenson*, Penguin Books, London, 1978

Rolt, L. T. C., *Isambard Kingdom Brunel*, Longmans, Green & Co., London, 1957

Rolt, L. T. C., *Red for Danger*, Pan Books Ltd, London, 1966

Rolt, L. T. C., *Thomas Telford*, Longmans Green & Co., London, 1958

The Future of the Railway Heritage (report of conference), The Royal Society of Arts, London, 1985

Scott, E. K. (editor), *Matthew Murray, Pioneer Engineer*, Leeds, 1928

Simmons, J., *The Railway in England and Wales 1830–1914*, Leicester University Press, Leicester, 1978

Simmons, J., *The Railways of Britain*, Routledge & Kegan Paul, London, 1965

Snell, J. B., *Early Railways*, Weidenfeld & Nicolson, London, 1964

Tomlinson, W. W., *The North Eastern Railway*, Andrew Reid & Co. Ltd, Newcastle-upon-Tyne, 1914

Transport Saga 1646–1947, Hay's Wharf Cartage Co. Ltd, London, 1947 (History of Pickford & Co.)

Vale, E., *The Mail-Coach Men of the Late Eighteenth Century*, David & Charles, Newton Abbot, 1967

Vignoles, K. H., *Charles Blacker Vignoles: Romantic Engineer*, Cambridge University Press, Cambridge, 1982

Warn, C. R., *Rails between Wear and Tyne*, Frank Graham, Newcastle-upon-Tyne, n.d.

Warn, C. R., *Waggonways and Early Railways of Northumberland*, Frank Graham, Newcastle-upon-Tyne, 1976

Webster, N. W., *Britain's First Trunk Line*, Adams & Dart, Bath, 1972

Westcott, G. F., *The British Railway Locomotive 1803–1853*, HMSO, London, 1958

Wilson, H. S., *T.P.O. A History of the Travelling Post Offices of Great Britain*, Railway Philatelic Group, Leicester, Part 1, *England – The Specials and Associated T.P.O.s*, 1979; Part 2, *England – South of the Midland T.P.O.*, 1979; Part 3, *Scotland and Ireland*, 1977

Wrottesley, John, *The Great Northern Railway* vol. I, *Origins and Development*, B. T. Batsford Ltd, London, 1979

Bibliography

Young, R., *Timothy Hackworth and the Locomotive*, Shildon 'Stockton & Darlington Railway' Jubilee Committee, Shildon, 1975 (first published 1923)

Periodicals

Nineteenth Century:

> *Blackwood's Edinburgh Magazine*
> *Engineering*
> *Illustrated London News*
> *Mechanics' Magazine*
> Minutes of Proceedings of the Institution of Civil Engineers
> *Punch*
> *The Engineer*
> *The Times*
> *Transactions* of the Institution of Civil Engineers

Recent:

> *Industrial Heritage*
> *Journal* of the Railway and Canal Historical Society
> *Newsletter* of the Friends of the National Railway Museum
> *Railway Magazine*
> *Railway World*
> *Transactions* of the Newcomen Society.

Acknowledgements

I am most grateful to the following for their assistance during the preparation of this book:

M. R. Bailey, Friends of Greater Manchester Museum of Science & Industry; Gordon Biddle; Harold D. Bowtell; J. I. C. Boyd; R. Bracegirdle, Leicester Museum of Technology; Geremy Butler, photography; A. J. Byrne, Bristol Marketing Board; E. F. Clark, Old Locomotive Committee; T. J. Edgington, National Railway Museum; Robert Excell, Science Museum; Mrs Jean Farrugia, Post Office Archives; Norman Gurley; A. Hall-Patch, Science Museum; Philip J. Kelley; Peter Johnson, Railway Philatelic Group; R. G. Manders, Greater Manchester Museum of Science & Industry; Don Martin; S. G. Morrison, Institution of Mechanical Engineers; D. Rendell, photography; Dafydd Roberts, Welsh Slate Museum; Frank Staff; R. J. M. Sutherland; Charles E. Taylor-Nobbs, Old Locomotive Committee; Norman Thomas, The National Trust; M. A. Vanns, Ironbridge Gorge Museum Trust; Charles Whetmath, Great Western Society Ltd; Gareth Haulfryn Williams, Gwynedd Archives; my wife for research, and my wife and children too for their continuing support.

INDEX

Index

Index

Index

275